Telecommunication Policy
for the Information Age

Telecommunication Policy for the Information Age

From Monopoly to Competition

Gerald W. Brock

HARVARD UNIVERSITY PRESS

Cambridge, Massachusetts
London, England
1994

To my wife, Ruth, and our children,
Jane, Sara, David, and Jimmy

This book is printed on acid-free paper, and its binding materials have been chosen for strength and durability.

Library of Congress Cataloging-in-Publication Data
Brock, Gerald W.
    Telecommunication policy for the information age : from monopoly
to competition / Gerald W. Brock.
      p. cm.
    Includes index.
    ISBN 0-674-87277-0
    1. Telecommunication—Government policy—United States.
I. Title.
HE7781.B75   1994
388'.068—dc20   94-3911
                                              CIP

Contents

Acknowledgments

This book developed out of my attempts to integrate what I understood about the regulatory process from the academic literature with what I observed in six years at the Federal Communications Commission. I am indebted to Tom Spavins and Peter Pitsch, who arranged for me to join the staff of the FCC's Office of Plans and Policy in 1983 to work under their direction, to then Chairman Mark Fowler and Common Carrier Bureau chief Albert Halprin, who provided me with a number of assignments that allowed me to see various components of the FCC's operation, and to Dennis Patrick, who provided me with the privilege of serving as Common Carrier Bureau chief after he assumed the chairmanship. FCC staff members Michael Wack, John Cimko, Evan Kwerel, Colleen Boothby, Mary Beth Hess, Mark Uretsky, Mary Brown, Ken Moran, Peyton Wynns, Carl Lawson, Gerald Vaughan, and Jane Jackson, along with many others, were influential in helping me understand the complex interrelated components of the regulatory process.

Christopher Sterling, my colleague, friend, and supervisor at the George Washington University Graduate Telecommunication Program, has been a constant source of encouragement, ideas, and sources for this book. His extraordinary personal library of works on telecommunication was a great benefit in my research, and his careful reading of the draft manuscript and advice at all stages of the work were extremely valuable. John Kwoka, Richard Caves, Tom Spavins, Carl Lawson, Tim Brennan, and Evan Kwerel provided very useful comments on the draft manuscript.

Many students in the Graduate Telecommunication Program at

George Washington University have read portions of the manuscript in various stages and provided responses that were helpful in the revisions.

Early stages of my work on portions of this book were sponsored by Unitel Communications Inc. I have benefited from discussions with Unitel staff members David McKeown, Michael Harburn, Gary Pizante, David Watt, Richard Stursberg, Janet Yale, Steve Guiton, Michael Ryan, and Mark Zohar.

The writing of this book was facilitated by a grant to George Washington University from the John and Mary R. Markle Foundation. I appreciate the assistance of Lloyd Morrisett, president, Dolores Miller, grants manager, and Jocelyn Hidi of the program staff at the Markle Foundation in making this book possible.

I am grateful to Michael Aronson at Harvard University Press for his support for the project over a long period of time, and to Mary Ellen Geer for her careful and insightful editing of the manuscript. Jennifer Sterling transformed rough drawings into finished figures.

None of the individuals or organizations named above is responsible for the views expressed in this book, or for any remaining errors in it. Some of the individuals have specifically expressed disagreement with certain of the interpretations developed in this book.

First-person accounts of selected regulatory issues by Bernard Strassburg are quoted from Fred W. Henck and Bernard Strassburg, *A Slippery Slope: The Long Road to the Breakup of AT&T*, copyright 1988 by Fred W. Henck and Bernard Strassburg, published by Greenwood Press, an imprint of Greenwood Publishing Group, Inc., Westport, Connecticut; reprinted with permission.

I am especially thankful for the love, encouragement, support, and patience of my wife, Ruth, and our four children, Jane, Sara, David, and Jimmy, throughout a long research and writing process.

Abbreviations

APA	Administrative Procedure Act
BOC	Bell Operating Company (after divestiture)
BSA	Basic Serving Arrangement (ONA structure)
BSE	Basic Service Element (ONA structure)
CAP	Competitive Access Provider
CCB	Common Carrier Bureau (of the FCC)
CCL	Carrier Common Line
CCLC	Carrier Common Line Charge (access charges)
CCSA	Common Control Switching Arrangement
CEI	Comparably Efficient Interconnection (ONA structure)
CPE	Customer Premises Equipment (terminal equipment)
CPNI	Customer Proprietary Network Information
DOD	Department of Defense
DOJ	Department of Justice
EIA	Electronic Industries Association
ENFIA	Exchange Network Facilities for Interstate Access
ESP	Enhanced Service Provider
FCC	Federal Communications Commission
FNPRM	Further Notice of Proposed Rulemaking
FTS	Federal Telecommunications System
FX	Foreign Exchange (type of long distance service)
ICC	Interstate Commerce Commission
IXC	Interchange Carrier (after divestiture)

LATA   Local Access and Transport Area
LEC   Local Exchange Carrier (after divestiture)
MFJ   Modified Final Judgment (divestiture decree)
MPL   Multi-Schedule Private Line (pricing plan)
MTS   Message Telecommunication Service (ordinary switched
             long distance service)
NARUC   National Association of Regulatory Utility Commissioners
             (state regulation)
NPRM   Notice of Proposed Rulemaking
NTIA   National Telecommunications and Information
             Administration (in the Department of Commerce)
NTS   Non-Traffic-Sensitive (the largest category of telephone
             plant and associated expense)
OCC   Other Common Carrier (small competitors of AT&T,
             especially prior to the divestiture)
ONA   Open Network Architecture
ONAL   Off Network Access Line
OPP   Office of Plans and Policy (of the FCC)
PBX   Private Branch Exchange
PCA   Protective Connecting Arrangement
POP   Point of Presence (post-divestiture connection point
             between LECs and IXCs)
SCC   Specialized Common Carrier
SLC   Subscriber Line Charge
SPF   Subscriber Plant Factor (a component of separations cost
             allocation formulas)
WATS   Wide Area Telecommunication Service

Part I / Analytical Framework

Policy making in the United States is more like a bar-room brawl: Anybody can join in, the combatants fight all comers and sometimes change sides, no referee is in charge, and the fight lasts not for a fixed number of rounds but indefinitely or until everybody drops from exhaustion.

James Q. Wilson, *Bureaucracy*

1 / Introduction

The process for making telecommunication policy in the United States often appears chaotic and disorganized, with overlapping responsibility and frequent conflicts among federal regulators, state regulators, executive branch leadership, congressional committees, and judges. Parties disappointed by the policy choices in one forum frequently seek redress in an alternative forum. Some decisions can only be made by the concurrence of multiple independent agencies. For example, the routine preparation of the U.S. position on issues before Intelsat is done jointly by the Federal Communications Commission (FCC), the State Department, and the Commerce Department. Other decisions are issued independently by multiple agencies even though the implications may be contradictory. For example, AT&T and the Bell Operating Companies are subject to the orders of the FCC, the state regulatory commissions, and Judge Greene (the administrator of the AT&T antitrust consent decree), with none of the three required to coordinate their actions.

Observers of the telecommunication policy process have frequently criticized this state of affairs and have called for greater centralization of power and long-term planning of regulatory policy. Henry Geller has provided a survey of past criticisms of the telecommunication policy process that includes the following:

> [The FCC] has been found to have failed both to define its primary objective intelligently and to make many policy determinations required for effective and expeditious administration. (1949, Hoover Commission)

3

The whole Government telecommunications structure is an uncoordinated one and will be even less adequate in the future than it has been in the past to meet the ever-growing complexities of telecommunications. A new agency is needed to give coherence to the structure. (1951, Communications Policy Board established by President Truman)

[The FCC] has drifted, vacillated and stalled in almost every major area. It seems incapable of policy planning, of disposing within a reasonable period of time the business before it. (1960, Landis Report for President-elect Kennedy)

[Telecommunication policy] has evolved as a patchwork of limited, largely *ad hoc* responses to specific issues, rather than a cohesive framework for planning. . . . The patchwork nature of the present structure is not conducive to optimum performance of the telecommunications activities and requirements of the Federal Government. (1968, Rostow Commission)

Inherent deficiencies in the commission form of organization prevent the commission from responding effectively to changes in industry structure, technology, economic trends, and public needs. (1971, Ash Council)

Geller then added his own voice to the many past calls for reform and centralization of authority:

The authority bestowed upon diverse executive departments and agencies is fragmented and has led to jurisdictional battles, delays, and confusion. The lack of focused responsibility becomes particularly acute in light of the independence of the Federal Communications Commission. This flawed policy process is especially egregious in view of the great importance of telecommunications in the information age and the difficult policy issues now confronting the United States, particularly in the international trade arena.[1]

A major Department of Commerce study of telecommunications issues in 1988 repeated many of the old concerns with decentralized decision making:

So long as ultimate responsibility for most communications and information policy is fragmented among a multitude of agencies, and between domestic and international policymaking, then short-term, makeshift solutions will too often emerge as a hastily-coordinated, lowest common denominator. . . .

In the final analysis the problem is that for most issues there is, at times, no one in charge, and the buck does not stop anywhere.[2]

As Wilson's analogy between the U.S. policy process and a barroom brawl suggests, the chaotic process of developing telecommunication policy is not unique to that industry. Much of the routine development of U.S. policy in many different areas is done through agencies with vague mandates and overlapping responsibilities. Statutes frequently contain general language that must be clarified through regulations and administrative practice. Those who are dissatisfied with the response of one agency to their concerns generally have alternative places to seek redress, through either a formal appeal process or another agency with potential jurisdiction over the issue.

Positive Results of the Decentralized Process

While the decentralized telecommunication policy process in the United States has often been criticized, the results of that process have been better than the results of the centralized process in many other countries. Until recently, the most common telecommunication structure outside of the United States has been a single government ministry which was responsible for telecommunication policy and the operation of the government-owned telephone network. Yet those centralized structures have tended to show even less ability to adapt to rapidly changing technological opportunities in telecommunication than the U.S. process. Many countries have carefully examined U.S. telecommunication policy over the past twenty years and introduced elements of it into their own policies in order to reform rigid and dysfunctional hierarchical structures.

U.S. telecommunication policy has evolved gradually over a long period of time, resulting in a cumulative major transformation. Although many policy makers have been dissatisfied with the state of telecommunication policy at any one time, there has never been a consensus on what changes were needed. The telecommunication policy process can be clearly distinguished from the airline policy process, in which a single drastic change was made in the late 1970s (from traditional regulation to deregulation) through a new law supported by the Carter administration, the Civil Aeronautics Board, and congressional leaders.[3] In contrast, telecommunication policy is still tied to the

Communications Act of 1934 despite repeated congressional efforts to create a new statutory framework. Even though Congress has been unable to update the basic law, the Federal Communications Commission, state regulatory agencies, the Department of Justice, and federal judges have all taken actions that have gradually moved policy from traditional public utility regulation of a monopoly to substantial reliance on market forces and encouragement of new competition. The policy that has resulted from the independent actions of several different power centers does not conform to the prescriptions of any single theoretical perspective, but it does incorporate elements from a wide range of political views and include adjustments for changing technological opportunities.

Potential Benefits of a Decentralized Policy Process

A centralized telecommunication policy agency would exert a great deal of power, including the power to confer or withhold vast amounts of money to individuals and organizations that seek licenses, permissions, or protections. American political culture is unwilling to trust such a degree of power to particular individuals without many opportunities for review and reconsideration of their decisions. James Q. Wilson notes that Americans are generally willing to accept reduced efficiency in government in exchange for protection against abuse of power:

> Inefficiency is not the only bureaucratic problem nor is it even the most important. A perfectly efficient agency could be a monstrous one, swiftly denying us our liberties, economically inflicting injustices, and competently expropriating our wealth. People complain about bureaucracy as often because it is unfair or unreasonable as because it is slow or cumbersome. . . .
>
> The checks and balances of the American constitutional system reflect our desire to reduce the arbitrariness of official rule. That desire is based squarely on the premise that inefficiency is a small price to pay for freedom and responsiveness. Congressional oversight, judicial review, interest-group participation, media investigations, and formalized procedures all are intended to check administrative discretion.[4]

During the economic crisis of the 1930s, there was widespread belief that drastic government intervention in the economy was necessary, and consequently an effort was made to create agencies that combined executive, legislative, and judicial functions within a single organization. As confidence in market processes revived, the traditional concerns with limiting abuse of power caused the development of many restrictions on the activities of regulatory agencies. However, potential abuse of power is not the only problem with concentrating the power to make policy. A properly functioning policy process must be able to cope with four different problems:

1. Controlling power to be certain it is used only in the public interest, given the limited number of saints available for government service (opportunism).
2. Defining the public interest on issues for which any decision helps some people and hurts others and for which there are differing political views among those who are not personally affected by the issue (differing political values).
3. Providing adequate information to make rational decisions when critically important information is either missing altogether or controlled by individuals or firms that have an incentive to misrepresent it (unavailable information or asymmetric information).
4. Guarding against errors caused by the policy maker's lack of expertise or inability to fully utilize the available information to devise policies that accomplish given policy goals (bounded rationality).

Formal models have been developed to illuminate methods of coping with various subsets of the four problems. For example, the large literature on information economics is concerned with methods of coping with opportunism and asymmetric information (problems 1 and 3) while assuming a single principal and unbounded rationality (assuming away problems 2 and 4). There are no formal models of optimal processes that cope with all four problems simultaneously.

The perspective of this book is that existing government institutions have evolved over time to cope with observed conditions, including all four of the problems listed above. It is a similar perspective to that taken by Alfred Chandler in his famous study of the development of American business structures. Chandler explained the development of new corporate structures as efforts to manage the increasing complexity of large corporations as they expanded into diversified integrated companies.[5] He made no attempt to prove that the observed structures were optimal, but showed the relationship between the problems faced by the business leaders and the organizational solutions they developed to solve those problems. Similarly, this study makes no claim that the observed telecommunication policy-making institutions are optimal, but it does seriously examine them as possessing potentially useful characteristics for dealing with complex policy issues subject to all four of the problems listed earlier.

The policy literature contains two very distinct perspectives on the rationality of the policy process. Much of the theoretical literature assumes that the process is (or ought to be) highly rational. Policy makers combine political preferences into well-defined goals, collect relevant information, and use that information together with appropriate analytical frameworks to achieve the highest possible accomplishment of the goals. March and Olsen summarize that perspective as follows:

> In contemporary theoretical political science, institutions and behavior are thought to evolve through some form of efficient historical process.
>
> An efficient historical process, in these terms, is one that moves rapidly to a unique solution, conditional on current environmental conditions, and is thus independent of the historical path. The equilibrium may involve a stochastically stable distribution or a fixed point, but we require a solution that is achieved relatively rapidly and is independent of the details of historical events leading to it.[6]

Writers who closely observe specific policy-making activities generally report a more confused and random process. Lindblom and Cohen have described the policy process as "unmanageable, fitful, erratic."[7] March and Olsen summarize the empirical perspectives as follows:

> Ideas of temporal sorting are attempts to comprehend the relatively confusing picture of collective decision making drawn from empirical observations. Many things seem to be happening at once; technologies are changing and poorly understood; alliances, preferences, and perceptions are changing; solutions, opportunities, ideas, people, and outcomes are mixed together in ways that make interpretation uncertain and leave connections unclear.... Decision makers ignore information they have, ask for more information, and then ignore the new information when it is available.... Participants contend acrimoniously over the adoption of a policy, but once that policy is adopted the same contenders appear to be largely indifferent to its implementation, or the lack of it.

The apparent disorderliness of many things in decision making has led some people to argue that there is very little order to collective choice and that it is best described as bedlam.[8]

The perspective developed in this book is intermediate between the ahistorical, highly rational view and the historically determined "bedlam" view of the policy process. It assumes that any individual decision is dependent upon the information, perspectives, and goals of that particular decision maker, and therefore may be unpredictable to an outside observer, but that the decentralized institutional process combines those individual decisions into an overall policy that is related to the distribution of political views in the society.

Plan of the Book

This book examines the evolution of telecommunication policy in relationship to changing technology, industry structure, and industry responses to previous policy decisions. The primary focus is on events of the 1980s, when policy makers attempted to transform a policy structure designed for monopoly into one compatible with substantial competition. This study emphasizes the development of policy through the combination of independent decisions by separate power centers.

Part I of this book develops the analytical framework used to understand the observed policy process. Chapter 2 summarizes selected influential thinkers who provide a context for this study. Chapter 3 sketches the beginning of a model of the decentralized policy process. Chapter 4 describes the institutions and legal framework that guide the development of telecommunication policy. Chapter 5 presents the historical development and economic characteristics of the industry that are important for understanding the policy issues.

Part II analyzes the early development of competition within the regulated monopoly structure of the industry and reviews the policy problems created by regulating a mixture of competitive and monopolistic services. Chapter 6 examines the development of competition in customer-owned attachments to the telephone network, beginning with specialized items and expanding to include ordinary telephone instruments. Chapter 7 considers the development of specialized competition in the long distance network as a result of liberal licensing of microwave frequencies. Chapter 8 examines the controversies over interconnection of the specialized microwave systems and the public switched networks and explains how interconnection rights made the specialized services competitive with most long distance services.

Part III reviews the efforts to avoid regulating a mixture of competition and monopoly by creating rigid boundaries between regulated monopoly services and unregulated competitive services. Chapter 9 examines the Department of Justice's attempt to develop a structural solution for the competitive problems in the industry through the divestiture of AT&T's monopoly services (local service) from its competitive services (long distance service, manufacturing, and customer premises equipment). Chapter 10 considers the FCC and congressional efforts to develop the rules for payments among companies for jointly provided service (access charges), while Chapter 11 discusses the problems of implementing access charges.

Part IV examines the breakdown of the divestiture model of strict separation between regulated monopoly and unregulated competitive segments of the telecommunication industry, returning to the earlier policy problems of regulating a mixture of competition and monopoly. Chapter 12 considers the development of policies favoring the expansion of regulated local exchange carriers into new competitive services integrated with their traditional local telephone services. Chapter 13 reviews the initial development of new competitors to previously monopolized local exchange services in major city centers. Chapter 14 examines the development of alternatives to traditional rate of return regulation ("price caps") as a method of managing mixtures of competition and monopoly. Chapter 15 concludes the book with a summary of the observed decentralized telecommunication policy process.

2 / Perspectives on the Policy Process

The literature on the policy process is vast, and no short survey can cover it comprehensively. A complete review of even a specific portion of the policy literature, such as the economic analysis of regulation, is a book-length project in itself.[1] Rather than attempting a comprehensive review of some particular portion of the relevant literature, this chapter selectively reviews some of the important ideas that illuminate the wide variety of approaches to how the policy process ought to work.

This chapter does not review works that provide specific policy recommendations within a given institutional framework, such as the literature concerned with cost allocation or computation of rates of return. Instead it focuses on works that deal with the broader issue of the methods by which policy is made. A primary concern of these works is whether the policy process can be explicitly optimized through rational planning or whether attempted optimization will lead to processes inferior to those that evolve through many different decisions over a long period of time. A second important issue is whether there is a single public interest that could be discerned through some method of reducing private interests, or whether there are only individual preferences that will always be in conflict.

Blackstone versus Bentham

In order to understand particular government policies, it is useful to consider the philosophical ideas that motivated the design of the in-

11

stitutions that created those policies. Several crucial issues of regulatory design were incorporated into the eighteenth-century exchange between the English legal scholar William Blackstone and the Utilitarian philosopher Jeremy Bentham.[2] Blackstone's four volumes entitled *Commentaries on the Laws of England* were published betweeen 1765 and 1769. Bentham's first attack on Blackstone was published in 1776, and his more complete analysis was published after his death.[3]

Blackstone described a complex system of institutions that distributed power in order to protect fundamental rights. English law in his time was primarily common law rather than statute law. In Blackstone's view, judges did not exercise their own personal preferences in deciding a case, but rather sought to recover the true and pure law of Saxon times that had been corrupted through the Norman invasion. Individual human ability to reason correctly was limited, but the combination of many different judges attempting to decide cases correctly led to a body of precedent that constituted good law. Richard Posner suggests that Blackstone's emphasis on the good law of Saxon times is an adaptation of the Christian theology of the Fall and the corruption of human intellect:

> The idea of the fallibility of human intellect has roots in Christian theology, which contrasts the impaired reasoning power of fallen man with the perfect reason of the angels. Blackstone echoes this notion in his discussion of immemorial custom. The Saxon period described in the *Commentaries* recalls the Garden of Eden, as described, for example, in *Paradise Lost*, where man exercised his mental faculties with a clarity and force never recaptured after his expulsion.[4]

Blackstone saw a limited role for statute law, preferring that statute laws be used to clarify conflicting rulings in the common law rather than to impose radically new laws. Because good law was recovering long-established rights and customs, radical changes through statute law would fail to uphold custom and therefore would not be good law. In his view, change should only come slowly with incremental adaptation of the existing precedent to new situations in order to preserve the wisdom of the past.

Bentham vigorously disputed Blackstone's approving analysis of the then-existing English institutions and laws. While Blackstone distrusted the ability of any one person to devise an improvement over the existing common law, Bentham was a reformer who placed great faith in human reason and believed that his proposals were superior to existing institutions. While Blackstone viewed the division of power among the monarch, the judiciary, the House of Lords, and the House of Commons as a protection for individual rights, Bentham sought a concentration of power in order to implement reform. While Blackstone viewed the common law as incorporating the wisdom of many generations, Bentham saw the common law as the creation of judges and lawyers with a vested interest in the status quo.

Posner summarizes the differences between Blackstone and Bentham as follows:

> Blackstone and Bentham typify polar approaches to the study of social phenomena. Blackstone studied the operations of an actual social system, the system of English law as it had evolved against the background of the nation's disordered political history. His study revealed a system of emormous intricacy, with impressive survival and growth characteristics and a significant capacity for reform—in short, a resilient, adaptable, viable social organism.
>
> Bentham never studied systematically any social or legal institution, English or foreign, contemporary or historical. He never tried to master the working principles of the institutions he sought to reform. Instead he deduced optimal institutions from the greatest-happiness principle and then tried to work out the details of their implementation.[5]

Blackstone's analysis was influential in the development of the American concept of separation of powers and limitations on the power of the government to intrude on the rights of individuals. Bentham's approach has been influential in the economics profession and in many other disciplines that propose reforms of existing policies and institutions. Economists routinely propose changes to existing policies to improve "allocative efficiency" based on reasoning from economic theory, an approach similar to Bentham's proposals to improve total utility based on his reasoning process. Neither Bentham nor the modern economist normally emphasizes limiting the rate of change in policy and preserving the wisdom of the past.

While mainstream economics has been more closely related to the intellectual tradition of Bentham than of Blackstone, Austrian economics has emphasized the value of observed institutions as Blackstone did. In his Nobel Prize lecture, F. A. von Hayek emphasized the limitations on human knowledge which prevent individuals from designing institutions superior to those that evolve from the combination of individual decisions:

> To act on the belief that we possess the knowledge and the power which enable us to shape the processes of society entirely to our liking, knowledge which in fact we do *not* possess, is likely to make us do much harm. . . .
>
> If man is not to do more harm than good in his efforts to improve the social order, he will have to learn that in this, as in all other fields where essential complexity of an organized kind prevails, he cannot acquire the full knowledge which would make mastery of the events possible. . . . The recognition of the insuperable limits to his knowledge ought indeed to teach the student of society a lesson of humility which should guard him against becoming an accomplice in men's fatal striving to control society—a striving which makes him not only a tyrant over his fellows, but which may well make him the destroyer of a civilization which no brain has designed but which has grown from the free efforts of millions of individuals.[6]

The issues of the Blackstone-Bentham debate frequently recur in debates over policies and policy processes. The two fundamental issues are the tension between guarding against the potential for abuse when power is concentrated versus providing the necessary concentration of power to implement reform, and the question of the ability of any particular individual to design a superior system to the one that has evolved over time. The U.S. policy system with its separation of powers, overlapping agency jurisdictions, and extensive procedural requirements protects against abuse of power but also protects the status quo and prevents radical reform. In the tradition of Blackstone, those who are satisfied with the status quo and worried about abuse of power tend to emphasize the value of checks and balances and the necessity of making change in a slow and incremental way through established procedures. In the tradition of Bentham, those who are anxious to implement reforms tend to see the complex set of institutions and procedures as obstacles serving only to protect entrenched interests and block changes that would improve the social welfare.

Landis versus Stigler

The Great Depression created a sense of crisis that allowed popular acceptance of radical change and increased government power after

Franklin Roosevelt's election in 1932. James Landis played a key role in the expansion of federal regulation, as academic theoretician, legislative draftsman, and regulatory administrator. Landis was first a protégé of Felix Frankfurter at the Harvard Law School, then a clerk for Supreme Court justice Louis Brandeis. He returned to Cambridge to join the Harvard Law School faculty, achieving a tenured professorship at age 28. Five years later, at the beginning of the Roosevelt administration, Landis accompanied Frankfurter to Washington to draft securities legislation for Roosevelt. Along with Thomas Corcoran and Benjamin Cohen (both former Frankfurter students and Wall Street lawyers), Landis drafted the Securities Act of 1933, the Securities Exchange Act of 1934, and the Public Utility Holding Company Act of 1935.

Roosevelt signed the Securities Act of 1933 in May 1933 and appointed Landis to the Federal Trade Commission to oversee initial securities regulation. While setting up a crash program for initial securities registration, Landis also worked on the more difficult and hotly contested Securities and Exchange Act of 1934. When that act was passed, jurisdiction over securities regulation was transferred to the new Securities and Exchange Commission, and Landis was moved to that commission to serve under Chairman Joseph Kennedy. The early SEC was a very intense place of extreme enthusiasm and hard work. Landis wrote of setting up cots in the building for the 30 people finishing registration statements so they could work around the clock, and the first annual report noted the 72,000 hours of unpaid overtime work performed in the first year.[7] Landis later succeeded Kennedy as chairman, and then in 1937 returned to academic life as Dean of the Harvard Law School. While dean, he performed a variety of government assignments during World War II, then resigned the deanship in 1946 to accept Truman's appointment as chairman of the Civil Aeronautics Board. After disputes with the airlines and other government agencies, he failed to get his expected reappointment.

Soon after leaving the SEC, Landis gave a series of lectures that explained his perspective on regulation.[8] These lectures are a classic in the regulatory literature for their optimistic explanation of the potential of regulation. They are based both on Landis's academic studies and on his experience in an unusually successful administrative agency. Part of that success was due to Landis's own efforts, but part to the special conditions of the 1930s and the unusually capable personnel attracted to the SEC by the economic crisis.

As Landis uses the term, the administrative process includes both a substantive and a procedural aspect. Procedurally, the administrative process is a combination of the executive, legislative, and judicial powers into a single agency rather than the traditional American separation of powers into distinct institutions. Substantively, the administrative process is a response to the need for much greater government intervention in an industrial than in an agricultural economy. The administrative process as Landis conceived it was a substitute for the market, which appeared to have broken down during the Depression. "And as the demands for positive solutions increased and, in the form of legislative measures, were precipitated upon the cathodes of governmental activity, *laissez faire*—the simple belief that only good could come by giving economic forces free play—came to an end." He saw the administrative process as growing out of an expansion of the powers of the government because of industrialization, changing from "the desire for sporadic intervention on the part of government to adjust a particular abuse" into "a view which conceives it to be a function of government to maintain a continuing concern with and control over the economic forces which affect the life of the community."[9]

Landis praised the formation of the Interstate Commerce Commission as "the deliberate organization of a governmental unit whose single concern was the well-being, in a broad public sense, of a vital and national industry."[10] He viewed the problem of regulating an industry as analogous to the problem of operating one, and noted that no industrial enterprise would arrange itself with a separation of powers. In order to properly regulate an industry, it is necessary to give a single agency the appropriate powers:

As the governance of industry, bent upon the shaping of adequate policies and the development of means for their execution, vests powers to this end without regard to the creation of agencies theoretically independent of each other, so when government concerns itself with the stability of an industry it is only intelligent realism for it to follow the industrial rather than the political analogue. It vests the necessary powers with the administrative authority it creates, not too greatly concerned with the extent to which such action does violence to the traditional tripartite theory of governmental organization. The dominant theme in the administrative structure is thus determined not primarily by political conceptualism but rather by concern for an industry whose economic health has become a responsibility of government.[11]

Landis shared the general Roosevelt administration view that extensive government action was necessary. He saw regulators as active participants in the management of the industry, not merely as policemen trying to enforce particular laws and correct abuses. In order to properly control the industry, the agency should be composed of experts. Landis contrasted his vision with an earlier theory of U.S. government that "lifted the inexpertness that characterized our nineteenth-century governmental mechanisms to the level of a political principle" and cited Andrew Jackson's effort to limit civil servants to short terms in order to improve the "official industry and integrity." In Landis's vision, expert leadership is necessary and

> ... springs only from that continuity of interest, that ability and desire to devote fifty-two weeks a year, year after year, to a particular problem. With the rise of regulation, the need for expertness became dominant; for the art of regulating an industry requires knowledge of the details of its operation, ability to shift requirements as the condition of the industry may dictate, the pursuit of energetic measures upon the appearance of an emergency, and the power through enforcement to realize conclusions as to policy.[12]

Landis saw the creation of separate administrative agencies as one way of achieving expert knowledge. He supported the creation of many new agencies to handle particular problems in order to allow the focus on a specific issue that could produce expert knowledge.

Landis's brief for the administrative process applied the Bentham tradition to the conditions of the Great Depression. He saw a great need for change and had faith in the ability of public-spirited experts to implement change in a socially beneficial way. He sought new institutions with concentrated power to replace existing institutions that diffused power and limited the rate of change. He was unconcerned about the potential for abuse of power.

In contrast to the Landis vision of government control of industry through commissions composed of public-spirited experts who perceived the public interest and imposed it, George Stigler and his colleagues at the University of Chicago developed the theory that most government interventions in the economy produced pernicious effects. Stigler studied under Frank Knight at the University of Chicago, where he received his Ph.D. in 1938. After serving on the faculty of Columbia University, he returned to the University of Chicago in 1957 and began an empirical examination of the effects of regulation. Stigler's empirical findings led to his famous 1971 article proposing a theory of regulation in which producers secure government regulation to advance their own interests. Stigler was awarded the Nobel Prize in economics in 1982 for "his seminal studies of industrial structures, functioning of markets and causes and effects of public regulation."[13]

Stigler shared Blackstone's concern for protecting individual rights against government intrusion and abhorred the activist proposals of both Bentham and Landis, in which government intervention was the solution for the evils of society. However, Stigler's preferred alternative to centralized interventionist government was not Blackstone's accumulated wisdom of the ages, but the free market. Stigler established his faith in the superiority of the market over government orders early in life. He opposed price controls during World War II and believed that many wartime issues could be solved through market processes. He recounts:

> I received a note from Tjalling Koopmans asking whether I had really said that if Manhattan was bombed, the best way to evacuate the population would be to use the price system. I was taken aback by his letter, because I had not even thought of that problem. But I told Tjalling that the first time Manhattan was bombed *any* system of evacuation would be grotesquely confused and inefficient. If the bombings became repetitive, however, I thought the price system could handle the problem well.[14]

In 1971 Stigler proposed a theory of regulation in which he developed the thesis that "as a rule, regulation is acquired by the industry and is designed and operated primarily for its benefit" and distinguished his theory from the view that "regulation is instituted primarily for the protection and benefit of the public at large or some large subclass of the public."[15] He argued that industries could obtain privately beneficial but socially harmful regulation in a democratic society because of the voters' inability to register displeasure with small losses through the political process. Stigler concluded that the difficulties of regulation were fundamental to the political process and not something to be corrected by reforms in the agencies. He stated:

The idealistic view of public regulation is deeply imbedded in professional economic thought. So many economists, for example, have denounced the ICC for its pro-railroad policies that this has become a cliché of the literature. This criticism seems to me exactly as appropriate as a criticism of the Great Atlantic and Pacific Tea Company for selling groceries, or as a criticism of a politician for currying popular support. The fundamental vice of such criticism is that it misdirects attention: it suggests that the way to get an ICC which is not subservient to the carriers is to preach to the commissioners or to the people who appoint the commissioners. The only way to get a different commission would be to change the political support for the Commission, and reward commissioners on a basis unrelated to their services to the carriers.[16]

The Landis and Stigler interpretations of regulation are generally referred to as the "public interest theory" and the "capture theory" respectively. A vast literature elaborates both approaches.

Although Landis was a vigorous proponent of regulation and Stigler was a similarly vigorous opponent of regulation, their arguments do not deal with exactly the same questions. Landis assumed that extensive government intervention in the economy was necessary and focused his attention on how best to accomplish that intervention. His recommendation of industry-oriented commissions with concentrated powers was an alternative to government control through the existing executive, legislative, and judicial institutions, rather than an alternative to market forces. Stigler was unconcerned with the appropriate administrative institutions for regulation because he challenged the need for any government intervention.

Most of the literature on regulation prior to 1970 assumed that the basic purpose of regulation was to correct some market failure. Many difficulties with the operation and staffing of regulatory agencies were noted, and many proposals for improvements were suggested, but the public interest *goals* of regulation were seldom challenged. Stigler lamented in 1972:

> There is widespread agreement on the regulation of economic and social affairs in the United States. The subject is a relatively uncontroversial one. . . . A few people, indeed, believe that almost all regulation is bad, and by a singular coincidence a significant fraction of the academic part of this group resides within a radius of one mile of my university. . . .[17]

However, many economists who accepted the public interest goals of regulation expressed extreme dissatisfaction about its operation. F. M. Scherer's widely used industrial organization textbook stated: "The Supreme Power who conceived gravity, supply and demand, and the double helix must have been absorbed elsewhere when public utility regulation was invented."[18] While the Chicago economists sought the removal of all regulation, other economists generally distinguished industries such as electricity and communications in which service was provided under regulated monopoly from industries such as airlines and trucking in which service was provided under regulated competition. Important early works that advocated the removal of regulation from relatively competitive industries included John Meyer's 1959 study of transportation and Richard Caves's 1962 study of airlines.[19]

Information Economics and Transaction Costs

There is an extensive technical literature on the optimal structure of regulatory policies and institutions under conditions of incomplete information and opportunism.[20] These models assume unbounded rationality so that all participants can costlessly comprehend the implications of the information they have. Models have been developed for a wide variety of specific conditions in which individuals have different access to information and are expected to use their private information to the disadvantage of others who lack that information. Many of the models in this literature are directly related to regulatory issues.

The simplest case is the principal-agent problem. One person (the principal) hires another person (the agent) to perform a task. The benefit received by the principal is dependent upon the agent's actions plus a random component. The principal cannot directly observe the actions of the agent, and cannot definitely infer the actions of the agent because of the random component of the results. With no compensation differences, the agent prefers to take actions less likely to produce good results for the principal than to take actions more likely to produce good results (that is, prefers to be lazy than to work hard). The problem is to define a compensation mechanism that provides an incentive for the agent to take the actions most likely to produce good results for the principal. The general solution is sharing of the benefits of the final output between the principal and the agent, with the sharing proportions dependent upon which party is more willing to bear the risk of the random component of the final output.

Generalizations of the principal-agent problem to more complex cases tend to generate complex contracts as the proposed solution. Small changes in the structure of the problem lead to substantial differences in the proposed solution. For example, models of optimal regulatory mechanisms when the firm has more information about its costs than the regulator differ according to whether the regulator knows the firm's fixed cost but not its marginal cost, or knows the firm's marginal cost but not its fixed cost, or knows neither the fixed cost nor the private cost.[21] The complexity of the proposed mechanisms and their dependence upon the precise structure of the problem considered distinguish them from the observed mechanisms in either the government or the private sector. David Kreps states: "The models we analyzed suggested that optimal incentive schemes will in general be very complex, depending on the very fine structure of the environment. This is not a prediction that is verified empirically; incentive schemes in practice are usually quite simple."[22]

One explanation for the divergence between observed institutions and the optimal structures derived from information economics is that individuals are not able to comprehend the complex contracts proposed in the information economics literature. Oliver Williamson's transaction cost approach substitutes the assumption of bounded rationality for the unbounded rationality of the information economics literature, while retaining the assumptions of opportunism and differing access to information.[23] Transaction cost economics assumes that individuals attempt to make rational decisions in order to advance their own interest, but that they have limited abilities. If confronted with very complex contracts of the type proposed in the information economics literature, they would incur significant costs in attempting to understand them and make appropriate choices, and might make errors in their choices. Consequently, contracts should be relatively simple, with provisions for adjustment to take account of unexpected circumstances.

The transaction cost literature takes observed institutions much more seriously than most other economic writings. It attempts to understand the properties of existing institutions as methods of dealing with a complex environment under bounded rationality. Williamson summarizes the transaction cost approach as follows:

Transaction cost economics is a comparative institutional approach to the study of economic organization in which the transaction is made the basic unit of analysis. It is interdisciplinary, involving aspects of economics, law, and organization theory.

. . . transaction cost economics maintains the rebuttable presumption that organizational variety arises primarily in the service of transaction cost economizing. That approach is to be distinguished not merely from the technological approach to economic organization but also from power approaches, which ascribe nonstandard forms of organization to monopoly purposes or class interests.[24]

Information economics ignores institutions and focuses on market solutions. Problems that cause simple contracts to fail are solved with complex contracts tailored to the specific problem. Unbounded rationality allows individuals to write and follow extremely complex contracts without cost. It is assumed that contracts can be enforced. The assumption of bounded rationality in transaction cost economics gives very different prescriptions. Problems that cause simple contracts to fail are solved through institutions that substitute hierarchical control for complex contracts.

Preferences and Principles

Most economic writings assume that individuals have well-defined preferences over all relevant possibilities. In market analysis, an individual consumer's preferences are assumed to be related only to the various combinations of goods potentially available to that consumer and are assumed to be independent of the consumption bundles of other consumers. In collective choice problems, each individual is assumed to have preferences defined over all possible states of society. Such preferences may be contradictory among individuals, and may include preferences over many situations that would commonly be considered "none of one's business," such as how other individuals behave privately. In the formal structure of social choice, no attempt is made to evaluate or reconcile preferences, but rather the goal is to satisfy all preferences of the individuals in the society as much as possible. The best-known result in that tradition is Arrow's Impossibility Theorem: no social welfare function meeting specified conditions exists when all possible combinations of preferences are allowed.[25]

Although Arrow's elegant mathematical result was not published until 1950, the underlying idea that political systems do not work well if preferences vary widely enough has been implicit in political writings over a long period of time. Most authors have sought some way to abstract from individual personal interest, either by subordinating personal interest to goals of the state or by looking for shared values. Many writers have developed some version of the related generalization approaches of putting oneself in the position of another, or choosing the shape of society without knowing one's position in it, or choosing general rules that must apply to all. In the economics tradition, Harsanyi developed the concept of "ethical preferences" as the rankings of states of society that a person would choose if he or she had an equal chance of obtaining any position in the society.[26] Buchanan and Tullock used a similar concept in the economic analysis of the creation of constitutions when they assumed "that the individual, at the time of constitutional choice, is wholly uncertain as to what his role will be in the collective-decision process in the future."[27] The philosopher John Rawls has developed the uncertain position approach in great detail through his concept of choice in an original position under a "veil of ignorance," where individuals choose the kind of society they prefer without knowing what position they will occupy in the society.[28]

Amitai Etzioni has developed a related approach without postulating decision making under ignorance of one's own position in society. He assumes that individuals simultaneously have personal preferences of the ordinary economic kind and moral values that are shared by others. The two kinds of preferences may lead to conflicting results.[29]

While preferences are purely individual and are expected to routinely conflict with the preferences of other individuals, the goal of the generalization or moral value approaches is to find concepts that are universally accepted. An intermediate concept is the idea of "principles" that are widely (but not necessarily universally) accepted as desirable attributes of law or public policy. There may be a large number of principles that are widely accepted when considered in the abstract, but must be interpreted and adjusted when they are found to produce conflicting implications.

A strong view of principles has been developed by the legal philosopher Ronald Dworkin, who defined a "principle" as "a standard that is to be observed, not because it will advance or secure an economic, political, or social situation deemed desirable, but because it is a re-

quirement of justice or fairness or some other dimension of moral-
ity."[30] In Dworkin's view, principles become law only after having
been enunciated by a judge in a specific case, but the judge is not
creating a new concept. Rather, he is providing a particular formulation of accepted values and may even use those values to overturn
specific statutory law. Dworkin illustrates the use of principles with an
1889 inheritance case. A grandfather's will named his grandson as heir.
The grandson murdered the grandfather and claimed the inheritance.
Contrary to a strict reading of the written law, the court refused to
grant the inheritance to the grandson:

> It is quite true that statutes regulating the making, proof and effect of
> wills, and the devolution of property, if literally construed, and if
> their force and effect can in no way and under no circumstances be
> controlled or modified, give this property to the murderer.
> ... all laws as well as all contracts may be controlled in their op-
> eration and effect by general, fundamental maxims of the common
> law. No one shall be permitted to profit by his own fraud, or to take
> advantage of his own wrong, or to found any claim upon his own
> iniquity, or to acquire property by his own crime.[31]

Dworkin's strong view of principles elevates principles to the level of
moral values that create rights that should not be abridged by judges
even if those rights are not written into law or past cases. A weaker view
of principles has commonly been used in the public policy process.
Under that weaker view, principles are broad goals of policy that are
valued for their own sake as distinguished from the specific policy
actions that are designed to accomplish those goals. Such principles are
widely accepted and therefore more influential in public policy than
personal preferences, but they do not create absolute rights as the
Dworkin view of principles suggests.

Principles are not decisive in themselves, but require interpretation
and application to specific cases. Individuals who subscribe to particular principles do not necessarily have a clear expectation regarding all
the implications of those principles, nor do they necessarily agree with
others who subscribe to the same principles on the proper application
of those principles to any particular case. Ignorance of the specific
applications may simplify the problem of agreement on a particular
principle. Thus congressional representatives may be able to agree on
the principle that rates shall be free of "unreasonable discrimination"

and enact it into law (leaving the interpretation and application to a separate entity) while they would not be able to agree whether particular tariffs that affected known constituents were consistent with that principle.

Conclusion

The Blackstone, Hayek, and Stigler approaches all caution against attempting to design an optimal policy process. Even though Blackstone's ideal was the recovery of the pure law of the Saxon times that had been corrupted by the Norman invasion, and Stigler's ideal was the recovery of the pure free market that had been corrupted by government intervention in the economy, they shared the confidence that no individual could create a system better than the one that had evolved through a vast number of individual decisions.

Bentham, Landis, and current information economics theorists all advocate replacing observed processes with ideal ones created through explicit reasoning processes. They share a higher view of human abilities and are less concerned about controlling abuses of power than the authors who emphasize the advantage of evolving institutions.

Williamson occupies an intermediate position between the two approaches. He examines existing institutions in the light of economic theory to clarify their useful characteristics. Williamson neither assumes that the observed institutions are the best possible (Blackstone) nor ignores them altogether (Bentham). Instead, he looks for how a particular institution may be useful in reducing transaction costs.

The position taken in this book on government institutions is similar to the Williamson position on corporate institutions. Existing processes and structures are not necessarily optimal but should be seriously examined for potential useful properties. Williamson found that many corporate institutions that appeared unrelated to proper business needs under the assumption of unbounded rationality and zero transaction costs could be seen as appropriate once bounded rationality and actual transaction costs were taken into account. Similarly, in this book the decentralized policy process appears more useful when the full complexity of the environment (opportunism, differing political values, asymmetric information, and bounded rationality) is taken into account than when some issues are assumed away in order to make a tractable mathematical model.

The standard economic views are divided on the range of preferences that must be taken into account in constructing public policy. On the one hand, most formal theoretical models assume a wide range of individual preferences, with nothing that necessarily causes individuals to desire the same policies. On the other hand, much of the applied policy-oriented economic literature seeks to maximize allocative efficiency as if that were a universally accepted value. Many political theorists, philosophers, and moralists have attempted to construct values that are or ought to be universally held. The concept of multiple, widely shared principles that may conflict is a weak version of the effort to construct unanimously accepted values. As discussed in later chapters, principles have been commonly used in the policy process to coordinate the choices of independent policy powers.

3 / A Model of the Decentralized Policy Process

The U.S. government structure clearly diffuses power with the separation of powers among the executive, legislative, and judicial branches of the federal government and the division of power between the federal and state governments. Samuel Beer emphasizes the distinction between the federal system and delegation of power to a subordinate entity:

> Federalism is not mere decentralization, even where decentralization is substantial and persistent. Any polity except the very smallest will have territorial subdivisions. In a unitary system the bodies governing these subdivisions will receive their authority from the ordinary statutory law of the central government. The distinctive thing about a federal system is that the authority of these bodies is assured by a law which is superior to the statutory law of the center and which indeed is also the source of authority of that law. Decentralization is constitutional, not merely statutory.[1]

The vast commentary on the theory and practice of federalism and separation of powers generally assumes that a particular power clearly belongs in a single category of government. Debates over the proper dividing line among the various power centers have been routine since the ratification of the Constitution, but the disputants have generally agreed that the power belongs in one category or the other and that multiple power centers should not be simultaneously making policy on the same issue.

As discussed in Chapter 2, the Landis theory of regulatory agencies

27

sought to centralize power by creating an agency that was outside of the existing three branches of the federal government and contained powers of all three branches. In actual practice, regulatory agencies have tended to diffuse power rather than centralizing it. In telecommunication in particular, the FCC is an additional power center that overlaps but does not replace efforts to make telecommunication policy in the executive, legislative, and judicial branches of the federal government as well as in the state government agencies.

The vague dividing lines among the various constitutional power centers, followed by an effort to centralize power through creating agencies outside of the three branches, followed by efforts to limit the power of those agencies and reassert the power of the three branches, have created the opportunity for policies on the same issue to be acted on simultaneously in multiple forums. Furthermore, policies on a particular issue within a particular agency are the result of the efforts of multiple actions by different individuals over a long period of time. FCC rules, for example, are modified individually in separate proceedings. A new leader may desire a change in policy but can only modify a small number of rules during his or her tenure, with the final result being a mixture of old rules created by others and a few new rules. The frequent changes in the persons occupying senior federal positions cause policies in a single agency to be the result of the actions of multiple people over time.

The model developed in this chapter departs from the classic debates over where a particular power should be located. Instead, it assumes that a large number of agents take independent policy actions. The agents may be spread among various branches of the government, but there are no clear dividing lines that limit the actions of a particular agent. Actions by one agent remain in effect until explicitly repealed by the actions of another agent. The final policy result is a mixture of the actions of agents spread across different agencies and different time periods. The properties of the model are not developed formally, and no mathematical expertise is required for understanding this chapter.

One way to visualize the policy model developed in this chapter is to consider the current policy as the location of a large boat in a body of water. Many swimmers are in the water, each with a different idea of where the boat should be positioned. Swimmers are randomly chosen and sequentially allowed to give the boat a push in that swimmer's preferred direction. If the boat is near the center of the preferences of the swimmers, the pushes will cancel over a period of time. The boat will not have any consistent direction, though it will move slightly in a random way as each swimmer attempts to position it in that swimmer's preferred position. If the average preferences change, then more participants will push in a single direction and the boat will eventually be relocated to the center of the new preferences.

The decentralized public policy process is analogous to the decentralized methods of academic research. In academic research, there is no central coordinating agency or clear lines of demarcation on the projects undertaken by various individuals and research groups. Multiple research groups may work independently on the same problem while no one is working on other important problems as a result of the choices made by independent decision makers. As a preface to discussion of the decentralized policy model, this chapter first reviews the efforts of Michael Polanyi to defend the decentralized scientific research process against efforts to provide centralized control of such research.

The Coordination of Decentralized Public Policy and of Scientific Research

During and after World War II there were numerous proposals in Britain for the rationalization and coordination of scientific research. The belief that Soviet science was advancing rapidly as a result of central planning, together with the observation that most British scientific projects were chosen primarily by the individual senior scientist without central control, led numerous scientists to believe that greater planning was needed. In opposition to that movement, Michael Polanyi developed a justification for decentralized scientific decisions modeled on the decentralized market process. Polanyi wrote:

> I have described how this movement evoked among many British scientists a desire to give deliberate social purpose to the pursuit of science. It offended their social conscience that the advancement of science, which affects the interests of society as a whole, should be carried on by individual scientists pursuing their own personal interests. They argued that all public welfare must be safeguarded by public authorities and that scientific activities should therefore be directed by the government in the interest of the public. This reform should replace by deliberate action towards a declared aim the present

growth of scientific knowledge intended as a whole by no one, and in fact not even known in its totality, except quite dimly, to any single person.[2]

In opposition to the calls for centralized control of scientific initiatives, Polanyi asserted:

Such self-co-ordination of independent initiatives leads to a joint result which is unpremeditated by any of those who bring it about. Their co-ordination is guided as by 'an invisible hand' towards the joint discovery of a hidden system of things. Since its end-result is unknown, this kind of co-operation can only advance stepwise, and the total performance will be the best possible if each consecutive step is decided upon by the person most competent to do so. . . .

I am suggesting, in fact, that the co-ordinating functions of the market are but a special case of co-ordination by mutual adjustment. In the case of science, adjustment takes place by taking note of the published results of other scientists; while in the case of the market, mutual adjustment is mediated by a system of prices broadcasting current exchange relations, which make supply meet demand.[3]

Polanyi claimed to show that decentralized scientific decision making creates optimal choices. Although he made an analogy to the market process, he did not develop his theory formally or provide a clear criterion for distinguishing optimal results from nonoptimal results. Polanyi's case for decentralized decision making rested on two foundations:

1. The necessary information for good decisions is dispersed among the individual scientists. No central coordinator will know enough about what problems are most important and what problems can be solved to perform a useful coordinating function.
2. The decentralized scientific effort is not random, but is coordinated by the common observation of published results and by shared beliefs and standards that determine what gets published and whose work is accepted.

Polanyi asserted that most scientists share three common criteria for evaluating scientific work and use those criteria to reach similar decisions regarding what should be published and who should be appointed to prestigious university positions. The first criterion is "a sufficient degree of plausibility." Polanyi suggested that both at the initial research proposal stage and at the publication stage, scientific research must be closely related to the currently accepted norms of "how the world works." He wrote:

> It is indeed difficult even to start an experimental inquiry if its problem is considered scientifically unsound. Few laboratories would accept today a student of extrasensory perception, and even a project for testing once more the hereditary transmission of acquired characters would be severely discouraged from the start. Besides, even when all these obstacles have been overcome, and a paper has come out signed by an author of high distinction in science, it may be totally disregarded, simply for the reason that its results conflict sharply with the current scientific opinion about the nature of things.[4]

The second criterion is a measure of scientific value determined by accuracy, systematic importance, and intrinsic interest of its subject matter, while the third is originality. Polanyi believed that the first two criteria tend to encourage conformity while the third encourages dissent, setting up a creative tension:

> The professional standards of science must impose a framework of discipline and at the same time encourage rebellion against it. They must demand that, in order to be taken seriously, an investigation should largely conform to the currently predominant beliefs about the nature of things, while allowing that in order to be original it may to some extent go against these. Thus, the authority of scientific opinion enforces the teachings of science in general, for the very purpose of fostering their subversion in particular points.[5]

Polanyi related his conception of science as a "dynamic orthodoxy" to the political conservatism of Edmund Burke (emphasizing respect for tradition and the accumulated wisdom of the ages, as did Blackstone) and the radicalism of Thomas Paine (emphasizing the ability of society to choose the current best solution independent of tradition, as did Bentham). He claimed that the scientific coordination process united parts of both traditions by using commonly accepted values to impose order on new approaches:

> This view transcends the conflict between Edmund Burke and Tom Paine. It rejects Paine's demand for the absolute self-determination of each generation, but does so for the sake of its own ideal of unlimited human and social improvement. It accepts Burke's thesis that freedom must be rooted in tradition, but transposes it into a system cultivating radical progress. It rejects the dream of a society in

which all will labour for a common purpose, determined by the will of the people. For in the pursuit of excellence it offers no part to the popular will and accepts a condition of society in which the public interest is known only fragmentarily and is left to be achieved as the outcome of individual initiatives aiming at fragmentary problems. Viewed through the eyes of socialism, this ideal of a free society is conservative and fragmented, and hence adrift, irresponsible, selfish, apparently chaotic.[6]

The view of regulatory policy developed in this book has many similarities to Polanyi's perspective on the decentralized scientific co-ordination process. In both cases there are multiple decision makers working from a common set of public information and combining that with their own private information. In both cases, the participants in the process have a mixture of individual freedom to follow their own goals and constraints in the form of commonly accepted values and norms of evaluation.

The Structure of the Decentralized Policy Model

The Nature of Public Policy

In this model, public policy is viewed as a continuous quantity rather than a single discrete decision. Policy is the output of a combination of public capital goods. It is convenient to think of each possible public capital good as a combination of rules. Once rules are passed, they remain in effect until they are repealed. It requires effort to pass rules, or equivalently, requires investment in the public capital good. It also requires effort (investment) to repeal a rule. An agent (administrator) who believes an existing rule is inappropriate cannot simply ignore or immediately repeal it. That agent must devote the same level of effort to repealing a rule as was devoted to passing it in the first place.

In economic terms, the passing of a rule is an investment in a public capital good. The quantity of that good may be increased by passing additional rules and may be decreased by repealing existing rules. The set of rules in effect is a public good because it applies to all people in the applicable jurisdiction. All individuals in the jurisdiction consume the "benefits" of the collection of rules, either directly through the operation of rules on various firms or indirectly through the effect of the rules on the prices and availability of goods that consumers desire.

For any particular person and particular rule, the "benefits" may be either positive or negative. The collection of rules is a capital good because it remains in effect until explicitly repealed. A future set of individuals continues to receive the effects of rules passed by earlier individuals unless they take explicit action to repeal those rules.

There are many possible types of public capital goods corresponding to different types of collections of rules. For example, in telecommunication, the "access charge rules" are one particular type of rules consisting of a large collection of specific rules relating to the payments of long distance carriers to local carriers. That set of rules may be increased or decreased through FCC action. The set of rules related to the allocation of licenses for cellular carriers would constitute a distinct public capital good.

The current state of public policy is the combination of the output of all of the capital goods. It is convenient to choose units so that the total quantity of all policy capital goods is 1. This convention requires thinking of the "repeal" of one rule as the investment in a rule with opposite effect. Thus when all investments have been made, the total set of capital goods adds up to 1 even though some rules may effectively negate other rules.

Agents

Agents are appointed to their positions rather than being elected officials responsible to a particular constituency. In practice, agents are appointed to various positions that influence telecommunication policy (FCC or state commissioner, senior commission staff member with decision-making authority, senior congressional staff, judges, subcabinet officials in the executive branch of the federal government, senior state officials) for a wide variety of reasons. In the model, agents are randomly selected from the population. Assume that n agents are randomly selected from the population, where n is large enough to provide a representative sample of the population.

Each agent is given an endowment equal to the investment required to purchase $1/n$ unit of a public capital good. The agents appear sequentially. Each agent evaluates the existing set of public capital goods (rules), invests the available endowment in the combination of capital goods that the particular agent prefers, and then disappears. Each agent's decision is made independently of that of other agents except as the previous agents' decisions are reflected in the existing stock of rules. There is no bargaining process or voting process among the agents. The process is analogous to the competitive market in which each consumer chooses independently of other consumers in accordance with the consumer's preferences, the budget constraint, and the existing set of prices. In the policy model, the agent chooses investments in a public good in accordance with that agent's preferences and endowment, and the cost of the public good.

In practice, different agents of the government can accomplish different amounts. They come to the process with different amounts of "political capital" which they can use to move policy in their preferred direction. However, the structure of the administrative institutions generally leads to slow changes in rules and rapid turnover of agents. Thus any agent must set priorities as to the most important things to initiate or change. This is equivalent to a limited endowment with a price of adding to any particular public capital good. A decision to change rules in one area effectively means a decision to leave rules in another area as they are even though the agent might prefer that they be changed.

An agent's decision to invest in particular kinds of public policy capital has two separate effects:

1. It changes the set of rules in the economy (changes the quantity of particular public capital goods).
2. It affects the personal welfare of the decision maker, through the effect of the decision on his/her business interests, reputation, or direct payments.

Preferences

Agents have two kinds of preferences corresponding to the two effects of their action:

1. Agents have preferences over the shape of society independent of the effect on them personally.
2. Agents have personal preferences based on the effect of action on them and their own concerns, for money, prestige, future job opportunities, and so forth.

The first type of preference corresponds to a decision maker's vision of the good society. It is generally expressed in general principles rather than specific policies. It corresponds to the principles discussed by Dworkin, or the "original position" discussed by Rawls, or the "ethical preferences" discussed by Harsanyi and Sen (see Chapter 2). It is the preference of the agent when abstracting from personal interest and looking to the interest of society as a whole, and will be referred to by Harsanyi's term "ethical preferences" to distinguish them from ordinary personal preferences.

For this model, assume that ethical preferences can be expressed on a limited number of dimensions. Individuals share the particular dimensions, but they may differ on how conflicts among the accepted principles should be resolved. For example, most individuals would agree that both equity and efficiency are desirable attributes of public policy, but there would be less agreement on how much equity should be sacrificed in order to gain a particular increase in efficiency. In the illustrations of the model, it will be assumed that efficiency and equity are the two relevant dimensions of ethical preferences, though it makes no difference if the dimensions are relabeled or additional dimensions of ethical preferences are added.

No assumption is made concerning the way in which agents trade off ethical preferences against personal interest preferences. Some agents may be entirely selfish (assigning zero weight to ethical preferences), while others are entirely public-spirited (assigning zero weight to personal interest preferences) and still others consider both the public and private aspects of a decision simultaneously (as Etzioni suggests in his discussion of conflict between moral values and personal interest).

The State of the World

The implications of individual rules are often obscure. For example, one particular rule related to the computation of payments from interexchange carriers to local exchange carriers states:

> The charge for an LS2 premium access minute shall be computed by dividing the premium Local Switching revenue requirement by the sum of the projected LS2 premium access minutes and a number that is computed by multiplying the projected LS1 premium access minutes by the applicable LS1 transition factor. The charge for an LS1 premium access minute shall be computed by multiplying the charge for an LS2 premium access minute by the applicable LS1 transition factor.[7]

The quoted rule was part of an effort to quietly provide particular advantages to certain companies that became so complex that the staff experts drafting the initial rule created language that had a different effect from the intended political deal.

Agents cannot pass rules of the form, "increase efficiency." If the agent's goal is to increase efficiency, that agent must pass a rule (or repeal an existing rule) that places a specific legal requirement on the firms in the industry and is expected to improve efficiency given the empirical conditions in the industry. In the language of the model, the agent must translate the potential investments in various types of policy capital into both personal interests and ethical space. In the example rule quoted above, one would need considerable information and analysis regarding the effect of the rule in order to judge its effect on efficiency and equity.

The effect of a particular rule may change when external circumstances change. A rule designed for a monopoly environment will not necessarily be changed when competition is added, but the effects of the rule on equity and efficiency will change. At the time a rule is passed, it is based on a particular evaluation of the "state of the world" at that time, and therefore on the effect the rule will have. Rules may become obsolete when the circumstances that led to their creation change, but they remain in effect until repealed.

Contingent markets and contracts based on the state of the world are a common structure in economic theory, and that is the essential concept used here. However, most theory assumes that the contracts themselves are contingent upon the state of the world. At some particular time, the state of the world is revealed and then contracts are fulfilled in accordance with that state of the world. In this model, the rules themselves are not contingent on the state of the world; they remain in effect from the time passed until the time repealed regardless of whether the state of the world changes during that time. Only the agent's evaluation of those rules varies with changes in the state of the world.

A change in policy induces an industry response, which may result in a new industry structure. A key theme of the empirical chapters of this study is the evolution of policy in response to changing industry structure while the industry structure is changing in response to earlier policy initiatives. In the model, industry responses are included as part of the state of the world.

Information

Information on the state of the world comes in the form of "signals" that suggest distinctions among various states of the world, but do not necessarily definitively distinguish potential states of the world. The determination of the state of the world for policy purposes is dependent both on the signals (information) available to the agent and on the agent's skill in interpreting those signals correctly. A great deal of expert study is devoted to determining the state of the world from ambiguous signals.

In contrast to the normal contingent markets formulation, no state of the world is ever clearly revealed so that all agree on the state of the world. Instead, different agents determine policies based on their view of the state of the world even though those views may be contradictory. For example, the Department of Justice and the FCC both sought increased efficiency in telecommunication, but disagreed on the degree of economies of scope among telecommunication services produced by local telephone companies. The Modified Final Judgment restrictions on local company activities are based on a state of the world in which economies of scope between allowed and prohibited activities are non-existent. The FCC's Computer III rules are based on a state of the world in which economies of scope are substantial. The available evidence is not definitive enough to convince all relevant parties of the true state of the world, and thus the independent policy makers adopt different policies based on their views of the true state of the world even when they are seeking to implement similar goals.

Even though decisions are made independently, an agent may attempt to influence another agent's decision by explicitly creating signals about the state of the world and the effects of particular policies. These efforts include all of the ordinary political communication tools for shaping a debate and justifying a particular policy. They may also include the commissioning of expert studies that are expected to confirm the agent's view of the state of the world and convince other independent decision makers of the correctness of that assessment. They may include specific policies designed to generate publicly available data that will support the current agent's policy choices. For example, as discussed in Chapter 11, the FCC's efforts during the mid-1980s to strictly regulate AT&T's prices (despite a general policy toward reducing regulation) were designed in part to generate rapidly falling long distance prices in order to increase the support of other parties for the continued implementation of the access charge plan.

Bounded Rationality

The model assumes that agents make decisions under bounded rationality. Many of the implications of limited information and bounded rationality are similar, which has caused some authors to propose that they be considered in the same category. However, limited information and bounded rationality have different implications for the design of a policy process. With limited information and unbounded rationality (the information economics case), individuals are able to correctly perceive all logical inferences in the available data and are not confused by apparently inconsistent information or the form in which information is packaged. In contrast, with bounded rationality, individuals may be influenced by the form in which information is presented and may be confused by additional noisy information. Bobrow and Dryzek present a colorful description of the use of information under bounded rationality:

> [The decision maker] ignores much pertinent information, treats the information he does use in odd ways, grossly oversimplifies problems and action alternatives, attends to only a few aspects of utility, and is highly selective in the lessons he learns from experience. He also gives undue weight to concrete examples in assessing probabilities of future outcomes. His most potent memories are vivid images of a few events. His information-processing capacity is highly limited; hence increased information may impair his decisions.[8]

Bounded rationality is the justification for the common legal requirement that regulatory decisions be based on a particular set of information put into the record of the relevant proceeding. With unbounded rationality, there would be no reason to structure the relevant information set because all decision makers could utilize all available information. Lobbying restrictions are potentially useful under bounded rationality because decision makers could be unduly influenced by the particular form in which information is presented, whereas such restrictions are harmful under unbounded rationality because they restrict the flow of information to the decision maker.
    Given an agent's policy goals and belief regarding the state of the

world, it still requires considerable analysis to relate any particular proposed rule to changes in the agent's ethical preferences. For example, the economic theory of the efficiency of marginal cost pricing was the connecting link between the policy action of the creation of the Subscriber Line Charge and the goal of increased telephone industry efficiency (see Chapter 10). With unbounded rationality, all agents automatically understand the implications of any proposed action on their policy goals. With bounded rationality, an agent's choice of policy instruments is likely to be influenced by that agent's professional training. For example, economists are more likely to understand the efficiency implications of a proposed action (and possibly to misunderstand other implications) than those trained in other disciplines because economics gives such extensive attention to efficiency.

The Operation of the Process

Individual agents appear sequentially as policy makers. Each has the power to independently implement a small amount of policy change by investing that agent's available endowment in one of the public capital goods. Each agent's decision is a function of:

1. The agent's ethical and personal preferences.
2. The agent's view of the state of the world.
3. The agent's view of the relationship between potential policy actions and the ranking of the resulting public policy on that agent's ethical and personal preferences, given the state of the world.

Agents may make errors in choosing policy to implement their preferences through lack of information or lack of skill at using the available information. The result of the process is a set of rules developed over time for different preferences, different states of the world, and different perceptions of the relationship between individual rules and final results.

Policy changes as new agents are appointed for three different reasons:

1. The new agent may have different preferences than the previous agent did.
2. The new agent may have a different perception of the state of the world or the relationship between policies and ethical preferences

than the previous agent, even though the actual state of the world remains the same.

3. The state of the world may have changed, and therefore even agents with the same preferences and correct perceptions of the state of the world will implement different rules.

Examples of the Decentralized Policy Model

This section illustrates the operation of the decentralized policy model with a series of examples, beginning with the simplest case and then adding various complications. Each case is based on the structure illustrated in Figure 1. Individuals have ethical preferences over two dimensions, efficiency (the horizontal axis) and equity (the vertical axis). Sixty percent of the population is concerned only with maximizing efficiency and is indifferent to the level of equity, while the re-

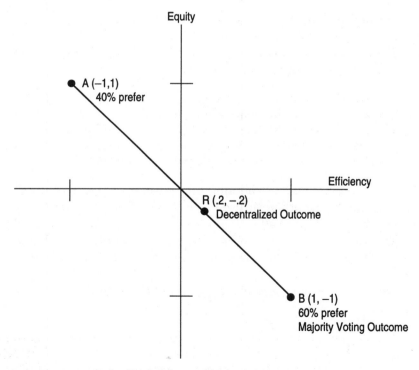

Figure 1.   Decentralized Policy Equilibrium

maining forty percent is concerned only with maximizing equity and is indifferent to the level of efficiency.

There are two types of policies available. Policy A maximizes equity at the cost of efficiency. One unit of policy A (meaning all agents choose A because the sum of all choices adds up to one) produces the result $(-1, 1)$ in efficiency-equity space, labeled as the point A on Figure 1. Policy B maximizes efficiency at the cost of equity, and one unit of B produces the point $(1, -1)$. The feasible set of policies in efficiency-equity space consists of all combinations of the results of A and B, represented by the line segment joining A and B. Society as a whole can be anywhere along that line segment, but cannot be above it. The line segment joining A and B is the policy equivalent of the production possibility frontier.

Under these conditions, the institution of direct majority voting would leave society at point B. Because sixty percent of the population prefers B over any other feasible point, the preferences of the minority for point A have no weight.

Case 1: No Complications

For this case, assume full information, unbounded rationality, constant state of the world, and no opportunism. Thus all agents correctly perceive the results of the policies and are only concerned with the social outcome. The only issue is the differing views regarding the type of policies that are socially beneficial. Under the decentralized process, 60 percent of the agents invest their endowment in policies of type B while 40 percent invest their endowment in policies of type A. The result is a policy mixture consisting of .6 unit of B and .4 unit of A. That generates the result $(.2, -.2)$, labeled as R in Figure 1. The result is a weighted average of the preferences of the population. Minority preferences count just the same as majority preferences. The final policy is more of B than A because a greater percentage of the population prefers B, but the minority views get implemented whenever a member of the minority population is chosen as an agent.

Case 2: Opportunism

Opportunism can be represented by adding a measure of the personal effect on the agent represented on the z axis. Thus to the vector $(1, -1)$

in Figure 1, we would add an additional dimension such as $(1, -1, .5)$ to show that choosing to invest all of an agent's endowment in policy B provides a private benefit of .5 to that particular agent. Suppose that there are now four possible types of public capital that produce the results:

> A: $(-1, 1, 0)$
> B: $(1, -1, 0)$
> C: $(-1, 1.5, .5)$
> D: $(-1, .5, 1)$

Types A and B are identical to Case 1; the zero in the third dimension indicates that the agent gains no personal advantage from choosing either one of them. Type C is a variation on A in which the social results are superior (same efficiency, improved equity) and for which the agent also gains a personal advantage. Type D is a variation on A in which the social results are inferior (same efficiency, reduced equity) but for which the personal advantage is maximized.

Clearly, type C is superior to A and ought to be chosen by those who prefer to maximize equity. However, agents primarily interested in personal welfare will choose D over either C or A because it has the maximum personal benefit even though it has a low social benefit. It is often difficult or impossible for society (other than the agent involved) to distinguish between policies of types C and D. An agent may choose D in order to maximize personal advantage and claim the choice was made in order to maximize social equity without the rest of society being able to evaluate the honesty of the agent.

In the economic literature, opportunism problems have been dealt with extensively. The most common solution is some version of a sharing mechanism in which the agent's incentives for self-dealing are recognized and incorporated into the mechanism. A wide variety of specific mechanisms have been proposed depending upon the precise structure of the problem. The government approach has been quite different. Rather than allowing any risk sharing or participation shares that might induce truthful activity, the government has attempted to eliminate all actions for which the agent benefits personally. That is, the entire range of complex rules regarding procurement ethics, stock ownership, post-employment restrictions, and so forth can be summarized as an attempt to create "disinterested" agents whose official actions make no difference in their personal welfare other than as related to their preferences for a desirable kind of society.

The observed institutional mechanisms applied to the above four social goods would simply eliminate C and D as feasible options. Types A and B would be allowed because neither produces any personal effects on the individual. Type C represents a "good" way to improve equity by going beyond the impersonal government structures, while type D represents a "bad" way in which overall equity is harmed in order to shift income to the agent. The inability to distinguish between the types has led to a broad-brush approach in which any decision that produces personal benefit is assumed to be taken for the wrong reasons. Ethics rules have become stricter in recent years than in the past, with a consequent reduction in the range of feasible government actions.

The proposals in the economic literature for dealing with opportunism violate the government ethics rules because the economic proposals are based on using self-interest to promote the interest of the principal. The weaker the self-interest, the weaker are the economic mechanisms. The government ethics rules assume that individuals with no self-interest in a proposal will evaluate it according to the public interest standards that they hold, but that self-interest will cause them to choose policies that are personally beneficial. The economic approach, on the other hand, assumes that individuals care only about self-interest and seeks to harness that self-interest to the goals of the principal. The economic approach would attempt to create personal responsibility for the outcomes of particular policies, with rewards for successful policies and punishments for unsuccessful ones. Such an approach is fundamentally different from the observed one, and is inconsistent with the overall decentralized process in which policies are a mixture of the decisions of many different people, with the outcome impossible to attribute to any one of them.

The effort to eliminate personal interest from government decision making does not mean that individuals have no reward for participating in government. Individual agents receive a salary and often receive later career benefits simply from having served in a responsible position. However, the existing system largely removes the economic link between compensation and accomplishments in the position. Essentially the same compensation is received regardless of the actual decisions made or the effort put into the position.

Compared to the standard economic prescriptions, the existing mechanisms for dealing with opportunism contain two faults:

1. They restrict the feasible set of actions and thereby potentially eliminate actions that would be socially beneficial.
2. They break the tie between personal action and personal benefit that is presumed to provide the incentive for intense work.

However, given the complex existing environment, it is not clear that a mechanism could be designed to provide a consistent positive correlation between personal benefit and public interest. In any case, the model is designed to represent existing institutions, and therefore will simply eliminate from the feasible set activity vectors that make the personal welfare of the agent depend upon the activity chosen.

Case 3: Changes in the State of the World

Assume that there are two possible states of the world, $s = 1$ and $s = 2$. The results of different policy actions must now be represented as vectors contingent upon the state of the world. Policy A of Case 1 is now divided into policy A1 (appropriate for $s = 1$) and policy A2 (appropriate for $s = 2$), with a corresponding division for policy B. The potential policies can be represented as follows:

A1: $\{(-1, 1)$ if $s = 1;$ $(-1.5, .5)$ if $s = 2\}$
A2: $\{(-1.5, .5)$ if $s = 1;$ $(-1, 1)$ if $s = 2\}$
B1: $\{(1, -1)$ if $s = 1;$ $(.5, -1.5)$ if $s = 2\}$
B2: $\{(.5, -1.5)$ if $s = 1;$ $(1, -1)$ if $s = 2\}$

The possibilities are illustrated in Figure 2. When the state of the world is correctly matched with the appropriate policies, the social possibilities are the same as in Figure 1. That is, the choice of policy A1 when the state of the world is 1 and the choice of policy A2 when the state of the world is 2 result in maximizing equity at the expense of efficiency. However, a mismatch of the policy type and the state of the world results in a shift downward and to the left (the dashed line in Figure 2), where both efficiency and equity are below the maximum possible. The choice of A1 when the state of the world is 2 or the

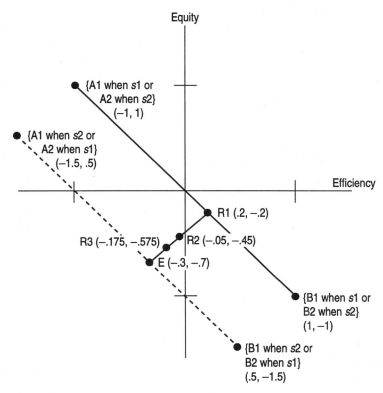

Figure 2.   Outcome Contingent on the State of the World

choice of A2 when the state of the world is 1 results in reduced social performance.

Assume that initially the world is in state 1, but that after half the agents have made a choice the world switches to state 2. Assume that all agents recognize the state of the world and recognize the relationship of policies to the state of the world. The first half of the agents will perceive that the state of the world is 1, and those who favor A policies will invest their endowment in A1 while those who favor B policies will invest their endowment in B1. The second half of the agents will perceive that the state of the world is 2, and those who favor A policies will invest in A2 while those who favor B policies will invest in B2. However, the rules adopted when the state of the world was 1 will remain in effect.

The final result is a combination of the results of all four types of social capital (.2 of A1, .2 of A2, .3 of B1, and .3 of B2). At the end of the process (when the state of the world is 2), the result will be at (−.05, −.45), labeled as R2 in Figure 2. The result is halfway between the result of Case 1 (R1 on Figure 2) and the result that would occur if all policies were chosen with the wrong state of the world (E on Figure 2). The individuals correctly perceive the state of the world and choose policies to correspond to it, but because old policies remain in effect until repealed, half of the policies in effect at the end no longer correspond to the current state of the world.

The above discussion assumes that individuals correctly perceive the state of the world but do not predict changes in the state of the world. Very knowledgeable agents might be able to predict that the state of the world would change to 2 and adopt "forward-looking" policies of type A2 and B2 even when the observed state of the world was 1. Policies based on predicted changes in the environment are often met with great skepticism and are difficult to defend against charges that they are "speculative" and not based on the record. Most policies are created either for current observed conditions or for conditions observed sometime in the past. Consequently, as the state of the world changes, the rules begin having a different effect from what was expected at the time they were developed.

The changing state of the world and the capital nature of the decentralized process represent an important limitation on the observed administrative process. The faster the state of the world changes, the less efficient the process becomes. The regulatory process, or the decentralized administrative process in general, is much better suited to a relatively stable environment than to a rapidly changing one. The decentralized process is an institutional mechanism for combining a wide range of opinion with slowly changing policies. It is not observed when quick decisions in response to a rapidly changing environment are imperative, as in military operations.

Case 4: Limited Information and Bounded Rationality

Consider the same situation as Case 3 (the state of the world is 1 initially and switches to 2 after half the agents have made a choice), but now assume that the early agents correctly perceive the state of the world, but that not all later agents recognize the shift from $s = 1$ to $s = 2$. The failure to recognize the shift may be a result of either incomplete information (signals not fully informative as to the state of the world) or bounded rationality (informative signals not completely understood), or some combination of both. As discussed in the previous section, limited information and bounded rationality are not identical. However, in the simple structure of this example they produce the same effect.

Assume that half of the later agents correctly perceive that the state of the world has shifted while the other half continue to believe that the state of the world has remained in its original position. Formally, this is equivalent to uninformative signals because there are only two states of the world and therefore random choice would generate correct choices half of the time. However, in the regulatory context considerable credible information would be necessary to cause even half of the individuals to adjust policies to a new state of the world rather than continuing with previously successful policies based on the old state of the world. Even the dramatic public event of the AT&T divestiture did not convince some FCC staff members that there was any need to change policies to accommodate a new industry structure.

The first half of the agents choose either A1 or B1 in accordance with their correct perception that the state of the world is 1 and according to their preference for policies of type A or B. Twenty-five percent choose either A1 or B1 in the mistaken belief that the state of world remains 1 when it has actually shifted to 2. Twenty-five percent choose either A2 or B2 in the correct belief that the state of the world has shifted to 2. The final result is composed of .30 A1, .10 A2, .45 B1, and .15 B2. The individual agents divide 40 percent to 60 percent over policies of type A versus type B in accordance with their ethical preferences. They divide 75 percent to 25 percent over policies of type 1 versus type 2 in accordance with their (not necessarily correct) perceptions of the state of the world and therefore with their perceptions of which policies best implement their ethical preferences.

Because the actual state of the world is 2 at the end of the process, the results in equity-efficiency space are determined for state 2. The result is labeled R3 on Figure 2. It is inferior to R2 on both dimensions because of the errors in choosing policies to match the state of the world. The point R3 is 75 percent of the way from R1 (all policies matched correctly to the state of the world) to E (all policies incorrectly matched) because 75 percent of the policy choices were based on a state of the world different from the one at the end of the process.

Conclusion

Most political writing assumes either a voting mechanism or a bargaining mechanism. The observed administrative process contains elements of both voting and bargaining, but it is particularly characterized by a large number of independent decision makers. This chapter has outlined a simple model of a decentralized public decision-making process. The essential idea is that policy is the result of a large number of past decisions that can be represented as investments in public capital goods. The decentralized process provides for representation of a variety of political viewpoints through the actions of a large number of agents, each attempting to implement his or her own political preferences. It also provides for representation of a variety of views on the state of the world and the appropriate policies to relate any particular state of the world to the desired political viewpoint.

The observed policy process is dominated by missing information and bounded rationality. There is rarely time available or information available to perform the rational computations advocated in economic and formal decision-making literature. An important source of political dispute is differing views on the state of the world and the effects that policies will have on that state of the world. The decentralized process allows many views to be partially implemented. It does not necessarily sort out the views or cause the best one to be implemented, but it causes the final combination of policies to be weighted toward the appropriate ones for accomplishing the mix of political objectives in the existing state of the world.

4 / Institutions of Telecommunication Policy

This chapter presents a brief overview of the main institutions responsible for telecommunication policy. The Communications Act of 1934 and the organization of the Federal Communications Commission (FCC) are discussed in some detail, followed by a review of other major institutions that contribute to telecommunication policy. The chapter does not provide a comprehensive explanation of the institutions or the relationships among them, but includes material selected to aid comprehension of the story of telecommunication policy development.

The Communications Act of 1934

Regulation of interstate telephone services nominally began in 1910 when the authority of the Interstate Commerce Commission (ICC) was extended to interstate telephone rates, but the ICC never took an active interest in communications or exercised effective power over the industry. Early in the Roosevelt administration, a committee was set up under the Secretary of Commerce to consider alternatives (including government ownership) to the existing communications industry structure. The industry was privately owned, with regulatory authority split into four different types: (1) the various state regulatory agencies, with authority over intrastate rates; (2) the ICC, with authority over interstate telephone common carriers; (3) the Federal Radio Commission (established 1927), with authority over the assignment of electromagnetic spectrum and the prevention of radio interference; and (4) the executive branch, with authority over cable landing licenses for international communications and shared authority with the Federal Radio Commission over radio matters. The committee recommended continued private ownership of communications subject to stronger and more centralized regulation. President Roosevelt transmitted their report to Congress in February 1934, and four months later Congress passed the Communications Act of 1934, which followed the general approach recommended by the President.

Although numerous minor amendments to the Communications Act of 1934 have been passed, the 1934 version of the act remains the basic law governing the regulation of communications in the United States. The law established the Federal Communications Commission and gave it broad discretionary authority to regulate communications. The frequently quoted statement of purposes said:

> For the purpose of regulating interstate and foreign commerce in communication by wire and radio so as to make available, so far as possible, to all the people of the United States a rapid, efficient, Nation-wide, and world-wide wire and radio communication service with adequate facilities at reasonable charges, for the purpose of the national defense, for the purpose of promoting safety of life and property through the use of wire and radio communication, and for the purpose of securing a more effective execution of this policy by centralizing authority heretofore granted by law to several agencies and by granting additional authority with respect to interstate and foreign commerce in wire and radio communication, there is hereby created a commission to be known as the "Federal Communications Commission," which shall be constituted as hereinafter provided, and which shall execute and enforce the provisions of the Act.[1]

The extremely broad purposes assigned to the commission were accompanied by great discretion in choosing how to best accomplish those purposes. Although some matters were specified in detail, the commission was given a broad grant of authority to carry out its purposes in matters not specifically legislated: "The Commission may perform any and all acts, make such rules and regulations, and issue such orders, not inconsistent with this Act, as may be necessary in the execution of its functions."[2]

The common carrier provisions of the Communications Act of 1934 were adapted from the provisions of the Interstate Commerce Commission Act originally written for the railroads. Compared to the ICC's authority over the railroads, the act provided stronger regulatory authority to compel interconnection and to suspend tariffs. In effect, telephone lines were treated like railroad lines, with similar tariff filing, nondiscrimination, and "just and reasonable" rate provisions.

The primary common carrier provisions of the act included:

1. Common carrier obligation to serve all who request service: "It shall be the duty of every common carrier engaged in interstate or foreign communication by wire or radio to furnish such communication service upon reasonable request therefor" (Section 201(a)).
2. Right of the commission to require interconnection with other carriers: ". . . where the Commission, after opportunity for hearing, finds such action necessary or desirable in the public interest, to establish physical connections with other carriers, to establish through routes and charges applicable thereto and the divisions of such charges, and to establish and provide facilities and regulations for operating such through routes" (Section 201(a)).
3. Rates to be just and reasonable: "All charges, practices, classifications, and regulations for and in connection with such communications service, shall be just and reasonable, and any such charge, practice, classification, or regulation that is unjust or unreasonable is hereby declared to be unlawful" (Section 201(b)).
4. Unreasonable discrimination prohibited: "It shall be unlawful for any common carrier to make any unjust or unreasonable discrimination in charges, practices, classifications, regulations, facilities, or services for or in connection with like communication service, directly or indirectly, by any means or device, or to make or give any undue or unreasonable preference or advantage to any particular person, class of persons, or locality, or to subject any particular person, class of persons, or locality to any undue or unreasonable prejudice or disadvantage" (Section 202(a)).
5. Publicly available tariffs for all communication charges must be filed and followed in a nondiscriminatory manner: "Every common carrier, except connecting carriers, shall, within such reasonable time as the Commission shall designate, file with the Commission and print and keep open for public inspection schedules showing all charges for itself and its connecting carriers for interstate and foreign wire or radio communication . . . No carrier shall . . . charge, demand, collect, or receive a greater or less or different compensation . . . than the charges specified in the schedule then in effect" (Section 203).
6. The Commission may suspend new tariffs for up to five months to

hold a hearing regarding lawfulness. If the hearing is not concluded, the tariff goes into effect (Section 204).

7. The Commission was given the power to prescribe tariffs after an appropriate hearing (Section 205).
8. The Commission was authorized to investigate complaints against carriers and, after a hearing, to award damages, as an alternative to filing such complaints in a U.S. district court (Section 208).
9. Extension of facilities can only occur after the Commission provides "a certificate that the present or future public convenience and necessity require or will require the construction, or operation, or construction and operation, of such additional or extended line" (Section 214).
10. The Commission was given the authority to prescribe the accounting system and to prescribe depreciation charges for the carriers (Section 220).
11. The Commission was given extensive rights to compel information from the carriers (Sections 213, 219, 220).[3]

The first reaction of an economist reviewing the substantive provisions of the act is that there is very little substance contained in it. The general order to the commission is to act "in the public interest" and to ensure that prices for communication services are "just and reasonable." Economists tend to think that acting in the public interest is simply a euphemism for doing whatever the individual finds in his or her private interest, and that serious efforts to find a just price have been out of style for the last five hundred years. Because many regulatory statutes are written with similar provisions and generality to the 1934 Act, many economists assume that members of a regulatory commission have full freedom in choosing policy. However, the provisions rule out many potential policy prescriptions. Furthermore, many of the principles have been given specific legal interpretation over the years and thus cannot be fully reinterpreted at the will of the agency.

The FCC and other regulatory agencies created during the 1930s mixed legislative, executive, and judicial functions. Fears that the agencies would abuse their power led to the passage of the Administrative Procedure Act (APA) in 1946. The APA established quasi-judicial procedures for rulemaking and the adjudication of disputes. Rulemaking requirements included:

1. Publication of a notice of proposed rulemaking in the Federal Register.

2. Opportunity for "interested persons . . . to participate in the rulemaking through submission of written data, views, or arguments with or without opportunity for oral presentation" (553(c)).
3. Consideration of views provided and written statement of basis and purpose of rules adopted.

More extensive requirements were prescribed for adjudications.[4] The APA provided procedural protections against violations of individual rights, but it also limited the agencies' ability to respond to change, made the agencies more responsive to the regulated industry that provided many of the comments for the record, and helped establish the reputation of the agencies as slow-moving captives of the industry they regulated. The influence of procedural rules on the substantive decisions of the FCC is examined in detail in later chapters.

The Structure of the FCC

The Federal Communications Commission was originally established with seven members appointed by the President (and confirmed by the Senate) for seven-year terms, with one commissioner's term expiring each year. No more than four of the seven could be from the same political party. In 1983, the number of commissioners was reduced to five but the same structure retained: five-year terms with one term expiring each year and no more than three from the same political party. Commissioners are full-time political appointees, paid at the same rate as executive branch subcabinet appointees (level III on the Executive Schedule for the chairman and level IV for other commissioners). They are prohibited from engaging in "any other business, vocation, profession, or employment," receiving honorariums for speeches, or having financial interests in the industries they regulate.

The President designates the chairman from among the commissioners. The chairman is designated the "chief executive officer of the Commission" and is given the authority to preside over commission meetings, represent the commission before Congress and in coordination with other government agencies, and "generally to coordinate and organize the work of the Commission in such manner as to promote prompt and efficient disposition of all matters within the jurisdiction of the Commission."[5] The chairman controls the agenda of the commission and selects the top staff officials, who must be approved by the entire commission. The chairman's powers are often used to exert a dominant influence on the functioning of the commission.

A President who serves two terms will have appointed all members of the commission by late in his or her term of office, including the three from his political party and the two that are not members of his party. If there are no vacancies when a new President takes office, his or her only guaranteed right is to designate the chairman from among the existing commissioners. In practice, a chairman who is expected to lose the chairmanship under a new President normally resigns his place on the commission and thus allows the President to initially appoint at least one commissioner as well as designating a chairman.

Each commissioner is entitled to appoint three professional assistants without regard to the civil service laws. The assistants are normally experienced attorneys either drawn from the commission's career staff or appointed from outside the commission. Initially one of the assistants was required to be an engineer, and at present engineers and economists are occasionally appointed as assistants. Commissioners' assistants are normally paid at the top of the regular civil service scale (level 15), but below the level of senior political appointees and career Senior Executive Service members. The assistants provide each commissioner with advice and assistance on the high volume of complex proposals flowing through the commission. The advice of the commissioners' assistants is particularly important because the recommendations of the regular FCC staff are normally filtered through the bureau chiefs and chairman before going to the other commissioners.

The Communications Act provided the commission with wide powers to choose staff and organize itself as it saw fit. Initially, the staff was organized by professional specialty into law, engineering, and accounting groups, each reporting to the commission. Commissioners could receive three different recommendations from the three separate staffs on a particular proposal.[6] The commission members and their congressional overseers were generally much more interested in the broadcast side of their responsibilities, including the awarding of lucrative radio licenses, than the common carrier side. In order to improve the commission's expertise on common carrier issues, several unsuccessful proposals were considered internally and in Congress to divide the commission into separate radio and common carrier portions, or to create panels of commissioners that would specialize in particular areas.

In 1949 the commission adopted the suggestion of Senator Mc-Farland of Arizona (then chairman of the Senate Communications Subcommittee) that the staff be organized into functional bureaus according to subject matter. The commission created a Common Carrier Bureau (CCB) that "develops, recommends and administers policies and programs for the regulation of services, facilities, rates and practices of entities . . . which furnish interstate or foreign communications service for hire—whether by wire, radio, cable or satellite facilities—and of ancillary operations related to the provisions or use of such services." Wide-ranging authority was delegated to the chief of the Common Carrier Bureau to act for the commission in many matters and to present recommendations to the commission for common carrier matters outside the scope of delegated authority.[7] Because the chief of the CCB supervises the staff working on common carrier matters (approximately 300 people during the 1980s) and controls the recommendations that go to the commission, the various chiefs have played a crucial role in policy formation. A similar bureau structure was created for broadcasting with parallel bureau chief authority. However, the greater interest of the commissioners in broadcasting matters, and the more technical and arcane nature of common carrier regulation, has tended to give the common carrier bureau chief greater freedom of action than the mass media chief.

In 1973 the commission created the Office of Plans and Policy (OPP) and assigned it "to conduct independent policy analyses to assess the long-term effects of alternative Commission policies on domestic and international communication industries and services, with due consideration of the responsibilities and programs of other staff units, and to recommend appropriate Commission action." The commission also assigned the chief of OPP "to recommend and evaluate governmental (state and federal), academic, and industry sponsored research affecting Commission policy issues" and "to review and comment on all significant actions proposed to be taken by the Commission in terms of their overall policy implications".[8]

OPP was far smaller than the operating bureaus (10–20 people rather than near 300 each for common carrier and mass media bureaus), and it was not given authority to conduct the many routine licensing, data gathering, and order writing functions of the bureaus. However, its broad grant of authority to conduct original policy research, review other outside policy research, and comment on all items coming before the commission, together with its organizational position reporting directly to the commission independent of the bureau chiefs, gave the small office an important voice in policy deliberations. It provided a counterweight to the dominant influence that the bureau chiefs gained through their control of the staff and information in their respective subjects. The OPP professional staff was interdisciplinary but weighted toward economists, in contrast to the heavy emphasis on attorneys in the professional staff of the Common Carrier Bureau and other units of the commission.

Non-FCC Policy Institutions

State Regulatory Commissions

Telephone rates were regulated by state commissions prior to the implementation of federal regulation. The Communications Act reserved the regulation of intrastate rates to the state commissions. Although organization varies from state to state, each state typically has a regulatory commission that regulates telephone, natural gas, electricity, and sometimes water or other utilities. They vary widely in staffing and expertise. Under certain conditions, the FCC can preempt state regulation.

The seemingly simple distinction between state regulation of intrastate rates and federal regulation of interstate rates is complicated by the fact that the same equipment is used for both types of service. Because both federal and state regulatory procedures require the rates to be related to total cost of service, the separate regulation of state and interstate rates requires a cost allocation procedure to determine which costs are treated as "jurisdictionally interstate" and which are "jurisdictionally intrastate" so that each jurisdiction can apply its own procedures to determine the appropriate rates to recover the costs allocated to that jurisdiction.

The separate agencies responsible for regulating intrastate and interstate rates, combined with the fact that both types of services are the joint products of an integrated network, have led to frequent conflict between the federal and state regulators over both jurisdiction and substantive policy issues. Each has the right to take action independently of the other. Some actions that affect both jurisdictions are coordinated through a Joint Board consisting of both state and federal regulators, but the decisions of the Joint Board are not binding on the agencies in either jurisdiction.[9]

Congressional Oversight

Congress can directly take action through legislation and could rewrite the Communications Act and even abolish the FCC if it so chose. However, as discussed in later chapters, the various conflicting interests in the industry have caused the failure of many attempts to pass controlling legislation for the telecommunication industry. The decentralized policy process as observed in telecommunication is in part related to the fact that Congress has not passed fundamental legislation to recognize the changes in industry structure and technology since 1934. Although it has the legal power to control telecommunication policy, Congress has not exercised that power and has therefore acted as one power center among many in influencing the evolution of telecommunication policy.

Both the House and the Senate have a subcommittee concerned with telecommunication issues. The subcommittees hold frequent "oversight" hearings to examine issues of current concern. In addition, there is routine frequent informal communication between FCC commissioners and staff and congressional members and staff. The oversight process in telecommunication is comparable to that for other agencies and has been extensively discussed.[10] The primary oversight activity is directed toward influencing the action of the regulatory agency, often with a threat of legislation if the agency does not conform. There are many different avenues for the expression of congressional interest short of a formal statute change: budget effects, confirmation of commissioners, negative publicity, conditions on operating authority.

Congress also frequently uses the power to take minor actions through attachments to budget or authorization bills. These actions do not go through the formal hearing process of major legislation and generally pass with little or no debate. For example, the budget bill may prohibit money from being used to examine a particular issue, thereby stopping action on it. Alternatively, a requirement may be inserted for fast action on a particular activity. These independent micromanagement functions allow individual senators or representatives (or their senior staff members) to function as independent telecommunication policy makers.

Judicial Review

Actions of the FCC and executive agencies can be challenged in the appeals court. The appeals court cannot review the factual determinations of the commission, but it can review the decisions for procedural correctness and relationship to the record and statute. The appeals court frequently overturns FCC decisions and enunciates principles that must be followed in new decisions. Because telecommunication policy over the past twenty years has departed substantially from the environment envisioned in the 1934 Communications Act, a strict interpretation of the act severely limits FCC freedom to substitute market forces for traditional regulation. Thus the court becomes an important telecommunication policy player itself. However, it can only rule on cases brought before it. Therefore the more effort the FCC makes to create a consensus decision, the less likely it is to be appealed and potentially overturned.

Appeals court cases are heard by panels of three judges, with each panel created specifically for a particular case. Consequently, even though judges have lifetime tenure, no single judge routinely oversees FCC decisions, and the judicial review is characterized by examining individual cases without regard for related cases that determine overall policy.

Department of Justice—Antitrust

Regulation does not exempt firms in the telecommunication industry from the antitrust laws. Antitrust suits may be brought either by private parties seeking damages or by the Department of Justice. Antitrust action has been a critical component of public policy in the telecommunication industry. Antitrust actions brought by the Department of Justice need not be coordinated with the FCC. When an antitrust action is settled by a consent decree (as happened in 1956 and 1982 in telecommunication), the decree is overseen by a federal district judge who retains jurisdiction to interpret and modify the decree. The judge administering a consent decree retains a continuing relationship to the issues, unlike the appeals court judges who see the issues in isolated cases. The judge administering a decree is not required to coordinate his orders with the orders of the FCC, and neither can overrule the other.

Other Executive Branch Agencies

The National Telecommunications and Information Administration (NTIA) within the Department of Commerce is responsible for coordinating the executive branch telecommunication policy. It supervises the allocation of spectrum for government use (while the FCC supervises the privately used spectrum). NTIA does not independently issue rules or orders to private firms, but it provides both formal and informal input to the FCC and congressional activities on telecommunication.

The Bureau of International Communications and Information Policy in the Department of State is responsible for coordinating U.S. positions regarding international telecommunication policy. For some activities, the FCC, NTIA, and the Department of State are required to coordinate their actions and develop a common position. As international trade issues in telecommunication have increased in importance, the office of the United States Trade Representative has begun to play a role in telecommunication policy as one part of its development of trade policy.

The critical importance of telecommunication to government operations causes many other agencies to exert influence on telecommunication policy, even though they do not have a specific mission of developing policy. Because the Department of Defense obtains many of its communications requirements from private firms rather than dedicated defense facilities, it has a continuing interest and influence in telecommunication policy matters. The General Services Administration, as purchasing agent for the federal government, has also participated in policy controversies in the role of a consumer.

Conclusion

The Communications Act of 1934 and the operation of the early FCC represent a combination of the traditions of strong centralized government and concern about abusive government power. The act was passed during the activist Roosevelt administration as an effort to centralize power that was diffused among multiple agencies. The commission was authorized to undertake a massive investigation of the telephone industry and recommend further legislative changes. Yet the reservation of the regulation of local telephone service to state commissions, the decision not to change the act after the telephone investigation was completed, and the limitation of commission activities through the Administrative Procedure Act all served to limit FCC control of the telephone industry.

Because Congress neither delegated full power to the FCC to make telecommunication policy nor exercised that power directly by revising the basic communication law, many agencies have been able to contribute to telecommunication policy. The institutional structures provide some boundaries on what may properly be decided by each agency, but the boundaries are vaguely defined and are subject to varying interpretations by the agencies involved. Policy makers may expand the jurisdiction of their agency by taking aggressive action or see the jurisdiction of their agency contracted by the aggressive action of others. Individuals frequently move among the various agencies and influence changes in the relative activity levels. Limited action in one agency may increase the efforts of other agencies, as it did when the two Justice Department antitrust suits against AT&T were inspired in part by perceptions that the FCC was not adequately controlling AT&T's market power. The vague boundaries among institutions and the many possible forums from which an aggressive individual can influence policy have created the conditions for the decentralized development of telecommunication policy.

5 / Economic Characteristics of the Telecommunication Industry

This chapter develops the economic characteristics of the telephone industry as it existed in the 1950s through a discussion of the historical circumstances that created them.[1] Those characteristics are a crucial component of the policy controversies discussed in the remainder of the book. The economic characteristics of the industry at that time came from a combination of managerial decisions, past policy actions, and the available technology.

The telecommunication industry is complex and does not neatly correspond to the normal expectations drawn from simple economic models. The complexity of the industry has been a critical part of policy controversies as different participants drew conflicting pictures of the industry from the ambiguous information available. Were MCI's early profits evidence of the company's superior efficiency, suggesting an absence of economies of scale and a potential social improvement through competition? Or were the profits evidence that MCI's inefficiency was masked by its avoidance of AT&T's settlement payments, suggesting that competition could increase total costs and cause local rates to increase? Were AT&T's pricing responses to early competition evidence of intent to exclude competitors, or were they necessary adjustments in the transition from a regulatory environment to a competitive environment?

The first economic characteristic that distinguishes telecommunication from most industries is that the value of telephone service depends on the number of people that can be reached through that particular service. A single telephone or a single fax machine unconnected with other telephones or fax machines has no value. This characteristic is known as the network externality and has been extensively studied in the economics literature.[2] Because the value of access to a network increases with the number of people that can be reached on that network, interconnection of two separate networks increases the value of both. Interconnection rights can therefore be used as crucial part of competitive strategy. There is also a social interest in interconnection issues because interconnection disputes can reduce total efficiency and exclude new competitors. A dominant theme in telecommunication policy is defining the rights and responsibilities for the interconnection of networks and the appropriate payments for interconnection under a wide variety of different conditions.

The second important economic characteristic was the revenue-sharing arrangements among companies in the industry prior to the divestiture of AT&T. A long distance call often traversed the facilities of more than one company. The customer paid a single charge for the call (generally collected by the originating telephone company), and the revenue was divided among the companies participating in the call. The revenue-sharing arrangements, which were determined by a mixture of privately negotiated contracts and public policy considerations, were a critical determinant of rate structures and of the availability of telephone service in sparsely populated areas of the country. The arrangements were based on complex cost allocation formulas that were difficult to fully comprehend. Differing views of the relationship of the revenue-sharing formulas to the industry price structure, to the provision of universal telephone service, and to AT&T's responses to competition have been a source of many of the public policy disputes in the industry.

The third important economic characteristic was the structure of the telephone industry as a vertically integrated effective monopoly controlled by AT&T. AT&T controlled long distance service, purchased its telephone equipment from its subsidiary Western Electric, and provided local telephone service to most urban areas of the country through its many Bell Operating Company subsidiaries. "Independent" telephone companies provided service to many rural areas of the country. Although they were not owned by AT&T, they followed Bell System standards, connected to AT&T for long distance service, and received much of their income from AT&T settlement payments to them. AT&T's huge bureaucracy controlled the operation of the telephone network with very little input from market forces. Prices were set by a combination of managerial and political decisions that were designed to produce total revenue equal to the total cost defined through the regulatory system, but not designed to relate the price of any particular service to the cost of that service. Interconnection of privately owned equipment or facilities with the telephone company network was prohibited.

The Development of Telephone Monopoly

Initial telephone service occurred under the Bell telephone patents that protected telephone *instruments*, not wires or switches. The very first service consisted of the company renting instruments to individuals who were responsible for providing their own connecting wire. That system was adequate for isolated pairs of individuals in close proximity, but was inefficient for connecting large numbers of individuals. Beginning in 1878, telephone exchanges were established in the major cities in which the company provided a switch and wires connecting the switch to each customer as well as the telephone instruments. Because of technical difficulties with long distance telephone communication, the initial exchanges were essentially isolated islands of telephone communication dependent upon the telegraph or mail for intercity communication. Service was not provided in the smaller towns or rural areas, nor was it provided outside of the densely populated core of the major cities. Although the number of telephones grew substantially in the early years, telephones remained rare for the general population. The number of telephones rose from 1.1 per thousand people in 1880 to 4.1 per thousand people in 1894 at the expiration of the basic Bell patent.[3]

In the initial organization of companies under the Bell patent monopoly, the parent company held the patent rights and franchised particular operating companies in individual cities. Licensed companies returned 30 to 50 percent of the stock to the parent company in exchange for patent rights; rented telephone instruments from the parent company; and were responsible for raising capital locally to establish the telephone exchange. Each local company was prohibited from building lines outside its assigned territory and was only allowed to connect to other exchanges through the parent company or its designated representative.

Although the early long distance technology was limited, the Bell parent company put considerable emphasis on developing long distance lines to control communication among the exchanges. In 1885 American Telephone and Telegraph Company was formed as a long distance subsidiary of the parent company, American Bell (later AT&T became the parent company), and developed service between New York and Philadelphia. New York–Boston service was established in 1889. Although the limited possibilities for long distance telephone service with 1880s technology together with competition from an extensive telegraph network made early franchisees unconcerned with long distance rights, the parent company saw the long distance rights as an important means of control. Theodore Vail, the chief architect of the Bell System both during its early period of patent monopoly and after a reorganization in 1907, stated:

> The first big effort was in multiplication of intensive local development and the conserving of the future, the preservation of all the future possibilities in a way to make them most effective when evolved. The telephone man of the day wanted the exchange rights. So he was given the exchange rights, and all other rights were reserved. I wish you particularly to note this in regard to interconnecting lines. In part payment for the exchange rights, . . . the right was reserved to run extra-territorial lines or toll lines into and connect them with any exchange.[4]

Long distance calls were charged by the minute, and all of the revenue went to the long distance company. The underlying concept became known as "board to board" long distance service. In other words, the routing of calls from individual subscribers to the local switch was a normal local function that did not involve long distance tolls, as was the distribution of the calls from the terminating switch to the final customer. The long distance toll was imposed for connecting service from one local exchange switch to the switch in a distant city.

Early long distance telephone rates were far higher than the telegraph rate, particularly for the longer distances. In 1902 the minimum charge for a New York–Chicago call was $5.45, while the minimum telegraph charge for that route varied between $.40 and $.60 throughout the 1876–1919 period. When telephone service first became available between New York and San Francisco in 1915, it was priced at $20.70 for a three-minute call, compared to a minimum telegraph rate of $1.00 for that distance. Telegraph rates generally rose while telephone rates generally fell over the next fifty years, causing the minimum telephone rate to drop below the telegraph rate by the early 1960s.[5]

The fundamental Bell patents expired in 1893 and 1894, leading to the entry of many new competitors. The competitors first established exchanges in areas not served by the Bell System and later expanded to the major cities in direct competition with Bell companies. Initially, the new competitors grew rapidly as they offered telephone service for the first time to areas not served by the Bell companies. However, after 1907 the financial control of the Bell System passed to a group of bankers led by J. P. Morgan, who chose Theodore Vail to lead the company. Vail began an aggressive program to restore Bell System dominance through patent control, purchase of independent telephone companies, and support of limited regulation as a substitute for competition.

The competitors maintained isolated exchanges without connecting long distance service. There was no separate long distance network, and the Bell System network refused to connect with non-Bell exchanges. The Vail and Morgan efforts to restore monopoly caused the independents to seek antitrust relief from the Department of Justice. As a result of threatened antitrust action, the Bell System in 1913 agreed to interconnect with the independents as part of an arrangement known as the Kingsbury Commitment. The Bell System and independents then exchanged territories until there was effective monopoly in each local area. This transformed the industry structure from competition in the local areas and monopoly in long distance lines into a fully monopolized industry, as it had been during the patent period. In general, the Bell System served the major cities while the independent companies served the small towns and rural areas.

The early pattern of non-Bell companies concentrated in sparsely populated areas has continued to the present. Many small towns and rural areas are currently served by small telephone companies that have never been a part of the Bell System. By 1982, 25 Bell System operating companies served 81 percent of the telephone lines but only 41 percent of the assigned geographic territory in the United States. A total of 1,432 independent operating telephone companies served the remaining 59 percent of the geographic territory but provided only 19 percent of the telephone lines.[6] Consequently, policies designed "to promote rural telephone development" and those designed "to assist small independent telephone companies" are generally aimed toward the same group of beneficiaries.

Regulation and the Sharing of Toll Revenue

Initial telephone regulation was applied to local services, first at the city level and then at the state level. Interstate regulation was formally instituted in 1910 when the Interstate Commerce Commission was given authority over interstate telephone service, but no effective interstate regulation was implemented until after the formation of the FCC in 1934. Thus the situation in the early twentieth century (after the Kingsbury Commitment) was one of regulated monopoly at the local level with unregulated monopoly at the interstate level. The initial local regulation was of widely varying effectiveness and in some cases appears to have had little effect on the rates.

With regulation, political boundaries became an important characteristic of telephone pricing policies. Within a single political jurisdiction, there was considerable freedom to adjust rates in order to achieve political goals. The Bell company acted across political jurisdictions and therefore encountered different levels of restraint on its various prices. When the local service was subject to cost of service regulation (prices limited to the amount necessary to cover cost plus a reasonable return on investment) but the long distance service was unregulated, the company had an incentive to minimize the allocation of the cost of commonly used facilities to the long distance service. In economic terms, AT&T had an incentive to argue that the cost of local service should be considered fixed and that only the marginal costs of long distance service, given the existence of local service, should be allocated to long distance service. The state regulators had an incentive to argue that the long distance service is only possible because of the local connections and that part of the long distance toll revenue should be used to cover the cost of local service (or equivalently, that part of the costs of basic connections should be allocated to the interstate jurisdiction and therefore to toll service).

The economic issue is that there are large economies of scope between local and long distance service. Neither can be provided without costly connections to a large number of individual low-volume subscribers. Once those connections are provided, both services can be offered over the same telephone instrument, inside wire, and connections to the switch. If there is differential regulation, the monopolist has an incentive to maximize the allocation of costs to the tightly regulated jurisdiction in order to justify higher regulated prices, while minimizing costs to the unregulated jurisdiction in order to capture the potential profits.

State regulatory commissions demanded that some of the costs of local service be allocated to the interstate long distance service, contrary to Bell System practice, in order to reduce the recorded cost (and therefore the price) of local telephone service. In the famous 1930 case *Smith v. Illinois Bell,* the Supreme Court ruled that the local telephone network was used jointly for local and long distance service and that therefore some of the cost of the local network must be allocated to long distance service.[7] That decision provided the legal foundation for the practice of *separations,* which has played a crucial role in later policy issues in communications. Separations is a cost allocation process that divides the costs of commonly used plant into state and interstate jurisdictions. Each jurisdiction then sets its own policies for the recovery of those costs. If each jurisdiction is regulated under the same cost and rate of return principles, then a change in the separations formulas causes a change in the rate structure (long distance versus local) but no change in the overall profits of the firm. Separations affects both the price structure of the industry and the relative power of state and federal regulators. If all of the cost of local service were allocated to the state jurisdiction, then federal regulators would have no authority to set rates for the local telephone companies. Because part of the cost of local service is allocated to the interstate jurisdiction through separations, federal regulators gain authority over local telephone companies.

After interstate regulation was established under the jurisdiction of the FCC, separations became a source of controversy between state and federal regulators. The Communications Act prescribed that issues related to the separation of costs among jurisdictions should first be analyzed by a Joint Board of federal and state commissioners. The Joint Board presents a recommendation to the FCC for final action. The first formal separations manual approved by a Joint Board went into effect in 1947. It split the telephone plant into a number of categories and generally allocated them between federal and state jurisdictions on the basis of relative use.

In the years following the initial separations manual, inflationary pressures caused the local companies to request permission to increase rates from the state regulators. Technological advances in long distance service reduced the cost of that service, especially for dense routes where coaxial cable or microwave could supply the equivalent of large numbers of wires. When the FCC initiated an investigation of AT&T's interstate rates in 1951 as a step toward requiring rate reductions, the states protested that the high earnings indicated a need for a change in the separations formula rather than for a reduction in interstate rates. The state regulators generally attempted to keep local rates as low as possible by increasing the costs allocated to the interstate jurisdiction and consequently increasing the share of interstate revenue paid back to local operating companies.

If a greater share of costs were allocated to the interstate jurisdiction, then AT&T's recorded interstate earnings would fall and its recorded intrastate earnings would rise without any change in the rates. Such a move would eliminate the politically painful necessity for state commissioners to grant local rate increases to make up the earnings deficiency, while also eliminating the need for AT&T to reduce long distance rates. Although the FCC resisted the proposed separations changes, it received considerable pressure from Congress to accept the state plan, particularly from Senator McFarland, who was chairman of the Communications Subcommittee. McFarland argued that the FCC's plan to reduce long distance rates would shift the cost burden from the large corporations to "the average housewife and business or professional man who do not indulge in a great deal of long distance."[8]

Under pressure from McFarland, the FCC agreed to changes in the separations formula in 1951 (the "Charleston Plan") that shifted costs from the intrastate to the interstate jurisdiction and consequently increased the local companies' share of interstate toll revenue. The pattern was repeated several times, resulting in a number of obscure technical changes to the separations formulas that had the cumulative effect of shifting a substantial share of the cost of providing local service from the intrastate to the interstate jurisdiction. By the 1970s the "Ozark Plan" separations formulas still incorporated the principle of relative use, but the various adjustments effectively multiplied the interstate factor by three for the largest category of plant. Thus if 6 percent of the minutes passing through a local exchange were interstate, the "non-traffic sensitive" local exchange plant would be allocated approximately 82 percent to intrastate and 18 percent to interstate.

The revenue side of the cost allocation formulas was known as "settlements" when payments were made between unaffiliated companies and "division of revenues" when payments were made between affiliated companies. While the separations cost allocation formulas were contained in a public manual approved by a Joint Board and eventually incorporated into the FCC rules, the settlements and division of revenues were accomplished by private contracts among the companies. In general, the contracts provided for the local exchange companies to recover the portion of their costs allocated to the interstate jurisdiction from the interstate toll revenue. This process was equivalent to a nationwide pooling of the allocated costs of local exchange origination and termination of long distance calls. It was not a "fee for service" arrangement, in which individual companies would charge a price per minute to the long distance companies for origination or termination service. Rather, the companies were entitled to revenues equal to a specified portion of their costs regardless of how those revenues related to the service provided for long distance. AT&T described the arrangement as a "partnership" among AT&T Long Lines (the interstate carrier), the Bell-affiliated local operating companies, and the independent telephone companies. The effective price per minute of access service provided was far higher for small high-cost independent telephone companies than for low-cost urban companies, but such price disparities did not affect the interstate long distance rate structure that was set on a geographically averaged basis.

Although the rhetoric of those who supported the increasing allocation of local exchange costs to interstate service emphasized shifting the cost burden from small users to large corporations, the largest corporations escaped most of the cost burden. The process applied to switched long distance calls, not to those made over dedicated "private lines." The largest companies had extensive networks of private lines connecting their locations and could make calls over those networks without generating switched minutes, which were used as the basis for cost allocation. Thus the actual income transfer from increasing the interstate allocation in the separations formulas was to increase the total paid by medium-usage companies (which made heavy use of switched service but were too small for effective private networks) and to reduce the total paid by subscribers with a lower than average use of interstate service per telephone line.

The historical structure of the separations formulas with their relatively high allocation of local exchange costs to switched interstate service played a critical role in the development of services and policies in the industry. The separations and settlements arrangements caused interstate switched long distance prices to be far above the cost of providing transmission between the local central offices. The high prices created incentives for intense long distance users to find alternatives to using switched services (such as private line networks) and provided incentives for entry into the long distance market.

The interstate revenue sharing system was a particularly important source of support for the small rural companies. They often had a high ratio of long distance to local calls and could recover a large share of their costs (in some cases as much as 85 percent of their non-traffic-sensitive costs) from the pool of interstate toll revenue. Many of the policy issues in introducing competition were concerned with determining which revenue flows to protect and attempting to find ways of protecting those revenue flows from the market pressures that would have eroded them.

The 1956 Consent Decree

AT&T's size and efforts to dominate its market left it vulnerable to antitrust charges. AT&T avoided a formal case in 1913 through its agreement to interconnect with the independent telephone companies. In 1930, the government filed antitrust charges against AT&T, General Electric, and Westinghouse, charging that their restrictive cross-licensing agreement for a massive pool of radio-related patents was anticompetitive. That suit was settled with a consent decree in 1932. AT&T's ownership of Western Electric, its unregulated equipment supply subsidiary, created additional concerns. Prices paid by Bell operating companies to Western Electric for telephone equipment were internal transfer prices to the Bell System and were neither regulated nor determined in a competitive market. However, those prices determined the costs of the regulated operating companies and therefore affected the prices the operating companies were allowed to charge under regulation. That arrangement created the possibility that AT&T could avoid regulatory control by simply raising the Western Electric prices and taking Bell System profits through Western Electric rather than through the telephone operating companies. The problem of Western Electric's relationship to the regulated system was considered in the drafting of the Communications Act of 1934 and in a major FCC study of the late 1930s, but neither institution took action.

In 1949 the Department of Justice filed an antitrust suit that charged Western Electric with monopolizing the market for telephones and related equipment and asked for an end to AT&T's ownership of Western Electric, the dissolution of Western Electric into three companies, and an end to all restrictive agreements among AT&T, the Bell operating companies, and Western Electric.

AT&T's defense against the suit asserted that Western Electric was not merely a supply subsidiary providing equipment that could otherwise be purchased on the open market, but was a vital part of a fully integrated company that included research and development, manufacturing, and provision of service. AT&T argued that its ability to provide integrated control of complex systems was a vital national resource. AT&T's argument gained credence when the government asked it to take over management of the production of atomic weapons at Sandia Laboratories because of its experience in managing complex operations. Because AT&T was a major defense contractor at the time, the beginning of the Korean War caused the Secretary of Defense to request a postponement of the antitrust suit to avoid interference with the mobilization effort.

After the Eisenhower administration took office in 1953, the Defense Department continued to support AT&T's argument that its integrated status should be protected. The Secretary of Defense wrote to the Attorney General:

> Currently, Western has orders for equipment and systems for the armed services totaling over $1 billion . . . the severance of Western Electric from the system would effectively disintegrate the coordinated organization which is fundamental to the successful carrying forward of these critical defense projects, and it appears could virtually destroy its usefulness for the future. . . . It is therefore respectfully urged that the Department of Justice review this situation with a view of making suggestions as to how this potential hazard to national security can be removed or alleviated.[9]

After considerable delay, a consent decree to end the case was signed in 1956. The decree accepted the AT&T and Defense Department arguments that AT&T's vertically integrated structure was an important national resource rather than an illegal anticompetitive arrangement. The decree required liberal licensing of Bell System patents, including the critical transistor patent. It also generally restricted the Bell System to the provision of common carrier communication services and restricted Western Electric to the provision of equipment for those services.

The 1956 consent decree was generally considered a victory for AT&T. The company retained its integrated structure, with Western Electric as a fully owned but unregulated subsidiary. It gave up the right to use patents as a competitive weapon, but AT&T had already largely eliminated the aggressive use of patents to block competitors that it had practiced in earlier years. The restriction to common carrier services represented a potential barrier to future expansion but not a limitation on then-current services. However, the controversy over vertical integration in the telephone industry was not fully settled by the decree. The same fundamental issue of the relative advantage of arm's-length dealing mediated by market forces versus integrated managerial control of the telephone network was raised in the 1975 antitrust suit and in other policy forums.

Interconnection and the Network Externality

This section introduces the economics of interconnection with a series of two- and three-person examples. While these simple examples may seem far from the complexity of the telecommunication industry, they help clarify the significance of interconnection and the network externality for policy toward the industry.

Consider first the case in which there are only two people, A and B, and each values communication with the other at 2. In order for A and B to communicate, a telephone company must build a wire from each of them to a costless central switch. Each wire from a location to the switch costs 1. If only one subscribes, there are no communication paths and no value. If both subscribe, there are two communication paths (A to B and B to A) and a total value of 4, while the total cost is 2.

If this is a contestable market (no barriers to entry so that any pricing plan that yields total revenue above total cost will be eliminated by competition), then total revenue must be 2 and the natural price in this symmetric example is 1 per subscriber. A price of 1 charges each subscriber the cost created by that subscriber. However, because of the network externality, the cost-based price of 1 is not the only sustainable price even in a contestable market. Suppose, for example, that the telephone company charges 1.5 to A and 0.5 to B. Normally, competition eliminates price discrimination because the entrants attempt to serve the customers paying the high price and leave the customers paying the low price to the incumbent. That strategy is not feasible in this case because a competitor must attract both A and B. Although A would be pleased to switch to a system offering a price of 1, B would not and therefore the system would not be viable.

The discriminatory price would not be feasible against competitors if the incumbent were required to offer free interconnection. With free interconnection and the (1.5, 0.5) price vector, an entrant can compete for A alone by building a wire from A to the central switch at a cost of 1 and demanding interconnection. A prefers the entrant's price of 1 to the incumbent's price of 1.5 and receives the ability to communicate with B because of interconnection. The incumbent is left with a system consisting only of B that costs 1 and receives revenue of 0.5. The incumbent must consequently raise its price for B to 1, eliminating the discrimination. In this two-person case, and in general, a company can sustain price discrimination against entry if it retains control over interconnection, but cannot sustain price discrimination against entry if free interconnection is required.

Now consider the addition of a third person, C, to the network of A and B. C adds four new communication paths: A to C, B to C, C to A, and C to B.[10] Assume that each of those paths is valued at 0.4. In other words, A and B each value the ability to communicate with C at 0.4, and C values the ability to communicate with A and B at 0.4 each. The total value of the network increases by 1.6 when C joins, while the total cost increases by 1. Thus it is socially beneficial to have C on the network. However, from C's perspective, the value of subscription is only 0.8 (C's value in calling each of the other two people). Therefore, if the telephone company charges the nondiscriminatory price of 1 to all subscribers, C will decline subscription.

In a contestable market with no interconnection requirements, a nondiscriminatory price structure that excludes C is not sustainable against a discriminatory price structure that includes C. For example, a price vector of (1.3, 1.3, .4) will induce all three to subscribe, exactly cover total cost, and make each person better off than that person would be under the nondiscriminatory two-person network. However, that price vector is not sustainable under conditions of required free interconnection because an entrant would attempt to serve A and B at a lower price than the combined 2.6 that they pay the incumbent and then interconnect with the incumbent to reach C.

In this three-person example, there is no nondiscriminatory price that reaches maximum efficiency. There is a discriminatory price that reaches maximum efficiency and is sustainable against competitors when interconnection is not required. There is no price that reaches maximum efficiency and is sustainable against free interconnection.

Conclusion

The network externality, the historical pricing patterns in the telephone industry, and the unified integrated managerial control over the telephone network were critical components of the policy debates as competition was introduced to the industry. There were two different aspects to the network externality. First, it meant that individual pieces of telephone equipment or separate systems were either of no value or limited value without interconnection to the public network. As long as AT&T could limit entry into some part of the network and could prohibit interconnection, it could prohibit entry into any part of the network. The part of the network for which entry was most difficult changed over time. Initially, the most difficult area of entry was the telephone instruments covered by the original Bell patent. After the patent expired and entry was possible into instruments, the most difficult entry shifted to long distance service, which was protected by a number of patents. Later entry became easier in long distance service but remained difficult in local service because of franchise restrictions and technological conditions. However, AT&T's prohibition on interconnection and the economic requirement that all parts of the system must work together prohibited competition in any part of the system so long as there was blocked entry into some part.

The second aspect of the network externality is the increase in the value of telephone service to a particular subscriber that comes from extending the number of persons that subscriber can reach by telephone. The social value of subscribing to a telephone is greater than the private value because subscription increases the value of telephone service to others on the network. Taking proper economic account of the network externality requires ensuring that telephone service is made available to people for whom the social value is greater than the cost, even though the private value of the service may be less than the cost.

In policy debates, the economic concept of a network externality has been blended with the policy principle that universal service is desirable. That principle was incorporated into the Communications Act ("to make available, so far as possible, to all the people of the United States a . . . wire and radio communication service") and became a widely accepted policy goal. When it was useful to explain that principle in economic terms, it was identified with the network externality; universal service must be sought in order to maximize the value of the telephone network for all. However, the universal service principle is more comprehensive than the network externality and has been used to support very high cost telephone development in remote areas that would not qualify through an economic computation of the network externality.

The pricing patterns established by the separations process under regulated competition have complicated the process of introducing competition to the industry and evaluating the effects of that competition. The pricing patterns were determined by a combination of AT&T choices and political choices by the FCC, Congress, and state regulatory commissions. During the regulated monopoly period, there was considerable freedom to choose relative prices of various services through politics rather than market forces. Various social justifications were developed for the practice of providing large payments from long distance revenue to small rural telephone companies. The payments allowed rural local rates to be set below city local rates even though the cost of serving rural customers was far higher.

The complex system of revenue sharing among companies was not closely related to the cost of providing various kinds of service and therefore was not consistent with expected arrangements in a competitive market. Beneficiaries of the revenue sharing arrangements opposed initial competition as a threat to the established revenue flows. Difficulties in measuring and understanding the revenue flows created controversy over whether early competitors were more efficient than the incumbents or were merely underpricing because they did not make the same payments to other companies that AT&T did. Those measurement difficulties also contributed to the controversies over the interpretation of AT&T's initial competitive responses as either predatory in nature or the expected response as competition moves prices closer to cost. After competition was established, debates over the social benefits of the earlier revenue flows and efforts to protect portions of the revenue flows from being eroded away by competition were central to many policy decisions.

The 1949 antitrust suit was an attempt to substitute market forces for managerial control in the telephone equipment market. The 1956 consent decree that settled that suit dropped the original objective and accepted managerial control as appropriate to the integrated telephone network. The argument for managerial control was inconsistent with the argument for open entry conditions and competition in parts of the industry, and many of the arguments over early competition concerned the feasibility of maintaining a high-quality network made up of multiple suppliers without a single manager. The independent telephone companies generally supported AT&T in the debate over managerial versus market controls. Their financial dependence on AT&T settlement payments and their economic dependence on connections with the AT&T network prevented them from acting as catalysts for new competition in the industry.

Part II / The Development of Competition

6 / Competition in Terminal Equipment

This chapter examines the development of policy toward terminal equipment (also known as customer premises equipment or CPE and including ordinary telephone instruments) between 1950 and 1980. Over that 30-year period, policy changed from one in which terminal equipment was considered an intrinsic part of the network exclusively under monopoly control to one in which terminal equipment was provided on a competitive unregulated market separate from the telephone network. Terminal equipment is necessary for calls and is thus an intrinsic part of the telephone network. The effort to "carve off" terminal equipment from the regulated monopoly was the earliest effort to establish clear lines of demarcation (boundaries) between regulated and unregulated services. Terminal equipment was also the simplest case of boundaries and the most successful. The boundaries were defined in terms of physical location and technical standards with no regulated revenue flows across the boundary.

The terminal equipment issues were fundamentally concerned with interconnecting private communication systems with the public network. As discussed in the last chapter, interconnection issues are critical to competitive activities in telephones because of the network externality. In the extreme case, terminal equipment is a single telephone on a desk that is useless because it is unconnected to the network. However, the terminal equipment controversies also extended to the ability to connect an extensive set of private telephones through a private switch (a Private Branch Exchange or PBX) to the network. An internal telephone network for a business is of some

79

value even if not connected to the public network because it provides communication among all the individuals in that business, but it is of much greater value if it also is interconnected with the public network so that outside calls can be made from the same telephones used for inside calls.

Terminal competition was established through a long series of slow steps that allowed participants to evaluate previous steps and revise their views of what should happen next and that brought new participants into the policy process. Information was scarce, and the cost of mistakes was high because of the possibility that improper private terminal equipment could harm the functioning of the public network. Policy makers adopted a conservative course of action that gave the benefit of the doubt to the status quo. Although in hindsight terminal equipment could easily have been deregulated much sooner, the arguments of the various parties (particularly AT&T) convinced regulators that great care was needed to avoid harm to the network. Each successful step led to another small adjustment until it became conventional wisdom that terminal equipment was part of a competitive market.

Hush-A-Phone

AT&T prohibited customer-owned attachments to its network from the early days of telephones. Restrictions were included in customer contracts prior to regulation and were incorporated into tariff language in 1913. Tariffs constitute the contract between the regulated company and its customers. They are filed with the regulatory authorities and generally go into effect automatically unless specifically disapproved. The tariffs contain the rates to be paid as well as "terms and conditions" that constitute a detailed contract between the carrier and anyone who chooses to take service from the carrier.

AT&T enforced its "foreign attachments" ban vigorously though unsystematically. In at least one case, the telephone company prohibited customers from putting a cover on the telephone directory because a cover was an attachment to the telephone book, which was telephone company property. In another case, Michigan Bell initially refused to allow the connection of a telephone line to a public address system to allow President Hoover to address a National Association of Broadcasters convention in Detroit from the White House, but later allowed the connection after the personal intervention of AT&T president Walter Gifford. However, AT&T allowed many unauthorized recording devices to be attached to the network through haphazard procedures in enforcing its restrictions.[1]

Although several early controversies over AT&T's restriction on network attachments were presented to the FCC, none established a significant precedent until the Hush-A-Phone case. The Hush-A-Phone was a cup-like device that snapped onto the telephone instrument to provide speaking privacy and shield out surrounding noises. It was a passive nonelectrical device that directed the speaker's voice into the instrument, and it was sold through department stores for about $10 retail in 1950.

Harry Tuttle invented the device in 1921 and sold about 125,000 units over a 30-year period before the case came to the FCC. AT&T did not make a concerted effort to stop use of the device, but from time to time it warned the managers of stores selling the Hush-A-Phone that the device violated the foreign attachment provisions of telephone company tariffs. The warnings caused several stores to discontinue the product and induced Tuttle to file a complaint with the FCC in 1948 alleging that AT&T was interfering with his business. At the 1950 hearing on Tuttle's complaint, Tuttle's counsel, Kelley Griffith (later an important figure in deregulation as deputy chief of the Common Carrier Bureau under Bernard Strassburg) called expert witnesses to testify that the Hush-A-Phone could improve the intelligibility of conversations in a noisy environment, while AT&T emphasized the sound distortions that could result from the Hush-A-Phone and the long history of foreign attachment restrictions. FCC staff counsel Bernard Strassburg (later the long-tenure chief of the Common Carrier Bureau responsible for many pro-competitive actions) recommended in favor of AT&T.

The FCC's initial decision in 1951 (under Democratic control) emphasized the importance of maintaining telephone company control over all equipment used with the network:

> Where a device has a direct effect upon communication itself, as does the Hush-A-Phone, if we were disposed to do so at all we would require a showing far stronger than that made by Hush-A-Phone herein to warrant departure from the general principle that telephone equipment should be supplied by and under the control of the carrier itself.[2]

After a delay of several years, the FCC issued a final decision in 1955 (under Republican control) dismissing the Hush-A-Phone complaint and upholding AT&T's foreign attachment rules.

Much later Strassburg explained his reasons for upholding the foreign attachment rules:

> I served throughout the Hush-A-Phone proceedings as the FCC's staff counsel and recommended against authorizing use of the device . . . it was the conviction of the FCC and its staff that they shared with the telephone company a common responsibility for efficient and economic public telephone service and that this responsibility could only be discharged by the carrier's control of all facilities that made up the network supplying that service. Such control included not only transmission, switching, and the subscriber station used for basic end-to-end service. It also had to extend to any equipment a subscriber might attach to or interface with the basic service. Only by this comprehensive type of control could the quality, safety, and economies of network performance and design be assured.
>
> The Hush-A-Phone, by itself, posed no threat of any real consequence to the performance of the basic network. Nevertheless, authorization of its use could set a precedent for other, less benign attachments which individually or cumulatively could degrade network performance to the detriment of the public.[3]

Tuttle did not accept his loss in the seven-year FCC proceeding as final and appealed the decision to the appeals court, where he won a clear victory and set an important precedent on the limitations of the telephone companies and the FCC to restrict privately beneficial use of the telephone network. The crucial issue was that the only harms found by the FCC were private to the parties conversing with the aid of the Hush-A-Phone. The court delineated the customer's right to use the telephone in privately beneficial ways so long as they were not publicly detrimental and ruled that the telephone company could not interfere with that right. The decision stated in part:

> The question, in the final analysis, *is whether the Commission possesses enough control over the subscriber's use of his telephone to authorize the telephone company* to prevent him from conversing in comparatively low and distorted tones. It would seem that, although the Commission has no such control in general, there is asserted a right to prevent the subscriber from achieving such tones by the aid of a device other than his own body. Thus, intervenors do not challenge the subscrib-

er's right to seek privacy. They say only that he should achieve it by cupping his hand between the transmitter and the mouth and speaking in a low voice into this makeshift muffler. . . . To say that a telephone subscriber may produce the result in question by cupping his hand and speaking into it, but may not do so by using a device which leaves his hand free to write or do whatever else he wishes, is neither just or reasonable. The intervenor's tariffs, under the Commission's decision, are an unwarranted interference with *the telephone subscriber's right reasonably to use his telephone in ways which are privately beneficial without being publicly detrimental.*[4]

The Hush-A-Phone decision was a challenge to the power of the FCC to authorize AT&T to interfere in the rights of individuals. Even with changing leadership, the FCC twice voted unanimously in favor of AT&T and against Hush-A-Phone. The court pointed to no procedural flaws in the FCC's actions nor to specific statutes or precedents that had been violated. Rather, it made an equity judgment under the broad "just and reasonable" standard of the Communications Act that the AT&T foreign attachment prohibition was improperly restricting the rights of individuals to use their telephone service in privately beneficial ways.

Neither AT&T nor the FCC interpreted the Hush-A-Phone decision as a major precedent that required substantial changes in the then-current practices. Rather, they developed a narrow construction of the decision that allowed the Hush-A-Phone but very little else. Following the November 1956 court decision, the FCC adopted an order requiring AT&T and its associated companies to file new tariffs "rescinding and canceling any tariff regulations to the extent that they prohibit a customer from using, in connection with interstate or foreign telephone service, the Hush-A-Phone device or any other device which does not injure defendants' employees, facilities, the public in its use of defendants' services, or impair the operation of the telephone system."[5]

Prior to the Hush-A-Phone decision, the AT&T restrictive tariff provision had read: "No equipment, apparatus, circuit or device not furnished by the telephone company shall be attached to or connected with the facilities furnished by the telephone company, whether physically, by induction or otherwise."[6] Rather than deleting the provision, the company added an additional paragraph that said the restriction would not be construed to prohibit a customer from using a device that served his convenience so long as the device did not injure the telephone system, involve direct electrical connection to the system, provide a recording device on the line, or connect the telephone line with any other communications device. The new provision clearly allowed the use of the Hush-A-Phone but did not allow many other devices that could have come under the requirements imposed by the appeals court to allow devices that provided private benefit without producing public harm. The commission accepted the new AT&T tariff without specifically approving it or ruling on whether or not it complied with the court-imposed requirements.

Carterfone

Soon after the revised tariff went into effect, Carter Electronics Corporation began marketing a device called a Carterfone that connected mobile radio-telephone systems to the telephone network. The Carterfone contained a cradle into which an ordinary telephone handset could be placed. The Carterfone transmitted voice signals from the mobile radio transmitter into the telephone handset and converted the voice signals received from the handset into radio signals for broadcast to the mobile radio-telephone without the need for a direct electrical connection between the two. The device violated the AT&T tariff because it provided a connection between telephone lines and other channels of communication, but it at least arguably fit within the Hush-A-Phone requirements because it was merely receiving voice signals from the telephone set and transmitting voice signals back to the telephone set. In response to a Carter inquiry, the commission informed the company that the Carterfone appeared to violate the AT&T tariff. Carter continued to produce and market the device. AT&T asserted that the tariff prohibited the Carterfone and threatened to suspend telephone service to customers who used the Carterfone.

Carter again sought FCC assistance and was informed that the device appeared to violate the tariff and that the commission could only change a tariff after a hearing. Rather than requesting a formal hearing before the FCC, Carter filed an antitrust suit against AT&T. The court then passed the matter back to the FCC for action rather than proceeding directly with the antitrust suit. In 1966 the commission instituted an investigation into the Carterfone, including its effect on the telephone system, whether it violated the tariff, and whether the tariff itself was lawful. The telephone companies suggested a variety of methods in which the Carterfone could cause harm to the network, but they were not able to specify actual problems that had arisen with the Carterfones in use. The hearing examiner found that the harms were speculative and of a nature that could be caused by the human voice as well as the Carterfone.

By the time of the hearing, Bernard Strassburg was chief of the Common Carrier Bureau and well aware of the potential significance of the case because of his prior involvement in the Hush-A-Phone controversy. Strassburg instructed the staff to take a broad view of the Carterfone issue and to use that case to eliminate AT&T's restrictive tariff provisions. In 1968 the commission unanimously accepted the bureau's position and found that the Carterfone violated AT&T's tariff but that the tariff itself was illegal and violated the requirements of the court and the commission in the Hush-A-Phone case. The commission ruled that the tariff "has been unreasonable and unreasonably discriminatory since its inception" and ordered the companies to file new tariffs to allow all devices that did not cause actual harm. The carriers were given permission to include restrictions on harmful devices and to specify technical standards to be met before a device was connected to the network.[7]

Protective Connecting Arrangements

Although the Carterfone case itself was about a specialized device with limited demand, it was decided in the context of a broader inquiry regarding the demarcation line between the regulated communications industry and the computer industry. Even without the court ruling in Hush-A-Phone as a guide, it was no longer possible for the FCC to take the mechanical approach of the earlier era that everything connected in any way to the telephone system was part of that system. The development of time-sharing computers in the mid-1960s created a need for joint use of telephone lines and computers to allow remote users to communicate with a central computer. A strict application of the original restrictive FCC and AT&T Hush-A-Phone approach either would have prohibited communication with computers over telephone lines or would have required AT&T to supply the computer. In practice, AT&T initially supplied teletypewriter terminals and modems as the terminating equipment for data lines, but did not attempt to stop the interconnection of an AT&T-supplied modem with customer-owned computers.

Both Strassburg and AT&T Chairman H. I. Romnes viewed the Carterfone case in the context of the computer/communications boundary issue, which was then under active FCC exploration in another proceeding. Both were looking for a way to open the network to connection with new types of equipment for computer usage and other purposes. Romnes chose not to fight the Carterfone concept and saw advantages for AT&T in allowing a wider variety of terminals to be connected to the system. AT&T could not supply all of the specialized devices that might be required by computer users and had no interest in forcing computer users off the public network. However, Romnes and other AT&T executives believed that centralized control of the telephone network and of the signals used to control that network was necessary.

An AT&T executive committee compiled a long list of potential harms that could result from freely interconnecting customer-supplied equipment. Most of the potential harms were related to network signalling. Telephone terminal equipment provides signals to the network that set up and discontinue the call and that provide for billing. Improper signalling from customer terminal equipment could cause the central office to fail to respond, to prematurely terminate a call, or to cause errors in billing. Consequently, AT&T sought to retain control of network signalling. Rather than promulgating standards required for attachments, AT&T offered a Protective Connecting Arrangement (PCA) that would isolate the customer equipment from the network. According to AT&T's post-Carterfone tariffs, any customer who wished to attach terminal equipment to the network was required to order a tariffed PCA from AT&T and attach the customer terminal equipment through the PCA. The PCA provided all network signalling.[8]

During the Carterfone case, the FCC staff had drawn a distinction between specialized equipment such as the Carterfone and ordinary telephone handsets and Private Branch Exchanges (PBXs) traditionally supplied by the telephone companies. The staff viewed the case as concerned with the customer's right to attach equipment to the traditional telephone service, not with the customer's right to substitute equipment for items traditionally supplied as part of telephone service. AT&T's post-Carterfone tariffs eliminated the distinction between specialized terminal equipment and traditional terminal equipment. Those tariffs allowed the connection of any customer-provided terminal equipment so long as it was done through a PCA. Strassburg was pleased with the initial AT&T response and later testified that the AT&T tariffs "went well beyond the requirements of Carterfone" by permitting customers "to substitute their own PBXs, key telephone systems, and even telephone sets for those provided by the telephone company."[9]

Although AT&T's offer of liberal interconnection of customer-provided terminal equipment through PCAs was accepted as a cooperative action going beyond the minimum legal requirements at the time, it did not constitute a stable position. AT&T viewed the PCA tariffs as a dramatic opening up of the network beyond what many of its executives thought desirable. The FCC viewed the PCA tariffs as an appropriate interim measure while the desirable long-term arrangements were being developed. The FCC dismissed objections to AT&T's PCA tariffs and allowed them to go into effect without formally approving them, thus reserving its right to find them unlawful at a later date. Strassburg testified that there were unresolved questions "with respect to various specific features of the protective connecting arrangements of the tariffs" and that "although the new tariffs complied with the Carterfone ruling and, in addition, liberalized customer interconnection beyond the purview of expectations of that ruling, we did not feel that we had a basis for formally approving the tariffs."[10]

The Carterfone ruling and AT&T's response transformed the ongoing policy issue from the question of what kinds of terminal equipment could be connected to the question of what conditions would be imposed for interconnection. AT&T conceded the customer's right to connect any terminal equipment with its PCA tariffs, but sought to retain control of network signalling and to impose a charge (around $2.00 per month) for each PCA provided. The relaxed barriers to entry brought many new suppliers into the market for modems, key telephone systems, and PBXs. Those suppliers considered the PCA unnecessary and anticompetitive.

The cost of the PCA reserved the market for inexpensive equipment such as ordinary extension telephones to AT&T because the charge for the extension telephone was less than the charge for the PCA required for connection of a privately supplied telephone. The competitors could supply more expensive equipment only if they provided enough cost advantage to overcome the cost of the PCA. In some cases the PCAs were unavailable, and thus attachment of competitive equipment was delayed. In other cases, a non-AT&T company manufactured terminal equipment to AT&T standards that was purchased by the Bell Operating Companies. When that equipment was supplied through the Bell companies, no PCA was required, but if the identical equipment was provided directly to the customer, a PCA was required. Furthermore, a great variety of equipment was attached to the network through interconnections with independent telephone companies and through special military arrangements without using either PCAs or formal protective standards.

Controversy over AT&T's PCA requirement caused the FCC to initiate an inquiry into desirable methods of protecting the network and to arrange with a panel of the National Academy of Sciences to evaluate the information submitted. The Academy's Computer Sciences and Engineering Board, led by Harvard professor Anthony Oettinger, set up a fourteen-member panel to provide technical assistance to the FCC. The panel concluded that network protection was necessary and that protection could be adequately provided by either PCAs or a program of standards and certification of equipment. The panel declined to choose between the two possibilities on the grounds that such a choice would be determined by nontechnical factors outside of the panel's particular expertise.[11]

Opposition to Terminal Competition

As the FCC moved toward a program of certification that would allow competition in all terminal equipment, opposition to the FCC policy direction developed at both AT&T and the state regulatory commissions. The original Carterfone decision was viewed as a reasonable accommodation to changing technology that required some means of connecting specialized equipment to the telephone network. AT&T's efforts to accommodate the policy with its PCA tariff that allowed any kind of equipment to be connected had created controversy over the imposition of the PCA rather than credit for opening up its network. AT&T's opposition to further liberalization was strengthened when John deButts succeeded H. I. Romnes as chairman in 1973. Chairman deButts was a vigorous proponent of the traditional end-to-end service responsibility of the telephone company. He probably would not have approved the PCA tariff if he had been chairman at the time and certainly was not willing to accommodate more competition. He established a high-profile program of intensive opposition to the FCC's efforts to further liberalize interconnection.

The deButts case against terminal competition was built on two foundations:

1. Network harm—the telephone companies must have complete control over the equipment attached to the network in order to properly manage the network for the benefit of all users.
2. Economic harm—competition in terminal equipment would upset the established system of revenue and cost sharing across the country, leading to savings for some large customers at the expense of local rate increases for most customers.

DeButts expressed both concepts forcefully in a famous 1983 speech to the National Association of Regulatory Utility Commissioners (NARUC) in which he publicly challenged the FCC policies:

> For some five years now, we have pursued our announced aim of facilitating the connection of customer-provided equipment by making interface devices as simple and inexpensive as possible. To pretend, however, that our experience thus far has been satisfactory—to us or to all our customers—would be just that—to pretend. . . . But we cannot live with the deterioration of network performance that would be the inevitable consequence of "certification" and the proliferation of customer-provided terminals that would ensue from it. No system of certification we can envision—and no interface requirement—can provide a fully adequate alternative to the unequivocal and undivided responsibility for service that the common carrier principle imposes. . . .
>
> For where will the burden of increasing interconnection fall? . . . the burden will fall on the average customer, the users of the basic services that it has been regulatory policy from time immemorial to keep as inexpensive as possible. . . . By one estimate, a ten percent loss of the terminal market by the common carriers will increase state revenue requirements by almost $220 million a year, a 50 percent loss by more than $1.0 billion. . . . The ultimate effect of this shift is not hard to see—a shutoff of service to people with marginal incomes.[12]

The AT&T argument that terminal competition would raise local prices was primarily based on the separations and settlements system. In 1973 about 18 percent of terminal equipment costs were assigned to the interstate jurisdiction through the separations system. At the end of 1973, the telephone companies recorded $6.3 billion in station apparatus and $3.0 billion in large PBXs in their regulated accounts, accounting for 12.0 percent of total communication plant in service.[13] The interstate share of the revenue requirement associated with that plant (including depreciation, rate of return, labor, and various other expenses allocated in proportion to plant) was recovered out of interstate long distance revenue. Substituting customer-provided station equipment for carrier-provided equipment would reduce the local operating companies' share of long distance revenue and therefore increase the local revenue requirement, assuming (as AT&T did) that the total revenue requirement was fixed.

AT&T's argument that terminal competition would increase local rates was well received by the state regulatory commissioners. They knew that revenue sharing was especially critical to the small independent companies that serviced sparsely populated areas, and they found AT&T's argument that introducing competition would reduce the revenue flows to small companies plausible. By the early 1970s, the state regulators had established a 40-year history of advocating the allocation of continually larger shares of the telephone company costs to the interstate jurisdiction in order to reduce basic local rates. They were consequently receptive to AT&T's argument that the federal plans for terminal competition would reduce the flow of long distance revenue to local companies.

The FCC's movement toward terminal competition originated from an entirely different line of reasoning than did the state opposition to competition. The Carterfone case was based on implementing the Hush-A-Phone principle of allowing actions that were privately beneficial without being publicly harmful in the context of growing interdependence between computers and communications. AT&T then voluntarily created additional rights of interconnection through its PCA tariffs, and the FCC was forced to judge disputes between AT&T and its competitors over the PCA requirement. The early FCC proceedings considered questions of technical harm to the network and did not focus on separations effects or other questions involving economic impact. The initial specialized equipment considered in Carterfone could have no significant economic impact because it was such a tiny fraction of the telephone company plant. AT&T's PCA requirement shielded single-line telephones from competition, but the PCA was justified on purely technical grounds and not as a barrier to competition.

As the FCC began shifting to certification standards as an alternative technical protection, the entire terminal equipment market became potentially subject to competition. However, AT&T found it difficult to refocus the federal proceedings on economic issues after they had been established to examine technical issues. In part, AT&T's inability to refocus federal attention on economic issues was due to its loss of credibility from overstating the technical harm problem. AT&T's Alvin von Auw recounted:

> Candidly examined, the history of AT&T's representations on the issue of terminal interconnection is one of position after position adamantly taken and then, each in its turn having proved unpersuasive, reluctantly—anxiously is a more accurate word—abandoned.[14]

Terminal equipment was clearly used jointly for the origination and termination of both interstate and local calls. That joint use was recognized through the separations process, which assigned a fraction of the costs associated with the equipment to the interstate jurisdiction and the remainder to the intrastate jurisdiction. So long as all terminal equipment was provided by the telephone companies under regulation, jurisdictional disputes simply concerned the appropriate share of cost to be paid by each jurisdiction. However, with the possibility of competition, shared jurisdiction without shared policies led to direct conflict.

The North Carolina Utilities Commission disagreed with the FCC's movement toward terminal competition and decided to nullify the action within North Carolina. It issued a proposed rule to prohibit customer-provided equipment and to require telephone companies to own and maintain all equipment used in intrastate telephone service. Because the same equipment was used for interstate and intrastate service, the North Carolina requirement that telephone companies own equipment used in intrastate service would have prohibited competition for any terminal equipment in that state. On behalf of a North Carolina equipment firm, Telerent Leasing, the equipment suppliers trade association, North American Telephone Association, asked the FCC to issue a declaratory ruling preempting state action. The FCC obliged and ruled in 1974 that no state could take action inconsistent with prior federal rulings on interconnection of customer-owned equipment. North Carolina appealed the FCC ruling, supported by other individual state commissions and NARUC. Many major corporations expressed views in the case, causing all but one of the Fourth Circuit judges to recuse themselves because of possible conflicts.[15] After developing a panel including two judges from outside the circuit, the court in 1976 ruled (two to one) in favor of the FCC preemption.[16]

The Telerent case was a critical step in the development of terminal competition. If the court had ruled against the FCC's preemption, then the FCC permission to attach terminal equipment would only have been meaningful in states where the state utility commission supported interconnection. Requiring agreement between the FCC and the state utility commission to establish competition would have protected the status quo, while the decision in favor of FCC preemption increased the rate of change. Although the Telerent decision was about jurisdiction rather than substance, it effectively focused the terminal equipment questions on technical harm (the federal concern) rather than on revenue flow and rate impact (the state concern). Had the two jurisdictions been required to negotiate a joint policy, revenue flow concerns would have played a much more prominent role than they did in the actual development of competition.

While the Telerent case was under consideration, the FCC ordered direct connection of equipment meeting prescribed technical standards. The commission concluded that the carrier-required protective connecting devices were unnecessarily restrictive on the customer's right to use the equipment and were an unjust and unreasonable discrimination among users and among suppliers of terminal equipment. The commission prescribed that terminal equipment should be connected through standard plugs and jacks rather than direct wiring and that all terminal equipment (including that manufactured by the telephone companies) would be required to meet specified technical criteria in order to prevent harm to the network. The carriers vigorously protested the requirement that their own equipment would have to meet the certification tests and claimed that it would impose unnecessary expense, but the commission upheld the requirement as necessary to avoid competitive misuse of the technical standards.[17]

The direct connection program was in direct opposition to the recommendations of AT&T and the state regulatory commissions. Both

AT&T and the state commissions appealed the program. The appellants lost the case but succeeded in obtaining a stay of the registration program until late 1977 when the Supreme Court declined review.

Computer II and Detariffing

By 1978 the controversies over interconnection of terminal equipment were settled. Customers had the right to interconnect any kind of terminal equipment that met the certification standards contained in the FCC rules and was compatible with the publicly available interface standards. The FCC rules were authoritative nationwide regardless of the policies of the individual state commissions. However, the settlement of the technical issues of interconnection did not settle the economic issues of competition in terminal equipment. The telephone companies continued to supply terminal equipment under tariff as part of their regulated communications service. The telephone-company-supplied terminal equipment was recorded on the regulatory books, allocated between state and federal jurisdictions, and used as a component of the regulated rate-making process in accordance with long-established procedures. Suppliers other than telephone companies were unregulated and sold their products through retail stores for simple items such as ordinary telephones and direct sales for complex items such as PBXs.

Although the competitive equipment market developed rapidly after interconnection rights were established, the mixture of regulated and unregulated products provided either individually by competitors or bundled with telephone services created confusion and complaints. The rates for most telephone-company-supplied terminal equipment were set by the telephone companies under the supervision of the state regulatory commissions. Because both the telephone companies and the state regulatory commissions had opposed terminal equipment competition, many competitors lacked confidence that the rates were being set in a fully compensatory manner that allowed fair competition between regulated and unregulated terminal equipment.

While the initial terminal competition with direct connection was developing, the FCC was engaged in a second attempt to develop a dividing line between regulated communications service and unregulated data processing service. The first attempt (which had been in progress during the Carterfone hearing) had ended in 1971 with a vague definitional dividing line based on whether a hybrid service was primarily data processing or primarily communications. As combinations of data processing and communications became routine during the 1970s, that definitional line became inadequate and caused the commission to initiate a second inquiry, which was known as the Computer II proceeding.

Among the specific reasons for the new inquiry was a piece of terminal equipment known as the AT&T Dataspeed 40/4. The Dataspeed 40/4 was a "smart terminal" designed to communicate with a computer and also to perform some processing functions on its own. AT&T filed a tariff for the Dataspeed 40/4 as a component of its Dataphone Digital Service, just as it had for a long time tariffed teletypewriter terminals as part of a communications service. IBM objected that the Dataspeed 40/4 was really a small computer designed to work with larger computers, just as IBM's unregulated smart terminals were designed to do. From IBM's perspective, AT&T was extending its regulated communications service into the data processing industry. The Common Carrier Bureau initially supported IBM and rejected AT&T's tariff. On review, the commission reversed the bureau and allowed the tariff to go into effect, but noted that smart terminals did not fit clearly into the existing rules and made the decision subject to new rules to be developed.

The confusion within the commission over how to classify the Dataspeed 40/4 occurred because the device straddled the line the commission had drawn in 1971. The smart terminal was an indication that computer technology was moving toward networks with intelligence widely distributed, rather than the initial time-sharing configuration of simple terminals communicating with a central computer. As that trend continued, any regulatory distinction between "computer-like" and "communications-like" terminals became increasingly artificial.

The initial goal of the Customer Premises Equipment (CPE) portion of the Computer II proceeding was to distinguish between telephone-type and data processing-type terminal equipment. The Notice of Proposed Rulemaking (NPRM) suggested that terminals performing a "basic media conversion" (similar to a traditional telephone set or teletypewriter terminal) would be classified as communications equipment, while terminals performing more than "basic media conversion" would be classified as data processing equipment. The commission's proposed distinction was opposed by a wide variety of commentators. While AT&T and GTE claimed that the proposed line provided too strict limits on what they could provide under regulation, IBM and other computer equipment companies challenged the proposed line for leaving too much flexibility to the regulated carriers, expanding the scope of regulation, and increasing the opportunities for cross-subsidy.

After considering objections to the proposed distinctions and the development of CPE competition during the late 1970s, the commission chose an unusual departure from the status quo by deregulating all CPE equipment in its early 1980 Computer II decision. Computer II was the first explicit deregulation in telecommunication. The earlier decisions had allowed competition but continued to regulate the equipment provided by the telephone companies. The earlier line of CPE decisions had been based on protecting consumers' rights to use their telephone service in privately beneficial ways rather than on efforts to bring market forces to the industry. However, the Computer II decision was explicitly deregulatory in nature. The commission sought to separate equipment that could be supplied on a competitive market from regulated monopoly services, and therefore to shrink the boundaries of regulation. The commission concluded:

> We find that the continuation of tariff-type regulation of carrier provided CPE neither recognizes the role of carriers as competitive providers of CPE nor is it conducive to the competitive evolution of various terminal equipment markets. We find that CPE is a severable commodity from the provision of transmission services. The current regulatory scheme which allows for the provision of CPE in conjunction with regulated communication services does not reflect its severability from transmission services, or the competitive realities of the marketplace. . . .
>
> Deregulation of carrier-provided CPE would separate the costs associated with the provision, marketing, servicing and maintenance of CPE from the rates charged for interstate common carrier services. Thus, the deregulation of CPE fosters a regulatory scheme which separates the provision of regulated common carrier services from competitive activities that are independent of, but related to, the underlying utility service. In addition, the separation of CPE from common carrier offerings and its resulting deregulation will provide carriers the flexibility to compete in the marketplace on the same basis as any other equipment vendor.[18]

Under the Computer II scheme, AT&T was allowed to provide CPE only under a "fully separate subsidiary" with strict limitations on the permissible interactions between the unregulated subsidiary and the regulated companies. At the time of the decision, the ability of AT&T to offer unregulated services at all was in question because of the 1956 consent decree that limited AT&T to common carrier (regulated) services. That limitation had influenced earlier considerations of the regulatory boundary because it appeared that eliminating regulation automatically eliminated AT&T's ability to provide the service or product in question. In the Computer II decision, the FCC construed the decree to allow AT&T to provide deregulated services through its separate subsidiary, but noted that it lacked the authority to definitively construe the decree. The commission announced that it would reconsider the decision if the court prohibited AT&T from providing unregulated services:

> We obviously cannot guarantee that the consent decree does not impose some constraint on their [Bell System companies'] activities in these areas. At the same time, however, removal of the uncertainty rests primarily with AT&T, should AT&T deem it necessary. As we perceive the situation, the choice rests with AT&T either to seek clarification from the judgment court as to the limits of permissible activity in these areas, or, weighing the risks, to proceed with its marketing plans for various types of CPE and enhanced services. . . . However, should a decision of the judgment court disagree with our reading of the decree and foreclose AT&T from the provision of enhanced services or CPE, we would feel compelled to reassess the situation to ascertain whether any revision to decisions made here would be warranted in light of our statutory mandate.[19]

The Computer II decision was a rare dramatic departure from the status quo. It was an attempt to eliminate regulated competition by reducing the scope of regulation and providing maximum opportunity for free market forces. The decision was influenced in part by a greater awareness at the FCC of competitive problems in the industry introduced by the appointment of Phillip Verveer (formerly a Department of Justice attorney on the AT&T antitrust case) as chief of the Common Carrier Bureau. At that time, the FCC, Congress, and the Department of Justice were all considering various methods of drawing structural boundaries between the competitive and monopolized portions of the industry.

The major changes ordered in the Computer II decision provoked great controversy in the industry and resulted in numerous petitions for reconsideration as well as requests that the appeals court overturn the decision. After two reconsideration orders and affirmation by the appeals court, the basic structure of the Computer II decision was implemented. The commission was particularly concerned about the valuation of the huge amount of CPE ($14 billion in AT&T book value) together with supporting facilities that would be transferred to the unregulated affiliate. Transfer of assets from the regulated company to the unregulated affiliate at too low a price, for example, would result in a competitive advantage for the affiliate compared to independent companies and create higher regulated rates than would occur under proper valuation. In order to allow time to conduct valuation studies and in order to minimize the effect on rates, a long phase-in schedule was developed. All new equipment installed after January 1, 1983, was to be provided on an unregulated basis, while "embedded" equipment (equipment already installed as of January 1, 1983) would remain on the regulated books of the telephone companies through a long phase-in, which was later modified by the divestiture agreement.

The Computer II decision completed the CPE policy story by shrinking the boundary of regulatory policy to exclude CPE. With that decision, the long-standing question of what attachments to the telephone network must be considered part of the regulated industry was definitively answered. The regulated industry was redefined to stop at the end of a wire on the customer's premises, and any equipment attached to that wire was excluded from the regulated industry. The boundary was defined with public interface standards. All equipment on the customer side of the boundary was for the use of that customer only and was excluded from the complex revenue-sharing and subsidy mechanisms of the regulated telephone industry.

Although Computer II was a major change in industry practice, the FCC was able to implement it despite many objections. The courts upheld the FCC's preemptive authority over the state regulatory commissions, and the congressional oversight committees were more sympathetic to the FCC action than to the telephone company and state regulatory commission opposition to that action. The state concerns that deregulation of CPE would create higher local rates were assuaged with a long phase-in schedule for embedded CPE.

The FCC's ability to implement the Computer II decision was aided by the fact that the argument for severability was simple while the argument for continued regulation was complex. Once interface standards had been established and customers had the option of purchasing CPE on an open market, it was easy to argue that the relationship between CPE and the telephone utility was comparable to the relationship between light bulbs and the electric utility. In both cases, the consumer must supply a piece of equipment to utilize the utility, but the equipment is used only by that particular consumer and need not be supplied by the utility. On the other hand, the argument for maintaining regulation in order to avoid disturbing the established revenue flows was complex and not especially appealing in the generally deregulatory mood of the early 1980s. Furthermore, although CPE was a significant share of the industry capital, it was possible to eliminate CPE from the revenue flows and still maintain the basic system. Thus the deregulation of CPE did not fundamentally threaten the system of payments that kept local telephone rates low in rural and other high-cost areas.

Conclusion

The terminal equipment policy was created by three types of policy institutions (FCC, state regulatory commissions, and appeals courts), with the FCC the leading actor. The dominating factors in the development of the policy were the search for information in a world of great uncertainty, the search for a policy equilibrium as each policy movement created an industry response that required further policy adjustments, and the search for a method to adjust old rules and procedures to changing technology. A secondary factor was differences in the definition of equity among the FCC, appeals court, and state regulators.

The initial situation was a stable equilibrium, with a well-defined telephone industry completely under managerial control with no attachments or interconnection allowed. All parties agreed that the protection of the network was a primary goal. Initially, all parties also agreed that the best method of accomplishing that goal was to give AT&T the freedom and responsibility to manage the network and impose any restrictions that it chose. The FCC initially rejected the Hush-A-Phone because it was unable to specify a proper dividing line between allowed and disallowed attachments, other than the AT&T line of prohibiting all attachments. Strassburg was confident that the Hush-A-Phone itself was not harmful but believed that overruling AT&T on that device could lead to other devices that would be harmful.

The appeals court intervention limited the FCC's discretion to uphold AT&T's restrictions without evidence that they were necessary. The court accepted the FCC and AT&T goal of prohibiting harm to the network, but required evidence that an individual device was harmful rather than the vague assertion that some device that could be allowed could cause harm. The court decision eliminated the simple solution of prohibiting all attachments and required an active effort to draw boundaries between allowable and prohibited attachments. Although there was great uncertainty about what would cause harm, the FCC gradually put less and less confidence in AT&T representations regarding the fragility of the network as initial competitive experiments produced no harmful effects. Because each effort to construct boundaries between allowed and prohibited equipment led to new problems, there was no new policy equilibrium until the Computer II decision deregulated all terminal equipment.

Many FCC and state regulatory rules were based on the assumption that all terminal equipment was provided by the telephone companies and that the boundary of telephone service was obvious. The development of time-sharing computers made the simple approach of telephone company responsibility for all equipment attached to the network obsolete. Rules and policies developed for an environment prior to time-sharing computers generated unreasonable results after that development. Continued failures in efforts to construct a meaningful boundary between unregulated data processing equipment and regulated telephone terminal equipment were an important impetus for the eventual deregulation of all terminal equipment.

The accounting and cost allocation rules created under an assumption of telephone company ownership of terminal equipment were no longer reasonable when some equipment was provided on a competitive basis. State and federal regulators both recognized the problem but came to different conclusions. The state regulators wanted to prohibit competition in order to maintain the old rules and the associated revenue flows, while the federal regulators wanted to change the rules in order to accommodate competition. The Telerent ruling upholding federal preemption together with later court support for Computer II allowed the federal perspective to be implemented.

The various policymakers used differing views of equity to determine their policy choices. The *Hush-A-Phone* court found that the restrictive policies of the FCC and AT&T were unfair to Hush-A-Phone and its potential customers. The FCC then adopted the court's reasoning as its own and attempted to protect the rights of competitive suppliers and users of terminal equipment to take any actions that did not result in harm to the network. The state regulators emphasized the rights of the beneficiaries of the revenue flows to continue to receive income from the separations process applied to terminal equipment.

The technological changes in the computer industry and its relationship to telecommunications also played a crucial role in the evolution of policy. Efforts to allow full utilization of the telephone network by computer users were behind both Strassburg's reasoning on Carterfone and AT&T's initial positive reaction to the Carterfone requirements. At the time, it appeared necessary to allow computer and other specialized equipment supplied by non-telephone companies to be attached to the network, but the focus was on additions to the network rather than substitutions for telephone-company-supplied equipment. As late as 1979, the commission continued its attempt to find a dividing line between ordinary telephone terminal equipment that should continue under tariff regulation and enhanced or computer-like terminal equipment that should be provided only outside of the regulatory boundary. It was only after continual failures to develop a defensible dividing line that the commission reached the conclusion that all terminal equipment should be deregulated. Although there were difficulties with the late 1970s competition between regulated and unregulated telephone terminal equipment, it is unlikely that AT&T's terminal equipment would have been deregulated as soon as it was without the pressure of distinguishing between telephone and computer-related terminal equipment.

Late in the process of terminal competition, the goal of substituting market forces for regulation whenever possible became important. The early decisions were based on protecting customer rights and adjusting the rules to new technologies, not on attempting to reduce regulation. However, as the early decisions brought competitors into the market, competitive controversies between the regulated and unregulated companies were presented to the FCC for resolution. Deregulating CPE was one way of dealing with those competitive problems.

From the current perspective, deregulation of CPE appears to be the obvious way to increase consumer choice in the terminal market. However, deregulating CPE required finding a way to "carve off" the CPE market from the rest of the regulated industry. The separation of CPE from the rest of the industry was accomplished in two stages. First, mandatory standards were developed for the interface between CPE and the telephone company so that any technically qualified company could manufacture CPE that would work with the telephone network. Second, the financial aspects of CPE were disentangled from the complex set of regulated revenue flows within and among the various telephone companies. The financial separation was more difficult and required more implementation time than the technical interface separation. Both technical and financial separation were accomplished successfully, but the total process of separating CPE from the telephone network required more than a decade and vast amounts of regulatory and industry time to solve the implementation difficulties.

Many of the changes in policy were the result of the availability of new information from sources separate from AT&T and the other telephone companies. The policy changes were initiated by companies outside of the regulated telephone industry that challenged the established beliefs shared by the telephone companies and the federal and state regulators. With no outside pressure, the regulators could accept the telephone company conception of the industry as necessarily composed of end-to-end service. When competitors challenged the AT&T conceptions of the industry and the FCC was given a legal obligation to protect individual rights that did not cause public harm, then the telephone companies were required to provide information to support their previously unquestioned claims. The inability of the telephone companies to support their earlier claims caused the commission to attribute more and more weight to the assertions of competitors and less and less weight to the assertions of AT&T. The commission gradually changed its attitude from one of believing that AT&T was sincerely attempting to protect the integrity of the network to a belief that AT&T was only opposing competition to maintain its monopoly position. That change in interpretation of AT&T's actions led to a regulatory emphasis on protecting competitors' rights and eventually to deregulation of the CPE market.

7 / Initial Long Distance Competition

Long distance telephone service remained an effective AT&T monopoly from the earliest days of the Bell patent monopoly through the 1950s. As early as the 1878 patent negotiations with Western Union over the conflicting patent claims, Bell manager Theodore Vail recognized the potential competitive importance of control over long distance lines. Vail refused Western Union's request to settle the outstanding disputes by assigning local rights to Bell and long distance rights to Western Union, even though long distance telephone service was not technically feasible at that time. Vail also reserved long distance rights to the parent company when licensing local operating franchises under the patent monopoly. During the competitive era (1894–1907), the inability of the independent telephone companies to develop an effective competitor to Bell's established long distance network left them limited to local service only. The Kingsbury Commitment of 1913 allowed all companies to interconnect with the Bell long distance network and eliminated efforts to develop a competitive network.

Despite the effective Bell monopoly, no formal government policy either in favor of monopoly or against monopoly in long distance service was adopted. The Bell monopoly was implicitly endorsed by the many different policy actions related to long distance that never sought to eliminate the long distance monopoly. The antitrust action settled by the Kingsbury Commitment of 1913 sought interconnection rights but not a competitive network. The state regulatory commissions sought a portion of the long distance revenues for the local companies, but accepted the existing market structure. The Communications Act of 1934 prescribed regulation for "every common carrier engaged in interstate or foreign communication by wire or radio" but provided no explicit discussion of the desired market structure. The early FCC accepted the existing effective monopoly without either formally endorsing monopoly as in the public interest or making any effort to create competition.

Although AT&T had an effective monopoly on long distance telephone communication, it did not have a total monopoly. Western Union continued to control the telegraph business ("record communication") and provided limited voice service as well. Several different carriers provided international record communication. Right-of-way companies such as pipelines and railroads provided their own private communication systems for internal communication separate from the AT&T long distance network.

Over a 20-year period (1959–1979), competition was gradually introduced into the long distance network through the interaction of FCC decisions and federal appeals court decisions. At no time was there a comprehensive plan for the phased introduction of competition to long distance. At each stage, decisions were made with extremely limited information. There was inadequate information to make a defensible case for either competition or monopoly. Thus under a procedure of making a comprehensive policy, whichever market structure had the burden of proof would have failed. If the FCC had been required to make a fully documented case that competition was superior to the then-existing monopoly structure, it could not have done so, and would not have adopted competition. However, the actual course of policy was determined by narrowly focused decisions guided by particular principles rather than by projections of what would happen under alternative policies. Acceptance of the principles by the policy makers substituted for extensive information and analysis in providing a basis for policy decisions.

This chapter and the next one trace the evolution of long distance policy from acceptance of monopoly through various forms of limited competition and eventually to full competition. That evolution was guided by four principles:

1. There should be no discrimination between similarly situated persons or companies.

2. Individuals or companies should have the right to meet their own specialized needs.
3. Interconnection of communication companies and systems is generally desirable.
4. The established practice of supporting part of the cost of local operating companies from long distance revenue should be protected.

The antidiscrimination principle is subject to an elastic interpretation and is potentially a very powerful determinant of policy. In its narrowest interpretation, it is the Communications Act prohibition of "any unjust or unreasonable discrimination . . . in connection with like communication service" (section 202(a)). More generally, it is a widely held ethical principle that all people should be treated equally under the law. Although an equal treatment or antidiscrimination principle is widely supported, it often must be restricted in scope in order to avoid conflict with other valued principles. Many conflicts in the development of long distance competition and pricing policy can be interpreted as efforts to make different compromises between the principle of nondiscrimination and the principle of protecting established revenue flows from long distance to local companies.

In addition to being valued for their own sake, nondiscrimination rules are used as a way to limit the opportunistic use of information. Policy makers cannot directly check the accuracy of detailed cost information supplied by industry participants. Because of the wide variety of accepted accounting practices, it is possible to tailor each information submission in a way that is favorable to the interests of the firm submitting the data. However, a regulator that cannot directly evaluate the reasonableness of data on the cost of providing service to a competitive system can impose a nondiscrimination rule such as requiring the carrier to charge the competitor the same rate as it charges its own affiliated operations. Such nondiscrimination rules are frequently used to cope with the regulatory problems caused by reliance on carrier-supplied information.

The second principle (the right to provide for one's own needs) is similar to the Hush-A-Phone concept of allowing actions that are privately beneficial without being publicly harmful. The burden is on the incumbent to show why a proposed action that it opposes would cause public harm.

The third principle (interconnection) is incorporated into the Communications Act requirement that "it shall be the duty of every common carrier engaged in interstate or foreign communication . . . where the Commission . . . finds such action necessary or desirable in the public interest, to establish physical connections with other carriers" (section 201(a)). Interconnection requirements have been implemented in many different contexts from the Kingsbury Commitment of 1913 onward. Interconnection can also be justified on efficiency grounds because it increases the value of the interconnected networks and reduces the incentive to build duplicate facilities for strategic advantage.

The fourth principle (protecting revenue flows) was particularly a concern of the state regulatory commissions but was supported by the FCC and congressional leaders as well. There was general satisfaction with the nationally averaged long distance rate structure, near-universal telephone service, and low telephone rates even in sparsely populated high-cost areas of the country. Most telecommunication policy makers other than those in the Department of Justice sought explicit protection for at least part of the established revenue flow system in order to avoid having it eroded away by competition.

The principles could be given an elastic interpretation adjusted to the particular issues in any specific problem. However, they played an important role in guiding and stabilizing policy across the many groups and individuals contributing to the process. While the principles were not binding rules, they were also not merely individual personal preferences. Widespread acceptance of the principles even among people who disagreed on their interpretation and implications provided a framework for policy arguments.

Bulk Private Service: "Above 890"

Prior to World War II, economical long distance communication required a physical connection (wire or coaxial cable) among the points served. Wartime efforts to develop high-capacity radio-based communication systems produced a microwave communication system used by the Signal Corps. Further development by the Bell System and others after the war created a commercial microwave system that could be used for either high-volume voice communication or transmission of video signals. Because microwave communication systems used radio frequencies, they required a license from the FCC. The FCC initially granted experimental licenses for microwave freely, and AT&T along with several other companies built early systems. However, the FCC's permanent licensing policy was more restrictive and favored AT&T provision of microwave service for both voice and video signals. Private microwave systems were allowed where AT&T did not provide adequate facilities. Private systems were established in remote areas for television transmission and were established by railroads and pipelines along their rights of way.[1]

AT&T's tariff structure during the 1950s caused users with a very high volume of communication among a few places to pay more than the cost of providing service privately through microwave. Applications to build private microwave systems to serve their own communication needs were filed by Central Freight Lines for a Texas system and Minute Maid Corporation for a Florida system. Motorola, a supplier of microwave equipment, pressed the FCC for broader authorization of private microwave systems.

In 1956 the FCC began a proceeding to develop policies for the allocation of microwave frequencies, known as "Above 890" because it was concerned with the allocation of frequencies higher than 890 MHz (above the frequencies allocated to UHF television). AT&T, Western Union, and the independent telephone companies argued that private microwave should be limited to areas where common carrier facilities were not available and should be abandoned when common carrier service became available. They argued that frequencies were scarce and could be most efficiently used by the common carriers. Furthermore, they argued that "widespread licensing of private systems would not only increase the cost of communications to the Nation's economy as a whole but would cast an added burden upon the individual and the small businessman who would continue to rely on common carriers."[2]

In contrast, the potential users and microwave equipment manufacturers argued that there should be no limitations on eligibility to establish private systems, that sharing of a system by more than one user should be allowed, and that the availability of common carrier facilities should not be a factor in licensing private systems. The microwave equipment manufacturers and potential users of private systems contended that although frequencies were not unlimited, there were adequate frequencies available for both common carriers and private users and that the commission had no duty to protect the economic interests of the carriers. The Electronic Industries Association (representing microwave manufacturers) presented an engineering study representing 6,000 person-hours of effort that indicated an opportunity for a 20-fold increase in the then-current number of microwave stations without interference even in the most congested areas.

In 1959 the FCC concluded that adequate frequencies were available for both common carrier and private microwave systems and that therefore private systems should be licensed. It sidestepped the questions of interconnection and economic harm by ruling that interconnection questions would be dealt with on a case-by-case basis, and that the demand for private microwave systems would be so limited that there could be no significant economic impact on the carriers.

The decision was not a determination to begin competition in long distance service. It did not authorize new companies to enter the communication business in competition with AT&T but only allowed individual users to build systems for their own use. The decision to license private microwave systems was framed as a frequency allocation issue, not as an issue of the market structure for long distance communication. The case was only before the FCC because of the commission's jurisdiction over the use of radio frequencies. Because it involved a frequency allocation issue, the key question was the availability of frequencies for the requested use. The Communications Act instructed the commission to "encourage the larger and more effective use of radio in the public interest" (section 303(g)). Any reasonable proposed use of the radio spectrum that did not interfere with other existing or proposed uses was generally approved. If two proposed applications interfered (as in two requests for the same broadcast frequency in the same city), a hearing was held to determine which application best satisfied "the public interest." Thus in the private microwave case, the EIA study showing that private and common carrier microwave systems could operate simultaneously without interference created a presumption that licenses should be granted to both types of systems.

Because the problem was framed as a question of frequency availability, the competitive impact and rate structure questions were largely ignored. No effort was made to predict the future course of prices with and without private microwave and to choose the preferred path. If the problem had been framed as a question of long distance market structure, much different data and analyses would have been used.

Private microwave systems required a substantial fixed cost per route and a low marginal cost per circuit. The systems were not competitive for users with traffic spread over many different locations. However, they were competitive for bulk users of "private line" service. The simplest private line service provided a direct circuit between two specific locations. At the time of the decision, AT&T charged a fixed rate per circuit for private lines (regardless of the traffic carried over that circuit), and charged multiple private lines at a multiple of the single-line rate with no volume discounts. The cost of private microwave systems relative to the then-existing tariff structure made common carrier service cheaper than private microwave for those with fewer than about 50 circuits between two specific points, but provided strong incentives for those with very high two-point demand to build a private system.

Immediately after the final decision allowing private microwave systems, AT&T filed a price response that largely eliminated the incentive for any company to build a private system where AT&T facilities were available. The new tariff, called Telpak, offered large discounts for groups of private lines: a discount of 51 percent for 12 lines (Telpak A), 64 percent for 24 lines (Telpak B), 77 percent for 60 lines (Telpak C), and 85 percent for 240 lines (Telpak D). For a set of 240 lines over a distance of 100 miles, a customer would have paid $75,600 per month under the old rates and $11,700 per month under the new rates.[3] The old rates were four times Motorola's estimate of the cost of a comparable private system, while the new rates were 30 percent below that cost estimate. The rates for a single private line were not changed.

The Telpak tariffs, as with most tariffs of the time, prohibited resale and sharing. The great differences between the cost per line for a single line and for a group of lines would not have been viable if a group of users could pool their demand to purchase service under the Telpak volume discounts. Telpak was a strong competitive response to the availability of private microwave. It largely eliminated the incentive of companies to build private systems where AT&T facilities were available.

The goal of large users in seeking authorization for private microwave was a reduction in the cost of their own bulk communication needs. They were not seeking to enter the communication business and were satisfied to remain with AT&T if the latter would provide attractively low prices. Consequently, many of the potential users of the newly authorized private microwave systems willingly abandoned planning for their own systems, signed up for Telpak, and supported the importance of Telpak in subsequent hearings. However, Western Union and the potential suppliers of microwave equipment saw the Telpak tariff as a discriminatory and predatory pricing scheme that would take away Western Union's private-line business through un-remunerative AT&T rates subsidized by its monopoly services, and would stunt the non-AT&T/Western Electric market for microwave equipment. Challenges to the lawfulness of Telpak led to extensive hearings, which became bogged down in interminable controversies over cost allocation methodologies. After extraordinarily complex litigation over a 20-year period (including one time when both the FCC and AT&T sought to eliminate Telpak but the appeals court ordered it continued to protect the interests of the customers using it), Telpak was finally withdrawn in 1981.[4]

Although private microwave was not competitive with common carrier services in the sense of providing the same service with a particular price structure, it did constrain the range of feasible price structures for the long distance service market. Because of the high value of communication relative to its cost and the lack of alternatives to AT&T services, AT&T's total allowed revenue could be recovered from many different price structures. Private microwave provided an alternative to AT&T for a particular set of bulk communication users, and therefore it was no longer possible to extract the revenue from those users as had been done before the private microwave authorization. Thus AT&T's choice was to lose those customers or to restructure its rates in order to make the AT&T network more attractive than the alternative of private microwave.

AT&T's Telpak rate restructuring created a regulatory quandary. The FCC did not have the information to evaluate AT&T's claim that the non-Telpak users were better off with Telpak than with maintaining the old rate structure and allowing some users to substitute private microwave for the common carrier services. The Telpak tariff created a legal problem of discrimination because AT&T was providing both low-volume and high-volume private line service under tariff at very different rates. Although the economic effect would have been the same if high-volume users obtained cheap service from private microwave while low-volume users obtained expensive service from AT&T, the legal issue of discrimination would not have been present in that case. The FCC had not previously been required to make detailed cost-allocation judgments or to evaluate the rate structure in detail; thus it did not have the staff expertise and operating procedures to evaluate the competing claims. Because of the FCC's inability to fully resolve the issues, AT&T's right to have its tariff go into effect unless found unlawful determined the issue.

Although the private microwave decision was framed as a narrow question of the availability of adequate frequencies for common carrier and private use, it was a crucial step in the evolution toward a competitive market. It provided the first alternative to AT&T services for long distance customers other than right-of-way companies such as railroads and pipelines. It induced a substantial restructuring of private line rates, with greatly reduced rates for large users. It forced the FCC to evaluate cost allocation issues and economic arguments that had not been necessary before.

The private microwave decision and the Telpak response increased the incentive to use private lines rather than switched service. Many large companies established systems of private lines as a replacement for switched voice service. The largest of these new systems was the federal government's Federal Telecommunications System (FTS), which established an extensive system of private lines connected by switches to provide the equivalent of switched long distance service for communication among government agencies. Because of the importance of FTS, the federal government entered the Telpak fights as a user of Telpak and by the late 1970s was arguing that the elimination of Telpak would increase the government's communication cost by $80 million per year. The development of extensive private line systems as a substitute for switched service reduced the separations payments to the local companies. The cost allocation formulas were based on the usage of switched services, and minutes carried over private line systems reduced the count of switched minutes.

The implications of the Above 890 decision were not known at the time, nor was there any effort to predict and evaluate those implications. If the commission had predicted the AT&T competitive response to Above 890 and attempted to judge whether the status quo or the predicted new situation was better, it probably would have declined to make private microwave available. When the question was framed as the right of private companies to use otherwise unneeded frequencies for their own private benefit, it was easy to grant the request on the basis of the general principles of allowing private choices and encouraging the use of radio frequencies. If the question had been framed as whether large users should be allowed to reduce their share of payments to AT&T while receiving the same service, the commission would not have had a basis for deciding one way or the other and thus would probably have allowed the status quo to continue.

Although the commission was skeptical about the legality of AT&T's Telpak response to Above 890, it lacked the information and analytical tools to make a definitive assessment of whether or not the tariff was illegally discriminatory. AT&T's right to have the tariff take effect while it was being investigated allowed it to continue the tariff for many years until the commission decided to eliminate all resale restrictions. Once resale was allowed, the many thousands of pages of arguments over whether Telpak was discriminatory or not became irrelevant. The clearly discriminatory nature of the tariff was shown in the incentive of people to arbitrage between the discounted Telpak rates and the much higher single line rates. Immediately after the prohibition of resale limitations, AT&T sought voluntarily to withdraw the Telpak tariff.

MCI Initial Application

The Telpak rate structure clearly indicated that the AT&T single line rates were far above microwave costs. If a company could purchase a set of 240 lines at the Telpak bulk discount rate and resell them to individual users who had been paying the single line rate, substantial profits could be made. Although the AT&T tariff prohibited the resale of Telpak lines, the fact that the Telpak tariff was designed to be competitive with private microwave indicated the potential profitability of setting up a private microwave system and sharing that system among users too small to benefit from the Telpak volume discounts. Providing service to unaffiliated companies over a microwave system removed it from the definition of "private" and thus was not directly authorized under the Above 890 decision. At the time, there was no explicit policy regarding the licensing of microwave for the use of new common carriers.

Three years after the Above 890 decision authorizing private microwave systems, Microwave Communications Inc. (MCI) filed an application for a public microwave system between St. Louis and Chicago. MCI was a new company founded by radio serviceman and entrepreneur Jack Goeken. Goeken proposed a limited microwave system costing about one-half million dollars that would have less capacity than many private systems. Goeken estimated that he needed to obtain 35 users to break even and presented a research report that concluded he was likely to obtain between 58 and 204 customers. Rather than supplying the capacity for a single company's intracorporate communication, Goeken's proposed system would provide low-cost, low-quality service for many different companies. The proposed system was designed to minimize cost and included low-bandwidth (and therefore low-quality) circuits, as well as limited provision for backup and servicing.

Because Goeken's proposal was for providing service to others, it could not be routinely granted under the private microwave policy. AT&T and Western Union along with the local carriers along the proposed route opposed MCI's application, complaining that the service would meet no demonstrated need, that it would result in wasteful duplication of facilities, that MCI did not possess the legal, technical, and financial qualifications to install and operate the system, and that the system would cause radio interference to existing and future facilities of the established common carriers. The opposition caused the FCC to refer the matter to a formal hearing. In such a hearing, the Common Carrier Bureau participates and makes a recommendation, but the decision of the Hearing Examiner rather than the bureau goes to the commission as a recommendation. MCI's limited finances and informal methods of operation as well as the actions of the incumbent carriers caused the hearing to be postponed several times; it was finally held in 1967.

Common Carrier Bureau chief Bernard Strassburg later recalled the case as a close call on a minor matter that was greatly influenced by the economists on his staff. He stated:

> There was a lot else going on, and what I had heard of the [MCI] hearings was mostly negative. Moreover, based on very few personal encounters with Goeken, I could not help but question his credentials to construct, own, and operate a common carrier system to compete with the likes of AT&T or Western Union. Certainly, he did not fit my stereotype of a successful entrepreneur. The case had been dragging on for a long time, and I didn't consider it a high priority item. A week before the proposed findings were due, I initiated getting together with two of the staff economists who had worked on the

case, Manley Irwin and Bell Melody, and discussed at some length what the case was all about with them.

Notwithstanding some personal misgivings, it looked like here was a legitimate opportunity to factor in a new supplier. The conventional thinking was still that the Bell System was a natural monopoly, but some changes in the demand side of the environment were beginning to show themselves. . . .

Jack Goeken's Chicago–St. Louis proposal looked like a safe and prudent guinea pig. I couldn't see any harm to be done by giving it a try to see what happened. We would find out whether there was [a] market for the specialized services he was proposing. So I issued instructions to rewrite the bureau's position, which had been drafted as a denial, to recommend a grant.

Still, wondering how the commissioners would react, I told the staff to make it clear we were not proposing a commitment to a new policy, but rather to put the applications in a "test tube" motif.[5]

In 1967 Hearing Examiner Herbert Sharfman adopted Strassburg's recommendation and found in favor of MCI. He found that despite the absence of AT&T-level care in the proposed construction, the system was likely to work, and dismissed the arguments of cream-skimming:

MCI sites are small; the architecture of the huts is late Sears Roebuck toolshed, and they are without the amenities to which Bell employees, for instance, are accustomed, and servicing and maintenance are almost improvisational; but there is no reason to believe that the system will not work, unless one is bemused by the unlikely occurrence of the catastrophes to which the carrier witnesses gloomily testified. . . .

Clearly, if the averaging doctrine is sacrosanct, and "cream-skimming" is an attendant horrific to the extent the carriers claim, they have insulated themselves against private line competition except from carriers with unlikely initial operations as widespread as theirs. They are like courtiers who deign to accept challenges for duels only from those of equal rank. But the efforts of a relatively impoverished newcomer, proposing a novel if by no means faultless service, to give battle on his chosen ground should not be impaled by this agency upon a principle devised by his opponent.[6]

By the time the appeal of Sharfman's decision was decided by the full commission in 1969, President Nixon had taken office but had not been able to make an appointment to the commission. None of the four Democratic commissioners who formed the majority under President Johnson had resigned, and their terms had not expired. In a rare split along strictly partisan lines, the four Democratic commissioners voted to uphold the examiner's decision in favor of MCI, while the three Republican commissioners voted against the decision.

The three dissenting commissioners viewed the case as a challenge to the established system of regulated monopoly communications services and nationwide rate averaging. They saw the case as prejudging major policy issues of interconnection and rate structure under the guise of a limited hearing for a small-scale construction application. Thus their opposition was based on a correct forecast that the MCI case provided an important precedent and was much more significant than the actual construction applications would suggest.

The majority emphasized the actual facts of the MCI applications rather than the significance of the decision for future policy. The proposal was to build a single-channel microwave over the single route of St. Louis to Chicago. The expected initial service was 75 voice circuits, and the expected maximum service was 300 voice circuits. Thus the proposed capacity of the new competitor was no more than would have been expected from a single private user operating under the 1959 private-user authorization. The majority was unwilling to deny what in effect was a shared private system that provided small users with the benefits of private system costs.[7] The commission's focus on the specific applications rather than the broader policy issues raised by new competition allowed it to experiment without determining an explicitly procompetition policy. The FCC dodged the issue of whether or not potential economic harm to established carriers was grounds for denying new competition by noting that the proposed MCI facilities were too small to have any effect on AT&T's financial results.

It is unlikely that MCI's application would have been approved if MCI had simply proposed providing identical service to that provided by AT&T at lower cost. Although there was no explicit grant of monopoly to AT&T, the commission had established a policy that duplication of facilities and services was generally unwise. The early microwave decisions had allowed private microwave only where common carrier facilities were unavailable. Near the time of the initial MCI decision, the commission had denied a request from GTE to build its own microwave system to carry toll traffic among its telephone companies because the proposed system would duplicate AT&T facilities. However, MCI proposed "specialized" services that would differ from the services provided by AT&T and would be customized to meet special needs. The differences between MCI's and AT&T's services were an important component in both the substantive reasoning and the legal justification of the decision. Strassburg was seeking ways to accommodate data transmission and "fill in the voids" of the AT&T services, rather than providing direct price competition.[8] Complaints from computer service companies and others about AT&T's inability to meet their specialized needs provided encouragement to the commission to allow MCI's proposed new services.

MCI's initial application was one example among many where "packaging" or "framing" of the issue was crucial. The services actually provided were essentially duplicates of the AT&T services at a lower price. However, MCI's formulation of the services as specialized services to meet needs outside of the AT&T range was designed both to appeal politically and to fit the legal definitions. It became possible to ignore the policy of avoiding duplication rather than changing it because of the claim that the services would not be duplicates. The computer companies' claims regarding AT&T's rigidity in providing services they needed also made it politically attractive to offer an alternative supplier.

It is easy to criticize the FCC majority's narrow interpretation of the MCI case as a small-scale construction application that was too small to have an economic impact on AT&T. Both staff and commissioners were certainly aware of the significance of precedent in regulatory policy and could have reasonably predicted that approval of the initial MCI application would encourage many similar applications. Peter Temin's history of the period reports: "AT&T told him [Strassburg] that he was opening a door he would not be able to close. But Strassburg insisted that approving MCI's application was just an experiment, a chance to try something that might not even work. Wishful thinking led him to ignore the clear signs of danger on that front."[9]

Most economists and other policy analysts would suggest that decisions should be made in a comprehensive way, taking account of all the relevant facts, rather than piecemeal. Yet it is important to recognize that the substantive regulatory decisions are affected by the scope. Even if Strassburg and the majority commissioners had worked out a policy of full competition in their own minds at the time of the MCI vote, they did not have the information to justify such a policy formally. Consequently, acknowledgment that the MCI application was a crucial policy change would almost certainly have required its denial. By framing the question narrowly, they could justify granting the MCI application without answering all the questions that a policy of full competition would raise. Commissioner Nicholas Johnson explained his support for the application as an attempt to try something new: "I am not satisfied with the job the FCC has been doing. And I am still looking, at this juncture, for ways to add a little salt and pepper of competition to the rather tasteless stew of regulatory protection that this Commission and Bell have cooked up."[10] A comprehensive proceeding to consider competition would have certainly delayed the application and probably would have raised so many issues on which only AT&T had detailed information that the application would have been denied.

Specialized Common Carrier Competition

Appeals and reconsiderations of the 1969 decision delayed final approval of the MCI application until January 1971. Meanwhile, the 1969 decision induced a large number of additional applications for similar service. Many of the applications came from MCI under the ambitious and aggressive leadership of William McGowan, who replaced Jack Goeken. With hundreds of applications on file, and each opposed by AT&T with essentially the same arguments, the commission decided to proceed by rulemaking rather than evidentiary hearing. The procedural difference meant far faster evaluation by settling the common issues through a notice and comment rulemaking rather than litigating each application in a trial-type proceeding. Over two hundred parties responded to the rulemaking notice with the predictable split of opinion. The existing common carriers were against any grant of new applications and challenged the right of the commission to authorize extensive new competition. They asked for delays of various kinds, ranging from individual evidentiary hearings on each application to a hold on new authorizations until the MCI facilities were actually in operation and could be evaluated. The carriers claimed that the new competition would cause great disruption in the established communications system and would lead to higher rates for customers, as well as causing frequency congestion and increased costs through duplication of facilities. The potential new carriers, their equipment suppliers, and their potential customers all supported new entry.

In May 1971 the FCC announced a fundamental policy decision in favor of increased competition. The new policy was recommended by the staff and approved unanimously by the commissioners, in contrast to the sharp divisions over the MCI application. The commission stated:

> We find that: there is a public need and demand for the proposed facilities and services and for new and diverse sources of supply, competition in the specialized communications field is reasonably feasible, there are grounds for a reasonable expectation that new entry will have some beneficial effects, and there is no reason to anticipate that new entry would have any adverse impact on service to the public by existing carriers such as to outweigh the considerations supporting new entry. We further find and conclude that a general policy in favor of the entry of new carriers in the specialized communications field would serve the public interest, convenience, and necessity.[11]

The proposed systems were trunk-line private line systems that did not extend to individual customer locations. Individual customers needed circuits from the local telephone companies to connect their premises with the proposed new systems. As part of the Specialized Common Carrier (SCC) decision, the FCC ordered that established common carriers would be required to interconnect with the new carriers to provide local distribution facilities. The decision did not define precisely what "specialized" services included or what the exact interconnection requirements were; it left those terms vague, to be settled by later decisions. However, the decision was understood by its authors to open up the existing private line market to competition as well as to allow new services by the new carriers. Under the decision, individual licenses for microwave routes were still required, but the issues for those licenses were limited to technical concerns such as the potential for interference with existing radio sources, rather than the policy question of whether to license new carriers that was considered in the initial MCI hearing.

The MCI precedent made it much easier to reach a procompetitive decision in Specialized Common Carrier than it would have been without that precedent. It was clearly within the legal authority of the commission to distinguish the case of hundreds of applications for a nationwide system from the case of a single application for a particular limited route. However, doing so would have required an explicit finding that the larger proposed systems were different because they posed economic harm to the existing carrier. The commission had dodged the question of whether or not it had an obligation to protect the economic interests of the incumbent carriers in the first case by finding that the system was too small to matter. The SCC case continued the same line of reasoning by asserting that the proposed systems were still too small to matter.

In the year of the SCC decision, the Bell System (including both AT&T and the operating companies) received $9.0 billion in local telephone revenue, $7.9 billion in switched long distance revenue (MTS and WATS), $0.3 billion in telephone toll private line revenue, and $0.4 billion in Telpak revenue. Because the Telpak rates were much lower than single line rates and the switched market was not open to competition, the $0.3 billion in telephone toll private line revenue was the primary competitive target. The telephone private line revenue constituted about 3 percent of the Bell System total toll revenue and 1.6 percent of the total operating revenue.[12] Thus it was plausible that competition for 3 percent of Bell's toll revenue while the other 97 percent remained a monopoly was unlikely to cause economic harm, though the argument was not so clear as it had been for the single St. Louis–Chicago route.

Given the MCI precedent, reaching an opposite conclusion for the additional applications would have required clearly distinguishing them from MCI's initial application. The most obvious distinguishing factor was the total size of the proposed systems. To use that fact to turn down the applications would have required a finding that the commission had an obligation to protect the economic interests of the Bell System and that the proposed systems were a threat to that interest. Those findings would have limited the commission's flexibility to encourage competition at a later date. MCI's aggressive filing of many new applications after its initial authorization limited the commission's freedom to try Strassburg's experiment of evaluating initial competition before deciding on the next step. The commission was forced to choose between denying the applications and developing a monopoly rationale to support its actions, or adopting a policy of open entry into specialized services. The commissioners who were unwilling to support the initial MCI action were also unwilling to defend an explicit grant of monopoly to AT&T. The vote on the SCC decision was unanimous.

The SCC decision departed from the implicit policy of monopoly service. It also introduced an important procedural innovation by using a notice and comment rulemaking to settle the policy problems of disputed license applications rather than holding a formal trial-type evidentiary hearing on each application. As in the case of terminal equipment competition, the state utility commissioners opposed the decision because they feared that it would upset existing revenue flows. NARUC unsuccessfully appealed the FCC's decision on both procedural grounds (formal evidentiary hearing required) and substantive grounds (no showing that AT&T services were inadequate). Although the state regulatory commissioners could file comments in the proceeding and appeal the outcome, they had no ability to take independent action. Radio frequency authorizations were explicitly reserved to the federal government and the common carrier authorizations were specifically for interstate service, eliminating the problem of joint authority over equipment used for both interstate and intrastate service that occurred with terminal equipment.

Conclusion

The events recounted in this chapter were driven by the necessity to decide specific requests brought before the FCC by industry participants. The commission did not decide on a policy of limited competition and then gradually implement it. Rather, it responded to particular requests in accordance with generally accepted principles. Each decision was made in a narrow context, but each decision helped shape the context for the next decision. The primary policy choice was to license microwave frequencies to companies other than the established common carriers. That decision was made in the context of spectrum allocation controversies of the past. Spectrum controversies generally occur when it is not possible to provide the requested spectrum to all contending companies without creating interference. Thus the factual determination that adequate microwave frequencies were available for both established common carriers and new companies, together with the established policy of encouraging use of the radio spectrum, suggested that the requests for private microwave should be granted. Denying the requests for private microwave when frequency was available would have required a policy of holding the private companies captive to AT&T and preventing them from satisfying their own communication needs in the way they considered best.

Although the economic effect of the decision authorizing private microwave was to initiate limited competition for long distance, from a regulatory point of view the decision was not establishing competition with AT&T. It was merely authorizing companies to use the radio frequencies to satisfy their own communications requirements. Those companies had the right to satisfy their own requirements without FCC authorization so long as they could do so without radio frequencies. Their need for FCC authorization was solely a result of their desire to use radio frequencies and not a result of the FCC's regulatory authority over communications common carriers.

Once private microwave and the resulting AT&T private line volume discounts were established, it was a small step to allow MCI to establish a microwave system and bring the benefits already enjoyed by large customers to smaller customers. The economic effect of the MCI authorization was equivalent to allowing the sharing of a private microwave system. The departure from the then-existing implicit policy of monopoly long distance service was disguised by the emphasis on MCI's "specialized" services and the experimental nature of the authorization. Insofar as MCI provided new and specialized services, it was not really a competitor of AT&T. With the Specialized Common Carrier decision, competition was explicitly encouraged in a limited segment of the market. That decision made a general policy of the MCI authorization rather than treating it as a unique experimental case. Although the decision did not specifically define the scope of specialized services, it was understood to authorize competition in private line services generally.

Under the end-to-end concept of service, individual services were defined and priced according to the expected customer valuation of the total service. Various combinations of terminal equipment, local connections, and long distance capacity could be used to provide a wide variety of services. The prices on the various services were set by business and regulatory criteria that did not correspond closely to the costs of the particular components of the services. The gradual liberalization of terminal equipment discussed in Chapter 5, together with the construction of bulk long distance capacity outside of AT&T's

control, provided building blocks for new competitive services at very different prices from those maintained by AT&T. Protection of the existing price structure depended on limitations on interconnection of the long distance capacity available from the new long distance carriers with the local operating companies. With the general authorization of competitive microwave systems, the battle for competitive advantage through the policy process turned to interconnection questions.

8 / Interconnection and Long Distance Competition

After the authorization of competitive microwave, the range of services the competitors could provide depended on the form of interconnection they received. Microwave provided bulk service between specific points. It was useful without interconnection for providing communication between two locations that had a high two-point demand, but that market segment was already supplied with private microwave and AT&T's volume discounts. MCI's plan depended on collecting the traffic of smaller users through the existing telephone facilities, carrying it over a distance on the MCI microwave network, and then distributing the traffic to smaller users through the existing telephone network. The Specialized Common Carrier decision in 1971 specified that interconnection would be required, but left the exact form of interconnection and the terms unspecified.

At the time, AT&T's pricing policies (and therefore the competitive opportunities) differed according to specific services that were differentiated by the types of connection between bulk long distance facilities and local distribution facilities. Although there were a large number of particular services, three were of primary importance. All three are illustrated in Figure 3, which is a simplified representation of the network. The customers are represented by the letters A through I, and the filled circles (B, E, H) represent large business customers that have a private switch (PBX) on their premises. Customers are connected to a local central office, and the central offices are connected to a toll office.

The simplest service is a two-point private line, represented by the

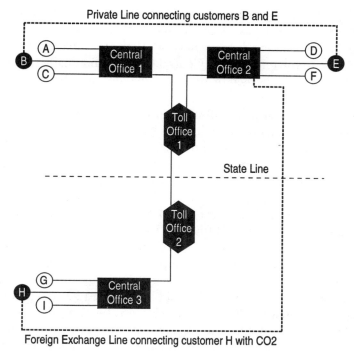

Figure 3. Network Services

connection between customers B and E. Although the private line would be physically routed along with other switched facilities (and in many cases was a capacity unit of a facility jointly used for private line and switched services), from a customer perspective, it is a separate line directly connecting the two customers. If the private line is connected to a PBX on each end, all extension phones served by one PBX can communicate with all extension phones served by the other PBX. Private lines were charged according to distance and capacity at a fixed rate per month, independent of the number of calls made over them. Thus a single voice grade private line between specified locations was charged at the same rate whether it was idle most of the time or used 24 hours per day.

An ordinary long distance call, commonly referred to as Message Telecommunications Service (MTS), allows service between any two customers through a system of interconnecting switches. A call from A to I, for example, proceeds from A's telephone to Central Office 1, where it is recognized as a long distance call and passed to Toll Office 1, then across the long distance network to the terminating Toll Office 2, and then to the terminating Central Office 3 and finally to customer I. MTS calls were charged by time and total distance, but not by actual location. Thus a three-minute call over a distance of 1,000 miles would be the same price regardless of whether it was between two small towns or two large cities, a practice known as "geographic averaging." AT&T was never specifically required to use geographic-averaged pricing for MTS, but it did so voluntarily and rural areas considered the practice vital to their welfare.

Foreign Exchange (FX) service is a hybrid of switched and simple private line service. It is represented by the private line connecting customer H with Central Office 2. By connecting with the central office rather than an individual, H receives access to all customers in local exchange 2. H receives a local phone number in exchange 2 and can make or receive calls as if H were physically located in the exchange 2 area. During the 1970s, AT&T classified FX as a private line service. It charged for FX based on the private line rates for service from H (the "closed end") to exchange 2 (the "open end"), plus the rate for local telephone service in exchange 2. If the FX service crossed a state line, as in the diagram, the private line portion of it was considered an interstate service and charged according to an FCC regulated tariff while the local service portion was considered intrastate and regulated according to the state utility commission regulated tariff. As discussed later in this chapter, the question of whether state or federal tariffs should be used for providing interconnection with competitors was an important issue in policy and competition.

The service distinctions were important because of differences in the way in which revenue was shared among the various components that made up the services. All three services used combinations of local and long distance facilities. The cost allocation formula for the simple private line was designed to recover the fully allocated cost share (including overheads) of the local equipment used for the private line service. The cost allocation formula for the MTS service was designed to recover much more than the fully allocated cost share of the local equipment used to originate or terminate long distance service. As the state regulators sought a greater share of the long distance revenues in order to hold down local prices, the allocation formulas were changed to increase the fraction of local costs recovered from the MTS revenue. FX service paid less than its fully allocated cost share because the open end received service at the local rate that was held below full cost by the revenue from MTS service.

At the time of the 1971 SCC decision, the FCC clearly intended to allow competition for simple private line service and clearly did not intend to allow competition for MTS service. The question of whether AT&T was required to provide interconnection for the hybrid FX service was not settled at that time. The dividing line between competition for private line services and monopoly for MTS services allowed the FCC to avoid dealing with the revenue flows from MTS to local service. As discussed in Chapter 5, those revenue flows had been created through a series of hotly contested political compromises over the years and were vital to the interests of many state regulators and independent telephone companies. Authorizing competition for all long distance services would have required making complex and politically controversial decisions about which revenue flows to protect and how to protect them. By limiting competition to private line services, the FCC could argue that the competition was an experiment that had no substantial effect on either AT&T's total revenues or the revenue flows to independent telephone companies.

Although the FCC made the distinction between private line and MTS services in accordance with then-existing practices in the market, there was little fundamental difference among the services. In Figure 3, the simple private line between customers B and E could be used to connect any person in exchange 1 to any person in exchange 2. Customer C, for example, could call B as a normal local call, be "patched through" the PBX onto the private line to E, and then dial a normal local call to reach F. That arrangement uses the PBX as the equivalent of a toll switch. Although there were a number of technical differences regarding line quality and signalling that made that arrangement of lower quality than an ordinary MTS call, the possibility of such nonstandard arrangements meant that control of interconnection was required to avoid having private line competition interfere with the revenue flows from MTS service.

This chapter examines the evolution of competition from simple private line to FX and MTS. The evolution occurred because of MCI's aggressive and innovative use of its private line and interconnection rights to create a substitute for MTS service. MCI's service innovations were protected against the FCC's attempt to limit competition by court interpretations of MCI's procedural rights.

The Private Line Interconnection Controversy

MCI's initial St. Louis–Chicago connection was built within a few months after final authorization, and service was initiated in January 1972. During 1972 the company built new facilities authorized under the SCC decision and by 1973 had established a basic network to many major cities. On April 1, 1972, AT&T CEO H. I. Romnes retired and was replaced by John deButts. While Romnes had sought ways of accommodating limited competition in the Bell system, deButts ordered an aggressive defense of AT&T's monopoly control. Even though public policy was becoming more favorable to competition after the Carterfone and SCC decisions, deButts moved AT&T into stronger resistance to competition, setting up a major clash with government authority.

The first substantial dispute occurred over interconnection rights. The SCC decision had ordered that "established carriers with exchange facilities should, upon request, permit interconnection or leased channel arrangements on reasonable terms and conditions to be negotiated with the new carriers" and had further specified that "where a carrier has monopoly control over essential facilities we will not condone any policy or practice whereby such carrier would discriminate in favor of an affiliated carrier or show favoritism among competitors."[1] The statement clearly established the new carriers' rights to interconnection, but left uncertain what would constitute "reasonable terms and conditions" and what would constitute discrimination "in favor of an affiliated carrier or . . . favoritism among competitors."

At the time AT&T provided long distance private line service in cooperation with local carriers through an interstate tariff that specified "rate elements" for the long distance portion and the local portion. Furthermore, AT&T provided facilities to Western Union at particularly favorable rates. Western Union had a limited network and was in chronic financial difficulty, which allowed AT&T to provide favorable interconnection rates to Western Union at little competitive risk to itself. However, AT&T did not want to provide connecting service to the new carriers at the Western Union rates or at the rate element specified in its interstate tariff. Although the new carriers sought those favorable rates, AT&T claimed that the Western Union contract was a special arrangement not applicable to any new carriers and that the rate elements for local distribution in AT&T's tariff were merely rate elements in a joint service and not rates for interconnected service.

Developing an appropriate rate for local private line connections through cost allocation procedures became a never-ending job. Neither the local rate elements in the existing AT&T tariffs nor the Western Union interconnection rates were meant to be cost-based. The FCC's goal was cost-based interconnection tariffs, but the interconnection required facilities that were used jointly for many services, and thus the "cost" was determined by the particular method of cost allocation used. AT&T had an incentive to show high interconnection costs in order to increase the costs of its competitors, and the FCC lacked the expertise to fully evaluate either the methodology or the results of particular cost allocation studies. At the time of the interconnection dispute, the FCC had been conducting the Telpak-related cost allocation proceeding for many years without resolution. In order to avoid a similar quagmire with regard to private line interconnection rates, the commission supervised negotiations among the parties to develop "interim" rates for private line interconnection while cost-based rates were being developed. Although the interpretation of the 1975 agreement was highly contentious and caused extensive controversy before the FCC and the courts, the interim negotiated agreement remained the basis for private line interconnection charges until after the divestiture.

The interconnection dispute concerned the types of services for which AT&T was required to provide interconnection as well as the rates to be charged for connecting service. It was clear that AT&T was required to provide interconnection for simple private lines that provided direct communication between two specified points. However, MCI claimed the right to interconnection to provide "foreign exchange" (FX) service, while AT&T denied that responsibility. A related private line arrangement used for configuring private switched networks for large organizations, known as Common Control Switching Arrangement (CCSA), was also the subject of disputed interconnection rights.

In February 1973 MCI informed FCC Chairman Dean Burch that it was having difficulty negotiating interconnection arrangements with

AT&T but did not ask for FCC intervention at that point. In August of that year MCI filed a complaint with CCB chief Strassburg, charging that the Bell companies were refusing to interconnect with MCI and that they were discriminating in favor of Western Union and AT&T in the services they did provide. AT&T's response denied the charges and indicated its intention to file interconnection tariffs with state authorities and to end its contract with Western Union. AT&T's proposed action would eliminate the discrimination between Western Union and MCI by raising Western Union's rates, and would end the discrimination between service provided to MCI and to AT&T Long Lines by treating them as jurisdictionally separate services. Filing the interconnection tariffs with state authorities would also take them out of the FCC jurisdiction and place them under the control of the state regulatory commissions, which were generally more sympathetic to the Bell view of proper policy.

In the midst of the interconnection dispute, AT&T chairman John deButts delivered a highly publicized speech (discussed in Chapter 6 with regard to terminal competition) to the National Association of Regulatory Utility Commissioners (NARUC) convention, in which he called for a "moratorium on further experiments in economics" and emphasized the Bell System's determination to oppose competition and espouse monopoly. Strassburg interpreted the speech as a direct challenge to his and the commission's efforts to initiate competition and adopted a more adversarial role toward AT&T as a result. Strassburg described the speech as follows:

> He [deButts] attacked the FCC's policies seeking to foster competition in both terminal equipment and intercity services. He made it clear that AT&T regarded accommodation or conciliation with those policies as heading down a path leading to destruction of time-tested principles of regulated common carrier monopolies as the best way to meet the nation's communications requirements. AT&T, he was saying, was now determined to actively resist further implementation or expansion of the FCC's policies.
>
> He received a rousing ovation of approval from his audience of state commissioners and regulated industry officials. Upon returning to his seat in the auditorium, he walked over to me. I knew he considered me the personification of misguided policymaking by the FCC. "No hard feelings, Bernie," he said, smilingly extending a handshake. I complimented him on the effectiveness of his delivery,

while expressing reservations about the substance of his talk and whether it was in the best interests of those affected.

Clearly, John deButts had thrown down a gauntlet of defiance on behalf of the most potent corporate power in the nation. It had ominous implications for the future implementation of the FCC's pro-competitive policies and the beneficiaries of those policies.[2]

A week after deButts's NARUC speech, MCI chairman McGowan met with Strassburg deputy Kelly Griffith to discuss a draft MCI letter formally requesting confirmation that FX and CCSA were authorized MCI services entitled to AT&T interconnection. The next day AT&T vice president George Cook met with Strassburg to formally notify him of AT&T's intention to file interconnection tariffs with state commissions rather than the FCC. Strassburg and Griffith concluded that MCI was entitled to FX and CCSA connections, in part because the services were classified as private line services in AT&T's tariffs. However, they advised MCI to wait for a commission ruling on the jurisdictional issue before filing a formal request for the FX and CCSA clarification.

The next week Strassburg met with the commission to discuss the jurisdictional issue involved in AT&T's proposal to file interconnection tariffs with the states rather than the federal government. Strassburg recommended rejection of AT&T's position, and a second meeting was scheduled the following day to finalize a response. Between the two meetings Strassburg met with McGowan and assured him that if the commission approved Strassburg's letter to AT&T the following day, he would then provide confirmation of MCI's right to provide FX and CCSA. The next day, the commission approved Strassburg's proposed response to AT&T. The response rejected AT&T's state tariffing approach and ordered AT&T to file interconnection tariffs with the FCC to allow the specialized carriers the necessary exchange facilities for their "authorized services." The commission did not specify what was included in "authorized services." As previously arranged, MCI then formally requested a clarification from Strassburg that it was entitled to interconnection for FX and CCSA service, and Strassburg confirmed that FX and CCSA were included within MCI's "authorized services."

In later explaining his actions that appeared to intentionally leave the commissioners out of the initial decision on the extent of MCI's authorized services, Strassburg emphasized his concern about the po-

litical forces attempting to influence those on the commission to re-
treat from the initial competitive policy:

> The commissioners, individually and collectively, were being increas-
> ingly buffeted by the telephone industry and state commissions. The
> latter were becoming more outspoken in their attacks on the FCC's
> policies of fostering competition in both specialized intercity services
> and customer premises equipment.
>
> John deButts's speech still reverberated and underscored the dif-
> ficulties that lay ahead for carrying out the FCC policies. In the wake
> of the intercity/state offensive, I sensed a growing uncertainty among
> some of the commissioners about the efficacy of competition. They
> were troubled that the new carriers had not made more dramatic
> progress in introducing new and innovative services, let alone com-
> peting for existing markets.
>
> The commissioners were creatures of politics—some more than
> others—and there were those who believed AT&T's goodwill, or the
> lack of it, could make a difference in realizing their political fortunes.
> It was not unknown for a commissioner to shade his or her voting,
> even if it meant the compromise of a personal conviction, to avoid
> incurring AT&T's antipathy.
>
> . . . I was concerned for the viability of the competitive policies I
> had been instrumental in shaping. I therefore felt justified in provid-
> ing the fledgling carriers with all the help I could extend within the
> limits of my authority and powers as bureau chief. The authority to
> interpret and implement FCC policies was, of course, my most im-
> portant and useful asset.[3]

AT&T appealed Strassburg's interpretation to the entire commission and continued its refusal to provide the requested interconnection. MCI then sought a court mandate to force AT&T to provide
connections. After a hearing, Judge Newcomer of the Philadelphia
District Court issued an injunction granting MCI's request on January
7, 1974. AT&T appealed the order and sought a stay while the appeal
was being heard. On February 4, the appeals court granted a stay.
AT&T then cut the connections for MCI's FX customers, leaving
them without service and raising questions about MCI's reliability as a
supplier. Later in 1974, the full commission confirmed that FX and
CCSA were included in MCI's authorized services, and the appeals
court upheld that ruling. FX/CCSA then became regular services of
MCI.

The FX/CCSA interconnection dispute is recounted here in some detail because it played a vital role in later policy issues. It was a substantive issue in itself because the outcome determined whether MCI would have access to the full range of private line services or only one part of those services. However, its greater significance was in setting a precedent for the future. The FX interconnection gave MCI access to the switch and thus allowed it to expand its services beyond those contemplated by either Strassburg or the commissioners. Furthermore, AT&T's aggressive actions in denying interconnection until absolutely forced by court mandate together with its elimination of service to the new competitors when the appeals court temporarily lifted its obligation played a major role in its antitrust difficulties. The incidents recounted above were examined in detail both in MCI's private antitrust suit against AT&T and in the Department of Justice suit that led to the divestiture. AT&T's opponents portrayed the events as proof that AT&T was determined to use its "bottleneck" control of local facilities to stop competition.

The FX interconnection dispute also contributed to a strong antipathy toward AT&T among many FCC staff members. AT&T's vigorous efforts to combat tiny MCI (which at the time of the Philadelphia court hearing in 1973 had revenues of $48,000 per month, amounting to 0.002 percent of the Bell System revenues of $2,000,000,000 per month) seemed heavy-handed and unfair. Strassburg's personal transformation over a 20-year period from the staff member who supported AT&T's right to refuse customers even the ability to use the innocuous Hush-A-Phone to the protector of MCI and other fledgling competitors was representative of the greatly increased suspicion of AT&T within the FCC. AT&T's decision to fight the FCC's policies vigorously in every forum available, including the state commissions, courts, and Congress, eliminated the protective feeling that regulatory agencies often have toward their incumbent carriers.

AT&T's Rate Response to Private Line Competition

MCI's ability to compete effectively with AT&T's private line services was determined by the extent of interconnection, by the prices paid for the interconnected facilities, and by the prices AT&T charged for services competitive with the MCI services. At the 1971 AT&T rates for private line services and at the 1971 prices that the Bell System charged Western Union for interconnection, there was opportunity for extensive profit. In addition to fighting the interconnection wars, AT&T sought to make its tariff structure a less attractive target.

When MCI's initial St. Louis–Chicago application was first approved, AT&T developed an "exception tariff" to reduce rates only on that route. However, AT&T's outside economic advisor, William Baumol, argued against filing the exception tariff. Baumol believed that a reasonable test for predatory pricing was the permanence of an incumbent's price reduction when faced with new competition. If prices remained permanently at the new lower level, the price reduction was an ordinary and desirable adjustment to more competitive conditions. If prices were reduced long enough to drive the competitor out of business and then raised again, the price reduction was predatory. Baumol was concerned that AT&T would only maintain the exception tariff while MCI was offering that particular service and then raise prices back to the normal schedule, creating a suggestion of illegal predatory pricing. After extensive high-level consideration of the exception tariff within AT&T, the company decided in early 1972 to forgo the special St. Louis–Chicago tariff and develop a more comprehensive plan for reducing vulnerability to private line competition. At the time MCI had only 14 customers using a total of 18 circuits, and AT&T decided that the benefits of an exception tariff were not worth the risks of adverse antitrust and/or regulatory action.[4]

The decision not to file the exception tariff was made under Romnes' leadership just before he retired. The issue was further discussed at the first "Presidents' Conference" (meeting of the leaders of the Bell Operating Companies and other high-level executives) after John deButts took charge. The minutes reported:

> A number of the conferees expressed disappointment that AT&T had not filed an immediate competitive response to MCI on the Chicago–St. Louis route. An immediate response, it was pointed out, would have provided clear notice of our intention to compete. To delay is to risk the prospect that, once one or more specialized common carriers become going businesses, regulatory authorities might seek to assure their continued viability regardless of the economic justification for their survival.

DeButts responded to the concerns:

> With respect to MCI, the EPC [Executive Policy Committee] did in fact decide at one point that as soon after their filing as practicable

the Bell System would respond with an "exception tariff" that would take account of the changed conditions in the Chicago–St. Louis route. The fact that on maturer reflection the EPC decided to defer this filing should not be taken as a sign of unreadiness to compete. The fact of the matter is that we realized we simply did not have the information on which to make an intelligent decision and in the absence of that information it didn't make sense to commit ourselves to a course of action, involving as it would a breach of so basic a principle as nationwide average pricing, from which there would be no turning back.[5]

In late 1973 (while the FX interconnection dispute was at its height), AT&T filed its new rate plan for private lines, known as the "Hi-Lo" tariff. The country was divided into regions of high-density lines and low-density lines. The new plan reduced the rates for high-density routes and increased the rates for low-density routes, resulting in the same expected total revenue for AT&T. The private line rate plan was a departure from the principle of geographic rate averaging (same rates for a particular length of call regardless of the actual route) that the Bell System and many regulators had long espoused. The monopoly switched services continued to follow geographic rate averaging.

MCI regarded the new plan as an illegal attempt to drive it out of business by reducing rates where MCI had or was building facilities and raising rates where AT&T did not face competition. McGowan visited deButts and threatened an antitrust suit. When AT&T refused to concede to MCI's demands, MCI filed its private antitrust suit and also began seeking a government antitrust suit. MCI and the other new carriers also challenged the new pricing plan before the FCC.

Under the Communications Act, tariffs are filed by a carrier and become effective automatically unless the FCC specifically stops them; they do not need explicit approval to become effective. A tariff can be suspended for a maximum of 90 days while the commission investigates it. Under the procedures used in the 1970s, investigations required far longer than 90 days to complete. Consequently, even tariffs opposed by the FCC staff would become effective until the investigation was complete. The Telpak cases had shown that a tariff investigation could drag on for years and result in long periods of operation under a tariff later found to be illegal. The commission suspended the Hi-Lo tariff for the maximum 90 days, and it then went into effect in 1974 while the investigation continued. After two years, the commission ruled that Hi-Lo was illegal and ordered AT&T to file a replacement tariff.[6]

AT&T's new private tariff was known as Multi-Schedule Private Line (MPL). MPL continued the Hi-Lo practice of separate rates for high-density and low-density areas of the country, and changed the previous flat rate per mile to a decreasing charge per mile with increases in the line distance. The rate taper increased the cost of short private lines and decreased the cost of long private lines. In a duplication of the Hi-Lo scenario, the commission suspended MPL for 90 days after complaints from AT&T's competitors and began an extensive investigation while the tariff went into effect in 1976. In 1979, the commission concluded that the MPL tariff was illegal and considered prescribing a tariff. However, because the commission lacked adequate information to meet the legal requirements for prescribing a tariff, it decided to allow the MPL tariff to remain in effect while it conducted a wide-ranging and time-consuming investigation of the general structure of AT&T's private line tariffs. The MPL investigation was still in progress when the 1982 divestiture agreement made many of the issues moot.

The Hi-Lo and MPL tariffs brought AT&T's private line price structure into closer alignment with its costs than the previous rate structures. The cost per line was less on a dense route than on a sparse route because of the economies of density in two-point communication paths. The cost per mile also decreased with the total number of miles included in a circuit. The tariffs were a departure from longstanding averaging principles, but those principles were not designed to provide cost-based rates. Because private lines are provided as one part of a large network, a determination of the cost of private line service over a particular route is an exercise in cost allocation. The tariffs did not comport with the particular methods of cost allocation favored by the FCC at the time and were therefore declared unlawful. However, the antitrust courts took a more positive view of the tariffs and did not find them predatory under the antitrust standards.

Just as the initiation of private microwave put a market restriction on the feasible range of price structures that would recover total cost, so the initiation of private line competition put additional restrictions on the feasible set of price structures. Because the initial private microwave decision was relevant only to high-volume customers, it placed a market limit on the prices that could be charged for large numbers of private lines but did not limit the price structure for small numbers of lines. When competition is allowed into a market priced at averaged rates, competitors will naturally attempt to serve the low-cost customers in order to maximize their profit. The averaged prices then become economically infeasible. They are changed either through a rearrangement of the prices by the dominant firm (as happened with Hi-Lo and MPL) or by the entrant taking the business away in the lower-cost routes and creating a differential between the prices there and the higher prices of those retaining the incumbent's service.

The private line controversies were a case of the regulatory agency attempting to maintain the status quo prices (by objecting to AT&T's proposed new tariffs), but failing to do so because of procedural limitations. AT&T was not required to justify the earlier averaged private line schedule, which was discriminatory in an economic sense because it contained the same rates for services with very different costs. AT&T did have to justify departures from that schedule under a strict standard in order to get FCC approval of the new rates. However, it had the procedural right to allow the rates to go into effect without FCC approval and wait out the extended investigation process. AT&T's freedom came from the difference in time allowed for suspension (90 days) and the time required for a final determination of lawfulness. At that time, the commission used formal trial-type procedures before an administrative law judge to determine tariff disputes. Later the procedures were streamlined in a way that allowed much faster investigations and therefore reduced the freedom for a carrier to implement rates opposed by the commission.

The private line tariff controversies contributed to a belief among Department of Justice staff that the FCC was unable to regulate AT&T. Walter Hinchman, who succeeded Strassburg as CCB chief during 1974 and supervised the private line tariff evaluations, testified at the government antitrust trial that the FCC was unable to regulate AT&T effectively. That belief created a desire to develop an antitrust solution to the competitive problems in the industry that would not be dependent upon FCC regulation.

Execunet and Switched Services Competition

In 1975 MCI began offering a service it described as "shared FX service" that it named Execunet. Under the Execunet service, the originating private line in FX service was shared among customers. A customer of Execunet called the MCI office as an ordinary local call and was connected to the "private line" through the MCI switch.[7] AT&T's version of FX service allowed interconnection of the private line to a company PBX so that the line could be reached by all of the extension phones of that company's location. MCI simply extended that approach by allowing the connection to be made with calls from the local area rather than only with internal calls. The Execunet service is illustrated by the FX line in Figure 3. There is no technical difference between Execunet and ordinary FX lines. The innovation was allowing customers such as G and I to access the service through a local call to the MCI office (H on the diagram), rather than restricting the use of the FX line to employees of H, and charging the users by the minute. It allowed the customer to access the MCI network through a local call to the MCI office, enter an identification code and the terminating telephone number, and thereby reach general terminating locations. It was essentially switched long distance service, though it required much more extensive dialing codes and provided a lower quality of service than the AT&T switched service.

The MCI Execunet service was a natural extension of the practice of sharing FX lines among employees of a single company to the practice of sharing FX lines among customers of MCI. In an ordinary competitive market, it would simply have been a response to pricing anomalies and would have eroded away the price discrimination implicit in the prior limitation on the sharing of FX lines to employees of a company. But because of the regulatory boundary that had been drawn between private line and switched service, with a far greater subsidy component built into the switched service, the Execunet service was a major challenge to the existing revenue flows. The Execunet service was of lower quality than the AT&T switched service, but otherwise was equivalent to switched service from the customer's point of view and was therefore far more competitive with switched service than previous versions of private line service.

MCI's Execunet service was a challenge to the regulatory boundaries drawn by the FCC, and if allowed to exist was a challenge to the price discrimination supported by those regulatory boundaries. The then-existing pricing practices allowed a far lower cost per minute for long distance communication between H and customers in exchange 2 through an FX line than through MTS. That discrimination was sustained by the practice of charging a fixed rate per month for the FX line that limited its use to companies with a high volume of calls. MCI's plan to subdivide the FX line and charge its usage by the minute would have eliminated the price discrimination between FX charges and MTS charges by allowing customers an MTS equivalent service at FX rates. However, the massive payments to local companies from long distance revenue flows were financed by high MTS rates that could not be sustained in an Execunet environment.

MCI's Execunet service in relationship to private line service was analogous to MCI's initial private line business in relationship to private systems. Prior to the MCI authorization, microwave was available to large businesses that could utilize the high capacity of a private microwave system. AT&T had responded to that competition with the Telpak tariff, which provided large volume discounts on bulk private line service. MCI's initial entry application essentially sought to share the capacity of a private microwave system among unrelated parties in the same way that the capacity of a private microwave system was shared among employees of a large company. The ability to share a bulk offering either through a separate company such as MCI or through resale of circuits obtained under an AT&T tariff broke down the barriers that allowed the maintenance of price discrimination between large and small users. Similarly, the Execunet "shared FX" tariff threatened to break down the regulatory barriers between voice and private line service and to reduce or eliminate the price discrimination between those two markets.

AT&T challenged MCI's Execunet tariff before the FCC, complaining that it was an unlawful entry into the switched voice market in violation of MCI's authorized services. Bernard Strassburg had supported MCI's private line competition but did not believe that MCI was authorized to provide competition to switched long distance service. He stated:

> In both the MCI proceeding and the specialized common carriers proceeding, MCI had explicitly represented to the Commission that it was not seeking authority to compete with AT&T's message toll service and wide area telephone service—AT&T's regular switched voice long distance services. Based on these representations of the limited nature of MCI's proposed service offerings, there was no need for the Commission in those proceedings to address the multiplicity

of difficult economic and public policy questions that competition with MTS and WATS so obviously raised. . . .

In the event that MCI had proposed Execunet service to the FCC while I was bureau chief—as part of the FX/CCSA interconnection dispute or independently of that dispute—I would have advised MCI that its facility authorizations and FCC policies precluded such a service.[8]

MCI's initial Execunet tariff was described as a "building block" tariff from which individuals could select the components they wanted rather than taking only the particular components bundled together by the company to make a complete service. Neither the FCC staff nor AT&T recognized the implications of the new tariff, and it went into effect routinely without opposition. However, once AT&T understood what the tariff allowed, it protested informally to the FCC and then filed a formal complaint. The FCC quickly found the MCI tariff improper (July 1975) and ordered it discontinued. After MCI succeeded in obtaining a stay of the FCC order from the Appeals Court, the FCC held more extensive proceedings on the issue and reaffirmed its finding that Execunet was beyond the scope of the MCI service authorizations.

MCI's appeal of the FCC order resulted in one of the most significant policy changes in the history of the telecommunication industry. In a famous decision written by Judge J. Skelly Wright, the Appeals Court found in favor of MCI on procedural grounds. The court looked for formal findings that AT&T's monopoly of switched service was in the public interest or that MCI's facility authorizations restricted it to particular services. Because there were no such findings, the court ruled that the FCC could not retroactively limit MCI's service authorizations over the existing facilities. The FCC appealed the decision to the Supreme Court, but the Court refused to hear the case.[9]

After the Appeals Court found that the FCC failure to explicitly limit MCI's authorization allowed it to proceed with Execunet over existing facilities, AT&T announced that it would not provide interconnection arrangements for MCI's Execunet service. The FCC supported AT&T's decision, leaving MCI's victory temporarily hollow. MCI returned to the Appeals Court and again won a resounding victory with a ruling that AT&T was obligated to provide interconnection for the service.[10] In part, the court decision requiring access was caused by Strassburg's 1974 strategy to guarantee MCI's right to FX interconnections. At that time he had asked the commission to affirm that AT&T was required to provide connections for MCI's "authorized services" rather than for specific named services, and had then interpreted the commission order to apply to FX. Once the Execunet court concluded that Execunet was one of MCI's "authorized services," then it naturally followed from the existing commission order that AT&T was required to provide connections for Execunet.

Interconnection Charges: ENFIA

In MCI's initial Execunet service, it ordered ordinary business lines from the state-regulated local tariff to connect its offices with the local central offices. MCI expected to receive the same service and pay the same rate for local connections between its switch and the local telephone office as any other business would obtain for local telephone service. That practice was consistent with the established pattern of charging for FX open ends at the ordinary local business telephone rate. MCI considered its Execunet service equivalent to FX with two open ends rather than the normal FX pattern of one open end and one closed end.

AT&T observed that minutes flowing between a local central office and an AT&T toll office effectively paid a very high rate for local service because of the way those minutes were used to allocate the costs of the local exchange to create a claim on long distance revenues. AT&T did not pay for access service by the minute but could compute an implied cost per minute by dividing the total revenue distributed to local companies through the settlements and division of revenues process by the total number of long distance access minutes used. After the Appeals Court ruled in 1978 that AT&T was required to provide interconnection for MCI's Execunet service, AT&T filed a new interstate tariff with the FCC known as ENFIA (Exchange Network Facilities for Interstate Access) in which it proposed to charge the new competitors the full amount of AT&T's estimated contribution to local exchange through the settlements and division of revenues process. AT&T claimed that MCI could not obtain interconnection facilities under the state-regulated local business rates but must obtain them from the far higher federally-regulated ENFIA tariff. The jurisdictional choice was contrary to AT&T's earlier position that private line connections should be tariffed with the states, but consistent with the FCC's ruling in that case that local connections for an interstate service were to be provided under federally tariffed rates.

MCI stridently opposed AT&T's proposed ENFIA tariff. It denied that there was any subsidy flow from long distance to local service and claimed to be simply providing a shared version of established private line service. It did not receive AT&T's "trunk side" connections that transmitted information for signalling and billing through the local switch. Consequently, MCI's service was lower in technical quality and required a long dialing sequence to convey the necessary signalling information to the MCI switch. MCI required ordinary local business lines for customers to call its office in order to initiate an Execunet call and claimed that it should pay the established local business rate. Furthermore, MCI supplied financial information to the FCC that indicated the ENFIA rates would convert its profits on Execunet into losses and asserted that AT&T was attempting to drive it out of business.

Because of the court-imposed necessity of establishing connections and the difficulty of fully resolving the controversy, the FCC accepted the suggestion of Henry Geller (then head of NTIA in the Commerce Department) that it supervise negotiations between the parties to develop an interim solution while an access charge proceeding was conducted. The ENFIA negotiations were modeled after the earlier negotiations that had worked out an agreement for private line interconnection rates in 1975. After extensive negotiations, a settlement was developed that both sides were willing to accept as an interim solution until the development of access charge rules. Under the 1978 settlement, AT&T computed an average cost per minute from the existing cost allocation process by which it shared long distance revenue with local telephone companies. The new competitors would pay 35 percent of the AT&T rate so long as their total revenues (as a group) were below $110 million per year; 45 percent when their total revenues were between $110 and $250 million; and 55 percent when total revenues were between $250 and $375 million. Despite the parties' hopes that the ENFIA arrangements would soon be replaced by access charges (which each side believed would be more favorable than the ENFIA agreement), the 1978 settlement remained the basic structure for payments between the competitors and AT&T until 1984.

Although it was established as an interim compromise settlement, the initial ENFIA agreement incorporated a major policy decision that has continued to dominate telephone pricing issues. Prior initiation of competition in specific sectors had resulted in a movement of prices toward cost in those sectors. Because the competitive potential was so circumscribed, the price changes had relatively little effect on the total system of revenue flows from toll charges to defray the cost of local telephone companies. With Execunet, the burden of the charges could no longer be easily shifted. Allowing MCI to provide Execunet by ordering connecting service from existing local tariffs would have pushed the price of long distance service toward the cost of providing service between cities and eventually eroded away the revenue flows to local telephone companies.

The ENFIA tariffs created a legal distinction between two physically identical services. If a person made a call to any local business not providing long distance service, the call was charged at the existing local tariff rate (often at a zero usage charge). If a person made a call to the local MCI office that was then relayed over the MCI network, the call was charged at the much higher ENFIA rate. The legal and price distinction between technically identical calls for local communication and for connecting with a long distance carrier has been maintained to the present in order to allow the local companies to share in the long distance revenue. Many of the issues discussed in later chapters are related to the tension between the desire of policy makers to maintain the legal price discrimination and the ability of entrepreneurs to profit by arbitrage among the discriminatory prices.

Competition under the ENFIA Agreement

MCI's court victories, together with the ENFIA agreement and a separate FCC decision that invalidated AT&T's restrictions on resale of its services, established the framework for early switched services competition. Although a large number of companies began service, the only two substantial early competitors were MCI and Southern Pacific Communications Company (later part of Sprint), the two established facilities-based private line competitors. Both companies put primary emphasis on developing the switched market and reduced their efforts in the private line segment.

The initial competition was a niche market for particularly price-sensitive customers who were willing to accept some degradation in quality and convenience in return for lower price. The competitors' primary market was small and medium businesses. The AT&T pricing structure provided volume discounted service (WATS) for large businesses and substantial evening/night discounts primarily for residential customers, but the moderate-use daytime caller paid relatively high rates. The new competitors first established their business among those moderate-use daytime callers who paid the highest per minute rates under the AT&T price structure. After first offering service only among selected cities, the competitors established resale facilities to allow their customers to terminate calls anywhere in the United States. They expanded the set of cities from which they offered originating service as they expanded their networks of physical facilities.

Although their initial market was daytime MTS calls, the competitors rapidly expanded their marketing efforts to include residential customers. An important component of the competitors' ability to pursue the residential market was the structure of access charges under the ENFIA agreement. Charges were based on the number of lines connecting the interexchange competitor and the local switch, rather than on the measured number of minutes between the two points. The necessary number of lines was largely determined by the peak demand. Consequently, off-peak calls incurred little or no additional access charge from the perspective of the competitive carrier. This feature of the access charge system made it much more attractive to service the off-peak discounted residential market than it would have been if the competitors had to pay a per-minute access charge for the off-peak traffic.

The competitive carriers, led by MCI, expanded rapidly from a small base during the early 1980s. MCI's gross revenues rose from $206 million in 1980 to $1521 million in 1983, an exponential growth rate of 67 percent per year for those three years. Southern Pacific Communications' total operating revenues rose from $153 million in 1980 to $740 million in 1983, an exponential growth rate of 53 percent per year. The $2.3 billion in 1983 revenue achieved by the two primary competitors was just over 6 percent of the total switched toll revenue reported to the FCC for that year.[11]

The companies continued to invest heavily in new facilities, initially building backbone networks among the major cities, then filling in with connections to smaller cities and overbuilding the backbone with higher-capacity facilities. MCI's annual investment grew with its gross revenue and remained at near 50 percent of gross revenues in the early 1980s, requiring continual infusions of new financing. Because MCI had no corporate parent, it was dependent upon public perceptions of its potential future profitability (greatly influenced by current profitability) in order to attract the necessary financing to continue expansion of its physical facilities and services. MCI was highly profitable during the early period. Between 1980 and 1983, MCI earned an average of 13.3 percent on total assets and 21.5 percent on stockholder equity.[12] Southern Pacific Communications was less profitable than MCI, but its return on total assets rose from near zero in 1980 to 19.4 percent in 1982, averaging 10.0 percent during the three-year period.[13] MCI's early profitability was adequate for it to attract the necessary external financing to maintain its growth rate and to improve its debt rating and reduce its interest costs.

Even though it was growing rapidly in revenues, plant, and net profits, MCI complained bitterly about the level of its ENFIA payments for local connections. In the 1981 Annual Report, CEO William McGowan explained his expectation of a future cost-based market:

> This means the end of all those strange and undocumented AT&T claims that local business rates subsidize local residential rates, that urban subsidizes rural, that long distance subsidizes local, and so on. . . .
>
> Because of the leanness of its operations and the trimness of its organization, MCI has been able to pass along the economies of its efficiency in the form of lower rates. However, as AT&T has been able to saddle MCI with the diseconomies of its own relative inefficiency by charging MCI above-cost access fees, MCI's genuine economies have been partially masked. But a cost-based market will remove that mask, and permit MCI's better ways of doing things to become more obvious.[14]

While MCI's McGowan expounded the view that the ENFIA rates were so high that they were hiding MCI's true efficiency advantage over AT&T, AT&T continued to assert that the ENFIA rates were far too low and that MCI was an inefficient company that could only compete because of favorable access charge payments relative to AT&T. The different views produced dramatically different forecasts of MCI's future profitability when the ENFIA agreement was replaced by access charges applied equally to all companies. Table 1 presents MCI's reported profit for the ENFIA years together with two alternative computations. The "24% Discount" column restates MCI's profits as if the company had paid access rates at a discount of 24

Table 1 MCI's Pre-Divestiture Pretax Profits (in millions of dollars)

Year	Reported Profit	24% Discount	No Discount
FY1979	7.10	−22.49	−37.93
FY1980	13.30	−37.30	−63.70
FY1981	23.50	−53.47	−93.63
FY1982	129.00	12.16	−48.80
FY1983	240.60	−24.21	−162.37

Source: MCI Annual Reports and author's calculations.

percent from the level AT&T computed as equal. The 24 percent differential was one FCC computation of the difference required to compensate for the inferior technical quality of MCI's access connections. The "No Discount" column represents MCI's profits if it had paid access at the AT&T requested rate equal to AT&T's implied cost per minute under settlements.

According to MCI's view, equal opportunity would have produced even better results than the rapidly growing profits shown in the first column. According to AT&T's view, equal opportunity would have produced results similar to those in the third column, with rapidly growing losses. The access payments were such a critical component of long distance financial results that the difference between the MCI actual results and the MCI results recomputed as if payments had been made at the AT&T requested rate constituted 37 percent of MCI's gross revenue.

Whether AT&T's or MCI's view was closer to the truth was important for both public policy decisions and investment decisions. The question of which company was competitively disadvantaged by the ENFIA agreements would appear to be a purely factual one that could be answered precisely. However, the differences in technical quality for access together with the complex cost allocation process used to determine AT&T's payments to the local companies made it difficult to determine the relative advantage of either company from the access arrangements. The limited information available and the complexity of the process by which AT&T's settlements were determined made it possible for participants to choose a view that fit their own interests or that they found plausible.

AT&T's record of overstating the dangers of any competition in the network, together with AT&T's control of the separations and settlements system, caused many policy makers to treat AT&T's claim of competitive disadvantage from ENFIA with skepticism. Investors generally accepted MCI's view that it was far more efficient than AT&T. MCI's stock price increased from a high of $6.50 per share during the quarter ending December 31, 1979, to a high of $55.50 per share in the quarter ending June 30, 1983, a compound increase of 61 percent per year over the 3.5-year period. The Department of Justice also accepted MCI's general view of the world and sought to protect long distance competition from AT&T's efforts to maintain control.

Conclusion

The FCC's efforts to implement its policy of private line competition by requiring AT&T to provide local connections allowed MCI the technical ability to provide a substitute for AT&T's MTS service. When the FCC sought to implement its implicit policy of MTS monopoly by prohibiting the MCI Execunet service, the appeals court struck down the action as procedurally incorrect. The appeals court gave no guidance on how the revenue flows within the industry should be maintained or rearranged under competition, nor did it even find that competition was in the public interest. It merely found that the FCC could not assume that monopoly was in the public interest and could not prohibit MCI's provision of services over its previously authorized facilities without going through proper procedures. Yet the ruling had the substantive effect of moving the huge message toll market ($20 billion in 1979, or 40 percent of total telephone company operating revenues) from protected legal monopoly to potential competition. Although the FCC could have attempted to make a properly justified finding that monopoly MTS was in the public interest, the court ruling that the burden was on justifying monopoly rather than on justifying competition effectively decided the issue.

Throughout the evolution from a monopoly long distance market to a competitive long distance market, the FCC was largely a passive judge of the specific issues brought before it by the parties. The commission never established a policy of monopoly, nor did it establish a policy of particular degrees of competition. It allowed tariffs to go into effect without either approving them or finding them unlawful. It frequently dodged important questions by declaring them insignificant at the time they were raised and not returning to them when the market events made them significant. Thus the change from monopoly to competition was not the result of a particular personnel change or new study that caused the FCC to adjust its policies. Nor can the policies easily be explained as a natural reaction to changing technology.

Although the commission was sympathetic to AT&T's claims that the market was a natural monopoly, it never fully accepted AT&T's views or made them a part of its rules. AT&T's frequent and extravagant claims about the harms of competition made it difficult to determine when the issues raised were significant. In the private microwave case, AT&T claimed both that there were inadequate frequencies available and that the private systems would harm its rate structure. When the Electronic Industries Association showed AT&T's claim of frequency scarcity to be false, it was easier to ignore AT&T's claim of economic harm even though there was little information available on that claim. Had AT&T acknowledged the availability of frequencies and focused its efforts on the economic effects of allowing competition, it is likely that its economic claims would have been taken more seriously.

As Strassburg describes it, the origin of the most significant FCC pro-competitive decision was quite casual. Just before the recommendation was due, two staff economists convinced him to recommend approval as an experiment, reversing the already drafted denial recommendation. Had Strassburg recommended denial, it is practically certain that the commission would have followed his recommendation. There was no extensive study of the likely consequences of the decision or consideration of the future problems to be solved if competition was allowed. Rather, it seemed innocuous to allow a small-scale experiment that promised specialized services for a very narrow segment of the market. Yet once the MCI application was approved, it was no longer easy to deny similar applications, and this eventually led to full private line competition. Because AT&T already had a partially switched service classified as a private line service (FX), it appeared only fair to allow MCI's private line services to be coterminous with AT&T's. Then MCI recognized that it could "share" the FX lines to make the equivalent of switched long distance service. The sharing required no new authorizations and was implemented through a tariff that even AT&T did not initially oppose. Because the new service was provided with existing facilities and authorizations, the court refused to allow the FCC to make the judgment call that the economic effect of the Execunet service placed it outside the class of MCI's authorized services.

Part III / Structural Boundaries

9 / The Divestiture

The last three chapters have examined the gradual development of competition in terminal equipment and long distance telephone service. During the 1970s, regulatory barriers to entry in parts of the market were eliminated, but those segments subject to competition remained dependent on interconnection with other segments in which entry was not possible. AT&T resisted the entry of new competitors into its formerly monopoly markets through pricing changes and interconnection limitations. In an effort to prevent its policies from being thwarted by AT&T's restrictive marketplace tactics, the FCC became deeply involved in managing regulated competition between AT&T and its tiny competitors.

Neither AT&T nor its competitors were satisfied with the commission's decisions in the competitive disputes. AT&T believed that the FCC's steps toward competition gave unfair advantages to competitors and unreasonably risked the practice of unified network control that had been developed by Theodore Vail at the beginning of the century and had continued with the acquiescence of policy makers ever since that time. The competitors believed that the FCC's slow response to what they regarded as outrageous AT&T competitive tactics prevented them from competing fairly. Both sides sought policy forums other than the FCC's slow case-by-case resolution of issues in order to develop a global solution for the industry's competitive disputes. AT&T sought congressional action to restore the monopoly policies of the past, while MCI sought Department of Justice antitrust action against AT&T in order to eliminate AT&T's anticompetitive actions.

This chapter examines the efforts to craft a global telecommunication policy through congressional action and through antitrust action. The congressional efforts failed because of the lack of adequate consensus on the appropriate overall policy toward the industry. The antitrust efforts led to the divestiture of AT&T's operating companies as the Justice Department's long-term solution to the competitive problems of the industry.

The Consumer Communications Reform Act

In the famous 1973 NARUC speech discussed previously, AT&T chairman John deButts based his call for suspending competitive experiments on the need for a major national reexamination of the policy toward the telecommunication industry:

> At issue in all these matters is the degree to which competition should obtain in a field that has been brought to its current state of development through the application of basic principles—end-to-end responsibility for service, the systems concept, the common carrier principle itself—that the doctrine of competition for competition's sake puts in jeopardy and could in time destroy. . . .
> The time has come, then, for a moratorium on further experiments in economics—a moratorium sufficient to permit a systematic evaluation—not merely of the question of whether competition might be feasible in this or that segment of telecommunications—but of the more basic question of the long-term impact of its further extension on the public at large, the adequacy, dependability and availability of its service and the price it will have to pay for it.[1]

DeButts suggested during the speech that the state regulators were the most appropriate ones to initiate the major reexamination of telecommunication policy. He knew that the state regulators were generally favorable toward AT&T's positions and hostile toward the competitive policies of the FCC. At the time of the speech, the power of the state commissioners to block FCC policies was unclear, but their power was severely circumscribed by the *Telerent* decision of the next year that upheld federal preemption of state terminal equipment policies. However, the state regulators had considerable influence in Congress, which did have the necessary power. AT&T enlisted the state regulators into a coalition of opponents of competition to support restrictive legislation. With the support of state utility regulators, independent telephone companies, and AT&T's two largest unions, AT&T drafted a bill known as the Consumer Communications Reform Act of 1976, or more commonly as "the Bell Bill," and lined up 175 members of the House and 16 members of the Senate as initial cosponsors.

The bill was formulated as a "reaffirmation" of the intent of Congress in the 1934 act, and was designed to eliminate the emerging competition in private line services and terminal equipment. With regard to private lines, the bill stated that "the authorization of lines, facilities, or services of specialized carriers which duplicate the lines, facilities, or services of other telecommunications carriers . . . is . . . contrary to the public interest."[2] In considering any authorization for construction, extension, or renewal of specialized facilities, the commission would have to hold an evidentiary hearing and establish that no increased charges would result, that the proposed services were not similar to any services provided by a telephone or telegraph carrier, and that the proposed services could not be provided by a telephone or telegraph common carrier. Because the burden of proof would be on the specialized carrier, it would be effectively impossible to show that the existing carriers could not provide the proposed services. With regard to terminal equipment, the bill provided that exclusive jurisdiction over terminal equipment would rest with the respective state commissions rather than with the FCC. That provision would have eliminated the FCC's then-proposed nationwide registration program and required terminal equipment manufacturers to seek permission from each state commission for attachment.

The Bell System established a massive public relations campaign in favor of the bill, including telephone bill inserts and lobbying at all levels. Although AT&T had gathered an impressive number of sponsors for the bill, it had failed to gain the support of Congressman Lionel Van Deerlin, chairman of the House Subcommittee on Communications. Van Deerlin decided to hold extensive hearings on a possible major revision of the Communications Act, preventing rapid movement of the Bell Bill through his committee. As the process expanded, objections to the Bell Bill were presented by a wide variety of parties, eliminating the possibility of quick passage.

In 1978 Van Deerlin introduced his own bill, which had a procompetitive thrust. The Van Deerlin bill proposed competition as a desirable goal and prescribed regulation only "to the extent marketplace

forces are deficient." The introduction of the Van Deerlin bill effectively ended the consideration of the Bell Bill or any bill based on
returning to the prior monopoly structure. Over the next four years,
several different bills to rewrite the Communications Act were introduced. Although they differed in important respects, they all shared
the basic approach of the 1978 Van Deerlin bill that accepted competition as desirable and sought to prevent the spread of monopoly power
from monopolized to potentially competitive aspects of the industry.

The various market-oriented bills of 1978–1980 were consistent
with the general deregulatory approach of the Carter administration
and of Congress at that time. Considerable deregulatory legislation
was passed during those years. However, the complexities of the telecommunications problem prevented passage of telecommunication
legislation. There was divided congressional authority between the
Commerce Committee (with jurisdiction over telecommunications)
and the Judiciary Committee (because of the possible impact of any
legislation on the antitrust suit). It was not possible to pass a sweeping
deregulation bill similar to the one for the airline industry because
local service was widely acknowledged to be an area of continuing
monopoly power. Consequently, any market-oriented bill had to find
a way to divide competitive and monopoly areas and prevent cross-
subsidy of competitive services by monopoly services. Strict separation
between monopoly and competitive sectors was opposed by the Bell
System as inimical to the economies of scope in the industry, while full
integration of the monopoly and competitive sectors was opposed by
the Bell competitors as providing insufficient protection for competition. The new entrants and the Bell System were frequently engaged in
litigation against each other, described each other in the most unflat-
tering terms, and lacked the trust and personal rapport necessary to
negotiate a compromise to their differences. Each proposed bill generated a coalition of opponents strong enough to block its passage
despite strenuous efforts to find a satisfactory legislative solution to the
various conflicts in the industry.

The Antitrust Suit

AT&T's aggressive actions to block MCI's initial competitive activity
revived longstanding antitrust concerns about AT&T in the Department of Justice (DOJ). DeButts's September 1973 NARUC speech

increased the concerns. According to Peter Temin, "In Washington, D.C., his ringing speech sounded more like a challenge to a duel than an invitation to talk."[3] Soon after the speech, Strassburg met with Department of Justice officials to discuss increased scrutiny of AT&T. MCI pressed for a DOJ antitrust suit against AT&T. Two months after the speech, the DOJ issued a Civil Investigative Demand to AT&T as the beginning of an investigation of AT&T's actions toward the specialized carriers. After the FX interconnection controversy indicated AT&T's continuing intention to resist further competition, MCI filed a private antitrust suit against AT&T in March 1974 and continued to press for a DOJ suit.

During 1974, AT&T's top legal officers met regularly with Thomas Kauper, the Ford administration Assistant Attorney General for antitrust, in an effort to derail a possible antitrust suit. On November 20, 1974, Attorney General William Saxbe informed senior AT&T officials of his intention to file an antitrust suit that day. AT&T unsuccessfully sought to reach President Ford. Intervention by Treasury Secretary William Simon on behalf of AT&T was also unsuccessful, and the suit was filed.

According to the DOJ economic conception of the industry, AT&T participated in three separate markets: local telephone service, long distance telephone service, and the provision of customer premises equipment (CPE). The local telephone service market was a natural monopoly subject to state regulation. The long distance and CPE markets were potentially competitive but were dependent upon interconnection with the local market. AT&T used its market power in local service to limit competition in the long distance and CPE markets. The AT&T opposition to terminal attachment was not motivated by a concern for protecting network integrity but by a desire to monopolize the CPE market. Although CPE was rapidly becoming a competitive market by the trial date, the CPE stories were used as an indication of a general corporate policy against competition. AT&T's refusal to provide the private line interconnection requested by specialized carriers, and AT&T's provision of inferior "line side" connection instead of "trunk side" connection for switched competition, were interpreted as efforts to extend local monopoly power into the long distance market.

The DOJ did not charge AT&T with predatory pricing as such (which would have required a showing of below-cost pricing to drive rivals from the market) but with a unique variant of predatory pricing called "pricing without regard to cost." The DOJ claimed that the Bell System neither knew nor cared about its own costs for specific services, but that it priced competitive services at a rate designed to deter rivals, secure in the confidence that it could gain revenue from other services in order to obtain its maximum allowed rate of return under regulation.

The government's case asserted not only that regulation had failed to prevent AT&T's competitive abuses but that regulation was a key component of AT&T's ability to commit those abuses. The FCC was not intentionally serving AT&T's interests, but the commission was hamstrung by AT&T's abuse of process. Roger Noll and Bruce Owen wrote:

> The essential points were that the Bell System had strategically withheld information that was harmful to its self-interested claims, had purposely entangled its competitors in numerous regulatory and judicial proceedings to inhibit their ability to compete, and had refused to comply with procompetitive regulatory policies that were clearly enunciated by the agencies.[4]

The DOJ claimed that AT&T's regulatory interventions and court appeals went beyond the legitimate exercise of its right to plead its case and constituted a pattern of engaging in litigation that it knew it would lose in order to raise the costs of rivals and prevent them from becoming active competitors of the Bell System.

AT&T's defense also put great weight on regulation, but with a very different perspective from that of the DOJ. According to AT&T, it was subject to pervasive state and federal regulation that controlled prices and entry and limited AT&T's total profits. Although AT&T had a high market share, it did not possess monopoly power in the legal sense (the power to control prices and exclude competitors) because regulators rather than AT&T controlled entry and prices. The entire telephone business was a natural monopoly with economies of scale, scope, and vertical integration that would be lost if service were provided by multiple companies. The Bell System had operated the telephone business as a regulated monopoly for many years with the approval of state and federal regulators. Particular problems cited by the DOJ were isolated incidents that occurred as a large corporation sought to accommodate to confusing and contradictory policy changes by state and federal regulators. AT&T engaged in neither predatory pricing nor pricing without regard to cost, but sought to maintain pricing policies and revenue flows that had long been approved by regulatory authority. AT&T's regulatory and legal activities were the legitimate exercise of its right to petition the government.

Attorney Phillip Verveer, who was a key participant in the early part of the suit, described its origin as the result of economic analysis of the industry:

> It is important to understand that the case was a child of the efforts of a very small group of economists: some like Bob Reynolds and Dan Kelly who worked inside the Department of Justice at the time, and others like Roger Noll and Bruce Owen who were outside the Department of Justice but had been retained as consultants. They did work out a theory which stuck and it is one that obviously appealed to Bill Baxter [Assistant Attorney General in the Reagan administration who settled the case], that he understood, and it's why Baxter essentially held firm for the kind of fairly global comprehensive resolution he did.[5]

Roger Noll and Bruce Owen summarized the economic structure of the DOJ case as follows:

> The essence of the government's case against the Bell System was that it had used its status as a regulated monopoly in most of its markets to erect anticompetitive barriers to entry in potentially competitive markets. The novel feature of this line of argument was that much of the Bell System's anticompetitive behavior was economically rewarding to the company only because it was regulated and, consequently, that one arena of public policy, economic regulation, was a cause of illegal acts in another area, antitrust.[6]

AT&T executive Alvin von Auw agreed that the lawsuit was the result of economic thinking and lamented that AT&T's economic advisors did not produce a better defense of monopoly control:

> Objection might be raised to the characterization of the current dispensation in telecommunications [immediately post-divestiture] as a triumph for economics on the grounds that AT&T had economists aplenty of its own. It did and it does. . . .
> What now in retrospect appears clear is that not even among its own most intimate economic counselors could AT&T generate the degree of enthusiasm for opposing competition that they now evi-

dence for maintaining it. Differ as they might on particulars—what is the relevant cost standard for competitive ratemaking, for example— AT&T's economists and those of its opposition shared a common philosophy—what here has been characterized as the economists's view of the way the world ought to work. Indeed, the layman is at a loss to discern any fundamental difference in the philosophies of, on the one hand, William Baumol, Alfred Kahn and Otto Eckstein, AT&T's original "board of economic advisors," and, on the other, the philosophies of William Melody, Bruce Owen or Manley Irwin, the company's *bêtes noires*.[7]

Initially, the suit moved slowly as AT&T unsuccessfully sought dismissal on the grounds that regulation precluded application of antitrust standards; documents were exchanged and positions were refined. In 1978 the case was reassigned from Judge Waddy (then seriously ill) to Judge Harold Greene. Greene established a strict timetable for trial, requiring the parties to develop stipulations and detailed pretrial contentions in order to begin the trial in September 1980 (later postponed slightly to the beginning of 1981).

AT&T's strident opposition to all forms of competition and its aggressive challenges to pro-competitive regulatory policy began to disappear after Charles Brown replaced John deButts as Chairman and Howard Trienens replaced Mark Garlinghouse as General Counsel. As the trial date approached, the parties began intensive negotiations toward reaching a settlement. In December 1980, the Assistant Attorney General for Antitrust, Sanford Litvack, and Howard Trienens reached agreement on the outline for a settlement. The proposal was a combination of limited divestiture, separate subsidiaries, and injunctive relief provisions designed to make the industry more competitive. The proposal did not have full support within the DOJ staff and was particularly opposed by Bruce Owen, then the head of the Economic Policy Office, and by other economists working on the case because of its insufficient attention to incentives. The negotiations were complicated by the fact that at the time the top DOJ officials were Carter administration officials likely to be replaced by the incoming Reagan administration.

AT&T and the DOJ asked for a delay in the trial date in order to convert the outline settlement into a consent decree. Judge Greene granted a short postponement to allow negotiations and to determine the position of the new administration, but the complexity of the proposed decree and the opposition of the economists slowed the process of reaching a settlement. When William Baxter was appointed Assistant Attorney General for Antitrust by the new Reagan administration in February 1981, he refused to endorse the Litvack approach to settlement and ended the negotiations on the details of that settlement.[8]

The Reagan Administration's Perspectives

The trial began in early 1981 while the Reagan administration was still formulating its policy toward the case. Baxter became the top DOJ person on the case when Attorney General William French Smith was recused from the case because he had been a director of Pacific Telephone and Deputy Attorney General Edward Schmults was recused because his law firm had advised AT&T. Baxter shared the general perspective of DOJ economists that the problems in the industry came from the combination of regulation and competition. He wanted to draw a clean line between the regulated monopoly parts of the industry and the potentially competitive parts of the industry. Baxter's general approach was consistent with the FCC's approach in Computer II, but Baxter wanted a stronger structural separation (divestiture rather than separate subsidiaries), and he drew the line around monopoly parts of the industry more narrowly (including only the local operating companies rather than all basic network services) than the FCC had done. Baxter placed no confidence in regulation or injunctive relief. His goal was to remove the structural problems of the industry and then allow the competitive market to work without further government intervention.

Baxter's distrust of regulation was a common theme of the Reagan administration, but his desire to perform radical surgery on the Bell System was not endorsed by other senior officials. Secretary of Defense Caspar Weinberger adopted the longstanding Department of Defense position that an integrated AT&T was desirable for national security. He urged the DOJ to drop the suit, just as an earlier Secretary of Defense had urged dropping the 1949 antitrust suit. Secretary of Commerce Malcolm Baldrige supported Weinberger's position that no substantial relief was needed. AT&T also enlisted the support of Edwin Meese, then President Reagan's Chief of Staff, to oppose the Baxter divestiture goal. The opponents of divestiture within the administration urged Baxter to drop the suit, but they were reluctant to try to force him to drop it because of the potential political problems it could cause for President Reagan. Reagan himself was noncommittal on the case when the issues were argued at a meeting of the Cabinet Council on Commerce and Trade on June 12, 1981.[9] Peter Temin describes the negotiations within the government as follows:

> The task force report [1981 Commerce Department–led effort] and its recommendation were discussed at a meeting of the Cabinet Council on Commerce and Trade on June 12. The President attended the meeting, as did Baxter, representing the Justice Department. Since all of the departments involved except Justice had helped to prepare the report, Baxter found himself a minority of one at this meeting. The full weight of the administration came down on his shoulders. Weinberger presented the Defense Department's position, insisting that the case should never have been brought in the first place and should be abandoned now. Baldrige also argued for dismissing the case. . . . Baldrige was wary of divesting the operating companies in order to throw the equipment market open to competing producers since many of the competitors would be foreign; many Japanese. . . .
>
> Baxter . . . emphasized his commitment to the ideals of the administration. The radical restructuring of the Bell System would promote competition, advancing one of the administration's primary goals. It would reduce regulation, another of President Reagan's objectives. Divestiture, Baxter said, was an alternative to more regulation. . . .
>
> There was little discussion by the Cabinet Council. The meeting was organized for formal presentations to help President Reagan reach conclusions about what should be done. The hope had to be that Baxter would feel the pressure from the Cabinet members and do the right thing—that is, give way on the case. But, of course, a direct command to do so was not going to be given. . . . The administration was anxious to avoid even the appearance of impropriety in this newsworthy case.[10]

The dispute within the Reagan administration reflected different conceptions of the industry and different policy goals. Baxter believed that there were no economies of scope among the various sectors of the industry and therefore no efficiency loss in separating the potentially competitive long distance and CPE services from the natural monopoly local exchange markets. His goal was maximum freedom for competitors and market-based consumer prices. He was unconcerned about either foreign competition or the maintenance of traditional patterns of subsidy in the industry. Weinberger shared the AT&T position that there were economies of scope in the industry and believed that defense communications required a unified company that could meet all requirements. Baldrige was particularly concerned about the advantages that foreign firms would gain from Baxter's divestiture plan. Baxter's effort to break the tie between Western Electric and the Bell Operating Companies and increase the diversity of sources meant that opportunities would be created for foreign firms to sell in the U.S. market while most foreign telecommunication equipment markets would remain largely closed to U.S. sales.

Baxter's inability to convince other senior officials of the wisdom of his plan and the inability of other cabinet members to convince Baxter of the wisdom of their plans caused the administration to proceed in two different directions simultaneously. The DOJ continued with the trial and the goal of divestiture as a "narrow antitrust" approach. The other agencies united on a new congressional effort to pass legislation that would solve the broad policy concerns of the industry. In the 1980 election the Republicans gained control of the Senate, and Senator Packwood became chairman of the Senate Commerce Committee. With Reagan administration (excluding the DOJ) support, Senator Packwood introduced a bill to provide a legislative solution to the telecommunication policy problems.

The FCC's Computer II decision had combined local and long distance service in the regulated basic service category. The DOJ divestiture proposal treated long distance service as competitive and sought structural separation between long distance and local service. The Packwood bill combined elements of both boundaries by creating separate subsidiaries to distinguish basic services from enhanced services and terminal equipment, and by imposing an equal access requirement without structural separation between local and long distance service.

The Packwood bill followed the FCC's Computer II lead in imposing strongly separated subsidiaries between AT&T's regulated basic services and its more competitive services. The bill required the FCC to prescribe accounting systems for the carriers and to prescribe cost allocation rules for the division of the costs of jointly used activities between regulated and unregulated services. Information on operational protocols and technical interface requirements was required to be filed with the FCC and made publicly available except in cases that affected national security. AT&T was prohibited from transmitting information on new protocols and technical interface requirements to its separate affiliates before it was transmitted to the FCC. Thus in general, AT&T was required to make its new requirements known to its competitors at the same time as it made them known to its information services or manufacturing subsidiaries.

The DOJ requested that the bill provide that customers could reach any long distance carrier by dialing the same number of digits, and that it provide a specific network plan for how equal access would be obtained. AT&T strenuously objected to those provisions while accepting the general concept of equal access, and the provisions were not included in the Senate bill as passed.[11]

The equal access issue was argued in the legislative efforts and in a related and simultaneous effort to draft an antitrust consent decree molded on the outlines of the legislation. Baxter interpreted equal access as requiring an equal number of digits and all traffic to flow from the local exchange switches to the AT&T toll office, where it would be divided into the AT&T traffic and competitive traffic. AT&T believed the explicit network plan embodied in Baxter's proposals was both unfair and unworkable. AT&T interpreted equal access as including the existing arrangements for its own traffic ("1+" dialing) and a longer dialing sequence for competitive traffic so long as the technical quality was the same. AT&T proposed that each interexchange carrier connect to each local end office as the AT&T long lines network did, or in the alternative that the competitive long distance carriers interconnect at a local tandem switch in order to avoid the inefficiency of lightly used lines to each end office.

After extensive consideration while the AT&T trial was in progress during 1981, the Packwood bill was approved by the Senate in a 90 to 4 vote in October 1981. AT&T supported the bill, while MCI opposed it. The FCC along with the Departments of Defense and Commerce supported the bill, while the Justice Department remained concerned that it did not provide strong enough controls on AT&T's market power.[12] Despite the overwhelming support of the Senate for the bill, the House version failed to pass and the bill never became law. The failure to pass the Packwood bill left the Commerce and Defense Departments without a method to implement their views on telecommunication policy and increased Baxter's freedom to pursue the divestiture solution. However, the concerns raised by the debate within the

Reagan administration continued to influence policy after the divestiture.

The Divestiture Agreement

When the DOJ finished presenting its evidence, AT&T requested a directed verdict. Rather than simply denying AT&T's motion, Judge Greene delivered an extensive opinion on September 11, 1981, reviewing the evidence in detail. Judge Greene's opinion indicated that he was convinced by the Justice Department's presentation of the case against AT&T and that AT&T would have a difficult if not impossible job of rebutting the case. Greene's opinion intensified AT&T's desire to settle the case.

Soon after Greene's directed verdict opinion, AT&T Chairman Brown wrote to Commerce Secretary Baldrige suggesting settlement negotiations on the basis of the Senate bill. Baldrige passed the suggestion on to Baxter, and Baxter agreed to pursue it. Baxter's staff negotiated throughout the fall with AT&T representatives on detailed provisions of a consent decree without divestiture. The proposed decree became very long and detailed, and was known as Quagmire II or the Telephone Book decree. AT&T continued to hope for a legislative solution less onerous than the consent decree being negotiated by Baxter's staff, but in December 1981 it became clear that no legislation was likely.

All through the pretrial and trial period AT&T had adamantly opposed divestiture and asserted that the proposed divestiture would cause "the destruction of the most advanced, efficient and successful communications system in the world," "would seriously inhibit, and perhaps even prevent, the planning and implementation of a host of networking principles such as the sharing of facilities and the efficient aggregation or alternate routing of traffic," and would cause the "reckless destruction of the world's most successful research institution and industrial laboratory."[13] However, by the end of 1981 the chances for a legislative solution were diminishing, the chances of winning the trial were also diminishing, and the Quagmire II negotiations were becoming so difficult that AT&T began to think a simple divestiture decree might be more satisfactory. Baxter had earlier asserted that he could settle the case with a two-page divestiture decree. After approval by top AT&T management and the Board of Directors, Trienens asked Baxter to draft a divestiture decree as the basis for negotiations. The DOJ prepared the first draft on December 21. After a short period of negotiations, the parties reached the settlement that eventually became known as the Modified Final Judgment (MFJ) because its legal structure was a modification of the 1956 consent decree between the Department of Justice and AT&T. The parties reached agreement on January 6, 1982, and announced the agreement publicly two days later.

The MFJ granted the DOJ proposal to separate AT&T's long distance business from the local exchange telephone service, but the Justice Department abandoned its earlier efforts to further divide the manufacturing business (Western Electric) from AT&T. The theory of the decree was to leave the competitive or potentially competitive businesses with AT&T, and to separate those businesses from the monopoly local telephone companies. The Justice Department believed that such a division would remove both the incentive and the ability of the Bell companies to discriminate against competitors because there would no longer be a single company providing integrated service. AT&T would be dependent on the local exchange companies for access to its long distance and enhanced services, and for connection of its customer premises equipment, just as any of AT&T's competitors were dependent on those operating companies. Because the operating companies were prohibited from participating in the competitive businesses, they would have no incentive to restrict their access services to their own operations.

Although the divestiture was designed to remove the ability and incentives of the local operating companies to discriminate among suppliers of long distance service, the Justice Department was still concerned that the former Bell Operating Companies would favor AT&T. It consequently demanded strict equal access provisions in the Modified Final Judgment. The DOJ had no authority over the actual charges for local exchange access (charges were under the jurisdiction of the FCC), but it could impose general requirements on AT&T as part of the settlement agreement. The DOJ wanted to assist the viability of long distance competition by ensuring that the competitive carriers paid no higher rates per unit of traffic for access to the local exchange than AT&T did. The Baxter proposal for the competitors to interconnect at the AT&T Class 4 toll switch was designed to utilize the existing connections between local exchange offices and AT&T toll switches for the benefit of all long distance competitors. AT&T

opposed the proposal as overly restrictive of its freedom to choose the best technical arrangements for the network.

The issue was settled by adopting a definition in terms of service quality (as AT&T wanted, rather than in terms of physical configuration as the DOJ wanted) but also imposing a rule that required local exchange carriers to average the costs of providing access and to charge all carriers the same amount per unit of traffic. Thus even if a local exchange carrier found it cheaper per unit of traffic to serve AT&T because of AT&T's higher traffic density, it was required to charge all carriers the same rate per unit until 1991. A related provision designed to eliminate the price advantage AT&T could have because its switches were sometimes colocated with those of the local operating companies provided that competitive switches located within five miles of an AT&T switch should be considered in the same tariff subzone as the AT&T switch. Thus a Bell Operating Company (BOC) could not charge AT&T a lower price than nearby competitors because the AT&T switch was located in the same building as the BOC switch.[14]

The MFJ required the Bell Operating Companies (BOCs) to "provide to all interexchange carriers and information service providers exchange access, information access, and exchange services for such access on an unbundled, tariffed basis, that is equal in type, quality, and price to that provided to AT&T and its affiliates."[15] Connections between BOC offices and interexchange carrier offices were required to "deliver traffic with signal quality and characteristics equal to that provided similar traffic of AT&T, including equal probability of blocking, based on reasonable traffic estimates supplied by each interexchange carrier." The BOCs were required to develop a presubscription system that allowed them to automatically route communications to the interexchange carrier chosen by the subscriber without using access codes. The presubscription system equalized the dialing requirements for using AT&T and competitive interexchange providers. The BOCs were required to achieve equal access implementation including presubscription by September 1, 1986, with exceptions for offices serving fewer than 10,000 lines and those served by nonelectronic switches.[16]

The MFJ requirements were a strong version of equal access. They not only prohibited favoritism to AT&T, but also sought to minimize the competitive advantages AT&T had gained from its historical position. The equal charge per unit of traffic and non-distance-sensitive nature of access charges for closely located offices reduced the advantages AT&T gained from its established market position, its volume of local exchange traffic, and its switches colocated with those of the BOCs. AT&T retained the advantages of name recognition and established reputation, and the advantages of economies of scale in its long distance network, but obtained access at the same prices and conditions as its competitors. The equal access concepts developed in the MFJ, including cost averaging, were significant both for their contribution to interexchange competition and for their influence on later considerations of nonstructural safeguards.

The DOJ did not provide an opportunity for the FCC to participate in its negotiations or to review the proposed agreement prior to its public announcement. Baxter appeared to believe that the MFJ had largely eliminated the FCC's role in telecommunication policy. In Senate Commerce Committee hearings immediately after the MFJ was announced, Baxter was challenged on the narrowness of his concerns in formulating the decree:

> Senator Schmitt: The consent decree, as I am coming to understand it, seems to have totally ignored Congress; in particular, what has been going on in the Senate. It appears to have ignored much that has been going on in the FCC. It also has ignored the Department of Defense's wishes on the subject. Why, if you will, have you been so totally self-centered on the issue?
> Mr. Baxter: Because this is an antitrust case, and our primary responsibility was to solve the antitrust problem. The decree does solve the antitrust problem.
> Senator Schmitt: . . . I think a much more open mind at the beginning, a recognition of what the interests of what our national defense are, a recognition of what the interests of the local communities are, as discussed by Senator Pressler and others, what the total interests of the people are in the case might well have taken you along a different path.
> Mr. Baxter: I suppose we may have different views about some of those things. It's quite true that I view the appropriate resolution of this case as the divestiture of the monopoly aspects of A.T. & T. from the potentially competitive aspects. That's what I wanted at the beginning and I am very pleased with the result. . . .
> Senator Schmitt: Did the Defense Department get as much time as the FCC got? [to comment on the proposed settlement]. I understand the FCC had an hour to comment.

Mr. Baxter: So far as I know, the FCC had no opportunity whatsoever.

Senator Schmitt: Then that's even more surprising. I would think that you might have sought their advice and counsel, since they do have some potentially overlapping responsibilities here.

Could you tell us how long the Defense Department had to study the actual proposed decree?

Mr. Baxter: I really can't. I was out of the city. And Mr. Brown, the chairman of the A.T. & T. Co., took the decree, I believe, to Secretary Weinberger.

Senator Schmitt: You left it to Mr. Brown to discuss this with the Secretary of Defense?

It seems to me that it might have been the responsibility of the Justice Department to communicate with the Defense Department.

Mr. Baxter: I understand. I left it with Mr. Brown.[17]

In order to partially meet the concerns of the Defense Department that divestiture would result in fragmented responsibility for responding to emergency communications needs, the MFJ required that "the BOCs [divested Bell Operating Companies] shall provide, through a centralized organization, a single point of contact for coordination of BOCs to meet the requirements of national security and emergency preparedness."[18] Immediately after the divestiture agreement was announced, General William J. Hilsman, Director of the Defense Communications Agency, testified that the Defense Department thought the decree could work but still preferred a unified system:

> Does Defense like the settlement? Well, frankly, we like today's structure better. I agree with what Mr. Brown said, this is second best. However, we also recognize there are different forces in this Nation, all of which need to be recognized . . . we are, today, moving from a system where, for national defense and emergency preparedness, we have an entity with economic and structural clout to do something right now. We are moving to a system where we will rely just a little bit more on good faith to kind of get these things done.[19]

Baxter's view of the divestiture agreement was that it provided a sharp structural dividing line between the monopoly local exchange services and the competitive or potentially competitive remainder of the industry. The local exchange companies would be restricted in their operations and regulated primarily by state utility commissions. The new AT&T (including long distance services, Bell Laboratories, and Western Electric) should be largely free of regulation, eliminating much of the FCC's role in telecommunication policy. Baxter testified soon after the agreement was announced:

> The case is now precisely in the posture in which I wanted it and tried to get it.
>
> . . . the basic thrust of the decree is to separate the natural monopoly functions of our telephone system off into a group of regulated enterprises. They will be regulated primarily by the State public utility commissions. In certain respects, the Federal Communications Commission, too, will continue to have a role.
>
> . . . A.T. & T. Co., after the decree is approved and the reorganization occurs, will be, for the most part, an unregulated, intensely technological and, I believe, a very vigorous competitor in a large number of markets going far beyond the markets in which A.T. & T. has heretofore participated.
>
> . . . the long lines division at present and in the immediate future will continue to be regulated by the Federal Communications Commission. That may seem like an exception to the proposition that the regulated segments have been separated from the unregulated segments, but in a very important sense, it is not an exception.
>
> Again, as Senator Cannon very rightly observed, it is the inevitably and appropriately regulated sectors of their activity that have been broken off from the potentially competitive sectors. There is nothing about the long lines business in most markets in the United States which makes continued regulation inevitable. Long lines transmission of messages is, to a substantial degree, and will be, to an even more substantial degree, a . . . workably competitive industry.
>
> . . . To be broken off from this surviving piece of A.T. & T. about which I have been talking, are the local operating companies. Unlike the long lines function, the provision of local telephone service is one of the best known examples of what economists refer to as a natural monopoly. Having pulled one set of wires through the streets and into our homes, the cost of pulling a second and parallel set of wires would cause it to be true that prices would be higher with two companies than with one. There is nothing to be gained from competition under these circumstances, and that is precisely what makes regulation appropriate . . . if the service were not regulated, there is an enormous potential for monopoly profits to be earned of staggering magnitudes.[20]

The settlement agreement was a private agreement between the DOJ and AT&T and therefore did not need the formal approval of

Congress or the FCC. However, the Tunney Act procedures required public disclosure of steps leading to a DOJ consent decree. Although the applicability of the Tunney Act to this settlement was in some doubt because the settlement was technically a modification of an old decree, Judge Greene invoked Tunney Act procedures on January 21, 1982, rather than merely entering the decree as negotiated by the parties. More than 600 parties filed comments requesting a variety of changes in the agreement. After making minor changes but rejecting major changes requested by both federal and state regulators, the parties signed a revised agreement in August 1982 that was accepted by Judge Greene.

Implementing the Divestiture

Baxter believed that the brief decree provided a clear guide to how the divestiture would occur. He testified that the decree would divide AT&T's assets and personnel into two piles, one for providing local exchange service and one for interexchange service. Local offices (Class 5 switches), tandem offices, and trunks leading to the long distance carrier would be part of local exchange. The dividing line between local and long distance would be "the wall of the class 4 switch." He testified that "it is not difficult to identify that equipment" and that the division "is well defined. There is no large, open ambiguity about what equipment goes in what piles."[21]

AT&T executive W. Brooke Tunstall reported a far different reaction from within AT&T when the news was announced on Friday, January 8:

> Inside the Bell System, the hours that followed the announcement were characterized by profound shock, disbelief, and often anger, soon to be followed by a rush of unanswered questions. . . . One Bell Operating Company (BOC) president, hoping to get some grip on the project, asked his staff to develop questions that would have to be answered before the terms of the decree could be executed. The response was a 2-inch-thick binder with thousands of them, organized by department.
> . . . the task of executing divestiture was such that normal modes of project management—say, those for a moon landing or transcontinental pipeline—would simply not suffice. . . . To Bell managers it was "like cloning a 747 seven times over in midflight."[22]

AT&T initiated a vast planning and implementation process to accomplish the divestiture. By the end of 1982, AT&T had transformed the general principles of the MFJ into a 471-page Plan of Reorganization. The actual network did not fit Baxter's simple conceptual scheme. With over one million employees and nearly $150 billion in assets, AT&T's operations were complex and interrelated. Many difficult problems, ranging from assignment of personnel, to division of jointly used assets, to reprogramming operational systems to work independently, had to be solved. The divestiture process was completed over a two-year period of intensive work and became effective on January 1, 1984.[23]

Conclusion

The MFJ did not follow the slow, consensus-building procedures of either Congress or the regulatory agencies. It was not based on evolutionary modifications to previous policies toward the industry. It did not take account of the many interest groups in the industry or of the many different centers of policy-making power. The MFJ would have had no chance in the ordinary policy-making machinery. Neither the FCC nor Congress even proposed a divestiture, and if they had it would certainly have been defeated. MCI's William McGowan, a strong supporter of the DOJ suit and its resulting divestiture, wrote soon after the announcement:

> Divestiture was the answer. It had eluded the Federal Communications Commission. The FCC had settled for "fully separated subsidiaries," a concept as internally inconsistent as it was inherently ineffective.
>
> Divestiture was never even broached by the Congress. Such an action was "not politically feasible," according to Congressional leaders active in telecommunications legislation. That the right thing to do was not a politically palatable course of action is proof positive that antitrust cases should not—no, really, cannot—be tried in Congress.[24]

The MFJ was an exception to the general rule that it is easier to block a major change than to implement one. Many different parties that would ordinarily have had "blocking power" actively opposed divestiture: AT&T, state regulators, the Department of Defense. The

Justice Department's ability to impose the divestiture was the result of a particular combination of unusual factors that came together at that time. As a legal matter, the DOJ had developed a persuasive enough case that AT&T risked a high probability of loss at the district court level and a more moderate probability of loss after appeals. A loss in the government case would have exposed AT&T to numerous private triple damage actions, with possible dire consequences to its finances. Furthermore, the uncertainty that would be caused by a loss in the district court while appeals were being heard would have made long-range planning very difficult. AT&T Chairman Brown later stated: "The factors that led me to make the decision centered around the very difficult situation AT&T was in at that time. What it amounted to was a series of alternatives; the divestiture was the least worst of them."[25]

AT&T's acquiescence to the divestiture as a private settlement agreement greatly relieved the burden on the DOJ to prove its case for the divestiture. The assets, personnel, and information systems used to provide services that overlapped the DOJ definitions of "exchange" and "interexchange" would have made defending any DOJ-created divestiture plan against critical attack very difficult. However, AT&T preferred a divestiture in which it could control the actual division of the company to risking an unworkable solution designed by either the DOJ or Judge Greene. After the divestiture agreement, AT&T made vigorous efforts to plan a reasonable division of the company, including sharing agreements for jointly used assets, and received approval for its plan even though the final result did not precisely follow Baxter's concept of division "at the wall of the class 4 switch."

The narrowness of the antitrust context allowed the DOJ to make a sweeping policy intervention in the industry. Had the divestiture proposal been structured as a blueprint for telecommunication policy, it would have gone through all of the normal political channels. It would not even have been proposed by the Reagan administration to Congress because of the narrow base of support for the proposal within the administration. However, antitrust is concerned with enforcing the laws, and there is a strong tradition that there should not be political interference in law enforcement activities. Thus the Reagan cabinet members were not free to simply order the suit dropped in the way that they would have ordered other administrative actions. By framing the issue of antitrust enforcement narrowly and as separate from the choice of telecommunication policy, the Reagan administration was able to pursue two parallel and inconsistent tracks: a DOJ antitrust suit aiming to impose divestiture, and an interdepartment task force seeking a unified system to promote American competitiveness and manage Defense communication needs. The inability of Congress to pass the legislation supported by the task force (the Packwood bill) together with AT&T's acquiescence in the divestiture determined that the divestiture option would prevail. Once the divestiture agreement was reached, other policy makers necessarily accommodated to the new structure of the industry.

The divestiture theory was relatively conventional economics applied to a specific conception of the industry. Economists have long opposed regulated competition and have disparaged the ability of regulatory agencies to make good decisions on complex issues. They have generally emphasized the importance of incentives and have frequently advocated structural relief as a solution to antitrust problems. The innovative part of the divestiture economics was its strong emphasis on potential competition rather than the more traditional emphasis on market shares as a measure of market power. Baxter declared the long distance market "workably competitive" even though AT&T had over 95 percent of the market because he believed that potential competition would restrain AT&T's ability to profit from its high market share.

The critical differences of opinion were over the conception of the industry rather than the economic theory applied to it. The DOJ economists viewed the industry in simple terms. There was a well-defined local exchange service that was a natural monopoly. There were many other sectors of the industry—customer premises equipment, manufacturing of communications equipment, and long distance service—that were competitive or potentially competitive. AT&T maintained monopoly control of all sectors by exploiting the monopoly power of the local exchange companies to thwart entry into the potentially competitive sectors. There were possible economies of scale within the sectors but no economies of scope among the sectors. In other words, there might be a loss of efficiency from horizontally dividing AT&T long lines or Western Electric into multiple long distance or equipment manufacturing companies, but there was no loss of efficiency from separating local exchange service from long distance service. Given this model of the industry, conventional economic reasoning would lead to a policy proposal similar to the divestiture one: separate the natural monopoly segment and regulate it, and allow market forces to control the remaining sectors without regulation and with equal access to the services of the monopoly sector.

The various opponents of divestiture had a different conception of the industry that included some or all of the following characteristics. Long distance and local service were not two different products produced under different competitive conditions and separate equipment. Rather, they were two aspects of the services provided by one unified network. There was no sharp dividing line between the two either in terms of the actual way the network was configured or in potential competitiveness. Competitors sought to serve long distance rather than local because long distance service was priced above cost and local service was priced below cost, rather than because of fundamentally different competitive conditions. There were substantial economies of scope among the various services produced on the single unified network. Efficient and reliable operation of the network required unified administratively determined standards rather than market forces. Dividing the network among separate companies would require arbitrary divisions and would decrease efficiency.

There was inadequate information to definitively distinguish the rival conceptions of the industry at the time of divestiture. Even seven years after the divestiture agreement, the principals in the action expressed very different opinions of the results of the action. Charles Brown (AT&T CEO at the time of divestiture) continued to view the divestiture in negative terms:

> The bulk of the residence and local small business customers have not seen net benefits from the upheaval. Their lot has been expense, confusion, and inconvenience in ordering service, getting repairs done, and generally dealing with the telephone system. This is what we expected and gave warning. However, it has been said you can even get used to hanging if you hang long enough, and so perhaps by the end of the century people will have learned to live with the current arrangements without making comparisons with the way things were.[26]

Judge Greene considered the results of the divestiture very positive:

> The greatest successes of the decree seem to me to have been, first, the burst of innovation in telecommunications, which benefited both

industry and the average consumer, and which far surpassed what the Bell monopoly had done in any comparable period; second, the appearance on the scene of a considerable number of vigorous, inventive, independent companies, particularly in manufacturing, but also in other telecommunications markets; third, the emergence of real competition in long-distance and the resulting substantial reductions in rates and the equally substantial increases in usage; and finally, the taking of the first steps toward the achievement of broad-based information services in this country.[27]

William Baxter continued to believe the decree was desirable, but was critical of the implementation. On the crucial question of economies of scope among allowed and prohibited services, he was surprisingly agnostic:

> The decree implicitly made a wager that the regulatory distortions of those portions of the economy, which could have been workably competitive, yielded social losses in excess of the magnitude of economies of scope that would be sacrificed by this approach. It was a wager, a guess. It would be absurd to pretend it was made on the basis of detailed econometric data. It was not; we did not have the data. Of course, all other courses from that point were also guesses. Clear proof was not about to become available any time soon. It was a judgment call, and I guess, in some senses, I do not yet know. Maybe we will never know whether it was right or wrong.[28]

There was not a full debate between rival conceptions of the industry. The information available was interpreted by supporters of each view as supporting that view. However, the Justice Department gained the power to implement its view, and thus its preferred solution of divestiture was adopted. That determined the framework in which future analyses would proceed, but the different views of the fundamental nature of the industry continued to play a major role in the later policy controversies.

10 / Access Charges: A Confusing Ten Billion Dollar Game

William Baxter and his colleagues at the Antitrust Division of the Department of Justice thought they had settled the major telecommunication policy problems with the divestiture agreement of January 1982. They had often contrasted the complex and confusing regulatory approach to policy with the simple, clean solution created by structural separation of the monopoly and competitive aspects of the industry. Although Baxter's initial boast that he could produce a two-page divestiture consent decree missed the final length by twelve pages, the Modified Final Judgment was still far simpler than the hundreds of pages of detailed regulations developed by the FCC or proposed in the non-divestiture "telephone book decree." However, the apparent simplicity came from setting out general principles that left many critical issues for later resolution. Rather than settling the telecommunication policy issues, the divestiture agreement initiated intensive activity in many different policy forums (DOJ, court, FCC, state regulatory agencies, Congress, and industry players) as the various industry participants and policy makers sought to implement their policy goals in the new environment created by the divestiture.

The most critical policy issue during the divestiture implementation period was the development of a method of sharing toll revenue between long distance and local companies that would fit the new industry structure and meet other policy goals. The development of an appropriate sharing mechanism had been an FCC goal ever since the Execunet court decision opened the long distance market to competition, but the proposed divestiture brought a new urgency and new constraints. The key aspect of the new price structure was the concept of "access charges." The MFJ specified that a system of access charges paid by long distance carriers to local exchange carriers for the service of originating and terminating long distance calls must replace the existing AT&T-administered system of settlements and division of revenues.

The MFJ agreement created confusion over the proper authority to specify access charges. The MFJ itself included significant requirements on access charges that were potentially in conflict with rules the FCC would specify. By separating AT&T from the local companies, the agreement also raised the possibility that the new Bell Operating Companies (BOCs) could escape FCC regulation altogether because they provided no physically interstate services, and that therefore access charges would be a matter for state regulatory commissions to determine. Furthermore, the revenue flows to be determined by access charges would create income distribution effects similar to those created by a change in income tax law, and therefore many congressional leaders believed that legislation was needed to determine access charge policy. General Hilsman's comment on multiple policy initiatives soon after the divestiture agreement succinctly characterized the confusion of the access charge development: "We've got an issue in the industry today with what I describe as three basketball games going on in the same court at the same time with all the players wearing the same uniforms, three basketballs flying around, and you're trying to watch with some pillars in front of you."[1]

The vague boundary lines around the jurisdiction of the various policy powers allowed multiple actors to each attempt to determine the policy. While the DOJ sought to minimize the role of the FCC after the divestiture, the FCC sought to reassert its authority and emphasized that it could not be preempted by an antitrust settlement. Immediately after the settlement was announced, Commissioner Fogarty circulated a memo among the commissioners and senior staff that stated:

> I want to emphasize that while AT&T and DOJ may have reached a reasonable and proper private accord under the antitrust laws, such accord, with or without judicial approval, cannot oust, supplant or modify this Commission's mandate, authority, and jurisdiction under the Communications Act of 1934. Indeed, in cases of irreconcilable conflict it is the antitrust law which must yield to this Commission's

broader regulatory jurisdiction. . . . I am . . . concerned that the Commission take pains to ensure that its existing congressional mandate and regulatory jurisdiction and authority are respected.[2]

The FCC's aggressive action made it the lead player in determining the final shape of access charges, with significant inputs added by the MFJ requirements, state regulators, and congressional leaders.

As discussed in Chapter 6, the transformation of customer premises equipment (CPE) from a part of the regulated monopoly telephone companies to a separate unregulated competitive market required two separate policy steps:

1. Specification of the technical interface, CPE standards, and right of the customer to connect any conforming CPE to the network.
2. Financial separation of CPE from the regulated revenue flows within and among companies.

In the CPE case, the financial separation was based on the principle of free interconnection. A customer could order any service from the telephone company and attach any CPE that conformed to publicly available technical standards to that service without any payment to the telephone company that was dependent upon the customer-provided CPE. The focus of state regulators' opposition to CPE competition was the free interconnection arrangement that reduced some financial flows to the local companies.

The theory of the DOJ case considered long distance service analogous to CPE. Both were potentially competitive markets dependent upon interconnection with the monopoly local companies. Both should be severed from the local companies and provided on a competitive market. The divestiture and the associated equal access requirements were designed to provide the same interconnection rights for long distance companies as had been provided earlier for customer-owned CPE. The technical interconnection requirements were the focus of considerable controversy during the negotiations over legislation and a possible settlement for the case, but the agreement to specify general characteristics of the interconnection requirements and leave the details to the companies simplified the implementation. Most but not all of the issues relating to technical interconnection of local and long distance companies were solved as engineering arrangements among the companies without detailed oversight by the various government agencies.

The MFJ did not specify how the financial arrangements between local companies and long distance companies should be disentangled, other than that the pre-divestiture settlements system should be replaced by a system of access charges applied uniformly to all long distance companies. The simplest approach would have been to follow the CPE model and allow any long distance company to connect to any local service with no payment other than the established local service charge. That was the approach originally sought by MCI with its Execunet service, in which it expected to consider the local connection to an MCI switch equivalent to the local connection to any PBX and pay the established local business rate for service received. However, the CPE approach to long distance financial arrangements would have eliminated the complex set of payments among telephone companies (established with extensive political guidance) under the separations and settlements procedure. It would have caused a substantial increase in local telephone rates as well as possibly threatening the availability of telephone service in high-cost rural areas.

State regulators and many congressional leaders were determined to maintain at least some of the established revenue flows from long distance to local service. They vigorously opposed any effort to impose the CPE model. Yet maintaining those revenue flows required creating a legal and pricing distinction between local services used to originate long distance calls and other local services. It also required vigilant regulatory oversight to maintain the resulting price discrimination.

While the overall level of access charges affected the distribution of the cost burden between local and long distance customers and between urban and rural customers, the precise structure of the access charges was critical to the competitive battle among long distance companies. For example, a volume discount on the connections between a local company and a long distance company would provide the divested AT&T with great advantages over its much smaller long distance competitors. The central importance of the size and structure of access charges to telecommunication policy caused vast efforts to be devoted to constructing and implementing an access charge plan. The plan constructed in 1982 and 1983 continues to have an important influence on telecommunication policy even though conditions in the industry have changed substantially. This chapter examines the efforts to construct the access charge plan, while the following chapter examines the implementation of the plan.

The First Plan: Pre-Divestiture Agreement

The Execunet court ruled that MCI must be allowed to provide Execunet service over its existing facilities because the FCC had made no specific finding that the switched long distance market should be a monopoly (see Chapter 8). It left open the possibility that the commission could examine the question and find monopoly in the public interest, though practically no one thought that was a likely outcome of a formal proceeding on the desirable market structure. During the initial period of competition with payments from entrants to the local telephone companies determined by the negotiated ENFIA agreement, the FCC began a proceeding to determine how a long-run compensation for local companies should be computed and to determine whether competition in long distance switched services was in the public interest. In April 1980, the commission adopted a Tentative Access Charge Plan for comments and refinements. That plan attempted to maintain then-existing revenue flows from long distance service to local exchange companies and to adapt the monopoly system to competition with minimal changes. On the basis of the assumptions of that initial access charge plan, the commission concluded that competition would not necessarily cause local rates to rise or cause MTS rates to be deaveraged. It therefore concluded that competition in long distance service was in the public interest.[3] The conclusion was essentially a finding that the proposed access plan would cause competition to have little effect and therefore could do no harm, rather than a finding that competition would cause more efficient pricing patterns.

The tentative access plan of 1980 described four kinds of access that were being provided at different rates:

1. MTS/WATS—switched service provided through AT&T for which local telephone companies participated in a "partnership" and divided the revenues according to the settlement and division of revenue formulas. The compensation was based on recovering specific percentages of each local telephone company's cost from toll revenue.
2. Private line services—provided by a combination of AT&T Long Lines and the various local telephone companies. Revenue was shared with the local companies based on the portion of their cost that was allocated to private line services.

3. FX/CCSA—mixed private line and switched services. FX included a private line from one location to the central office switch in a distant city, as illustrated in Figure 3 in Chapter 8. The charges included a private line charge (from the interstate FCC-regulated tariff) and a local exchange charge (from the intrastate state-regulated tariff) for the open end. A similar arrangement existed for off-network access lines (ONALs) used in sophisticated private networks. ONALs were charged at the local business rate (intrastate state-regulated tariff) just like FX open end lines.
4. ENFIA lines—switched access lines provided to competitive long distance companies at rates determined through the ENFIA negotiated agreement. The ENFIA lines were physically identical to the FX and ONAL lines but were charged at higher rates.

The legal basis for the abolition of the then-existing arrangements in favor of the proposed 1980 plan was the elimination of price discrimination. The FCC found the wide variety of rates charged for similar access service unreasonably discriminatory, in violation of the Communications Act. The goal of the plan was to eliminate discrimination while interfering with the existing division of revenue as little as possible, not to eliminate the inefficiency that came from pricing long distance services far above their marginal cost. The key elements of the 1980 plan included:

1. Continuation of the existing separations system and the development of revenue to meet the requirements determined by that cost allocation system.
2. Continuation of the pooling system by which the receipts of individual companies were based on that company's costs allocated to the interstate jurisdiction.
3. The assertion of federal jurisdiction over any service used to provide access to interstate communications, including FX open ends and CCSA ONALS previously tariffed at local rates under state regulatory supervision.
4. Non-traffic-sensitive (NTS) costs (the largest category of costs, including subscriber lines, station equipment, inside wiring, and parts of the central office equipment) would be distributed to the various access categories (including private line) on the basis of minutes of use.
5. Each access category would recover its costs through a charge per minute for switched services and a charge per line for private line services.

The most critical change from the status quo was the proposal to distribute NTS costs across all access categories on the basis of minutes of use. That meant a substantial increase in the revenue requirement assigned to private line usage, and would have implied a consequent sharp increase in private line rates under the rate of return regulation used at that time. The proposal was designed to eliminate the price discrimination between rates for private line and switched service, while maintaining a distinction between rates for access and rates for other local services.[4]

Although the 1980 plan was designed to eliminate price discrimination among various categories of interstate access service, it did not attempt to eliminate price discrimination between "access service" and physically identical "local service." That legal distinction between two physically identical services was necessary in order to fulfill the goal of maintaining the then-existing revenue flows from toll service to local, and the distinction has continued through all of the various access plans. The substantial price difference between local service defined as interstate access and technically identical or similar local service defined as intrastate service has made the definition of service an important issue of competitive strategy and of regulatory enforcement. If companies were allowed to simply select the physical service that met their needs at the lowest price, the access services would not generate enough revenue to meet the costs assigned to the interstate jurisdiction. The 1980 access charge plan was designed to generate the same revenue for local companies as the past practices through a per-minute charge that was equal for all long distance companies but much higher than the charge that customers other than long distance companies would pay for the same service.

The 1980 plan was designed to allow long distance competition in an industry dominated by the integrated AT&T. It was essentially a way of fitting the new entrants into a structure created for a monopoly. It would have raised the rates for the largest users with extensive private line networks, reduced the rates for the smaller long distance users whose subsidy burden would be spread out over a larger base, and left local rates unaffected.

Despite the FCC's assertion that final approval of an access charge plan should come quickly, no quick action was taken. Three different issues prevented quick adoption of the 1980 proposal:

1. There was extensive opposition to the proposal to assign costs to private lines in proportion to total usage. Many companies had invested in private line systems and were accustomed to the substantial reduction in price per minute available under private lines. They had a strong incentive to protect their privileges and to develop a variety of public interest arguments on why private lines should not be subject to the proposed rules that would cause substantial increases in private line rates.
2. The 1980 election with its accompanying change in personnel slowed action at the FCC. Incoming chairman Mark Fowler replaced the top staff officers of the commission and required some time to review existing proposals and make desired adjustments.
3. The announcement of the MFJ agreement in January 1982 meant that the proposed access charge structure needed reconsideration to ensure that it was compatible with the planned change in industry structure.

The 1982 Access Plan

The AT&T–DOJ agreement of January 1982 dramatically changed the context of the industry for which the 1980 access charge plan was designed and also gave a new urgency to developing a plan. Despite the complaints of both AT&T and MCI that it was unfair, the ENFIA agreement had provided a satisfactory method of compensating local carriers so long as the competitors were niche players in an industry dominated by AT&T. However, the proposed MFJ required an end to the existing separations and settlements system at the January 1, 1984, divestiture date. After that time, compensation of local companies from long distance could only come from access charges. The proposed new industry structure designed to replace regulatory controls with market incentives provided the opportunity to rethink both the feasibility and the desirability of the 1980 approach of minimal change to existing procedures.

The Department of Justice took the position that the divestiture did not imply any requirement for change in the existing local service rates. A critical point of contention in the litigation was how settlements payments affected the interpretation of the historical record. AT&T, supported by many state regulators, interpreted its actions as an attempt to preserve the set of social prices determined and approved through the political process that led to geographic averaging, large payments to rural companies, overpriced long distance service, and underpriced local service. From that perspective, entrants were simply parasites profiting from socially desirable differences between price and cost, and providing no useful economic function. MCI and the Department of Justice developed the theory that no subsidies had been proved and that all revenue flows were under AT&T's control and determined by AT&T in its own interest.

Many small company representatives and state regulators, who had no doubt about the existence and the beneficiaries of the revenue flows, feared that the MFJ would eliminate all subsidy flows and dramatically increase local rates while reducing the profitability of small telephone companies. Soon after the agreement was announced, Baxter defended the agreement against challenges that it would cause higher local rates with two different arguments: (1) the subsidy flows don't really exist; (2) if they do exist they can be maintained through a system of access charges:

> It is said that the profits of long-distance telecommunications have, in the past, flowed into and cross-subsidized and kept down the price of local telephone service, and that that situation will now come to a halt, with the consequence that local telephone rates will have to go up. That is not true . . .
>
> It is not at all clear to me that long lines' revenues presently perform any cross-subsidization function with respect to local rates. . . . [The] license contract fee is too large and . . . it has been a path through which the A.T. & T. Co. has siphoned out of the local operating companies revenues that ought to have stayed there . . . the basic operating companies have been paying unnecessarily high prices for the equipment they bought from Western Electric. After the reorganization is in effect . . . they will be able to buy it competitively from whomever offers them the best quality at the lowest prices.
>
> . . . the fraction of long-distance revenues which has been retained at the local operating company has been generous, resulting from a generous attitude in the way one allocates these costs that I've referred to. And that is the so-called subsidy for local rates. But it is not at all clear to me that the fund flow in the direction of the local operating company that results from this cost allocation process is substantially more than or perhaps more at all than the funds that flow in the other direction through the license contract fee and the purchase of equipment.
>
> . . . In the future the local operating company will impose charges on

long-distance carriers, through these access charges, for the service of either originating or of terminating long-distance calls within the exchange area. Those access charges are subject to the regulation of the local public utility commission on intrastate calls, intrastate long-distance calls, and they are subject to the regulation of the Federal Communications Commission on interstate long-distance calls. And those regulators have the authority to set those access charges wherever they choose to set them, and there is not the slightest doubt in the world that if they wish to do so, they can set them high enough to recapture for the local companies precisely those revenues that would have been received through the separations process under the old way of doing things.[5]

The access plan would have been far simpler if Baxter had been correct. If it were true that excess payments from the local companies to AT&T resulting from the license contract fee and inflated Western Electric prices balanced the local companies' share of long distance revenues, then the simple CPE model of interconnection could have been imposed with no significant disruption to the industry pricing patterns. However, as information was gathered for the access charge plan, it became clear that the Baxter theory was in error by several billion dollars. Baxter's fallback position, that regulators could impose access charges at whatever level they desired, was closer to the truth but still overstated. The ability to impose access charges was a function of the monopoly power of the local companies over the connections between individual customers and the interexchange carrier office (Point of Presence or POP in MFJ terms). Insofar as individual large customers had an alternative to the local exchange carriers for carrying their long distance traffic to the POP, they could avoid high access charges. As with any monopoly, there was a ceiling on the total amount of money that could be raised through access charges, though how that ceiling related to the then-existing settlements revenue was a point of dispute.

Baxter's second argument was consistent with the FCC's 1980 access plan, which assumed that the local exchange companies had full monopoly power and that any amount of revenue could be raised by setting the access charge at the necessary level. That plan was designed to work with the then-existing separations formulas or any revisions that might be made. Consequently, the consideration of an access charge structure was decoupled from the separations decisions regarding the total amount of local exchange cost that should be recovered from the interstate jurisdiction.

Even before the divestiture agreement, FCC staff economists objected to the 1980 plan and sought to convince the new FCC leadership of the Reagan administration (Chairman Mark Fowler and Common Carrier Bureau chief Gary Epstein) to revise it. The January 1982 divestiture agreement provided pressure to resolve the access charge issues and added strength to the economists' two fundamental objections to the 1980 plan:

1. The proposed plan continued the inefficient practice of recovering the non-traffic-sensitive costs through traffic-sensitive rates that distorted economic decisions. The plan attempted to protect the existing revenue flows against the movement toward cost-based pricing that was expected to be a major benefit of competition.
2. The monopoly power of the local exchange companies was not absolute, and the opportunity for limited local competition (bypass) would be used by the largest customers to avoid paying the access charges. This process would increase the burden on smaller users by decreasing the number of access minutes used to recover a fixed revenue requirement and could possibly make the access plan completely infeasible.

The pending divestiture also raised concern within the industry about the proposed pooling of revenues under AT&T administration. In an attempt to mimic the existing arrangements, the 1980 plan had proposed that AT&T continue to administer an access charge pool just as it had prior to competition. The consensus in favor of pooling evaporated after the divestiture agreement as the low-cost BOCs questioned the wisdom of agreeing to voluntarily send large amounts of money from their access charges to subsidize high-cost BOCs that would be independent from them. Furthermore, the new industry structure made AT&T one payer of access charges rather than the main payer and recipient, and thus made the proposal to have AT&T administer the entire system seem inappropriate.

The FCC needed to create an access charge plan that would work under the industry structure created by the divestiture (based on an assumption of maximum reliance on competition and cost-based prices) and would also survive the political review of many interested parties who were primarily concerned to maintain the benefits to them of the status quo. Thus the task of the FCC was to create a pricing structure that would radically change past arrangements in order to transform a politically determined monopoly pricing structure into a price structure compatible with competitive market forces while also maintaining the income distribution effects of past arrangements in order to avoid creating a political backlash. The impossibility of reaching the two incompatible goals created extensive controversy over how to construct a reasonable plan with an appropriate balance of the two objectives.

In May 1982, the commission adopted a further NPRM on the access charge plan. The most significant change was a new emphasis on the economic efficiency of the industry and on the sustainability of the access plan in the industry structure created by the divestiture. The earlier plan had not mentioned economic efficiency, and had assumed that whatever revenue was required could be raised by simply setting the charges at the appropriate level. The 1982 proposal noted the economic efficiency losses that arise from recovering non-traffic-sensitive costs with usage-based charges and the bypass incentives created by the 1980 plan. The 1982 notice acknowledged that there were technologies available that could allow some users to connect to long distance carriers without using the local exchange carrier. The notice attributed the commission's new concern about bypass to the divestiture because the separation of AT&T from its formerly owned operating companies increased AT&T's incentive to bypass the local carriers.

The 1982 notice observed that the discrimination problem between private line and switched services could be solved by treating all local access lines as private lines. In other words, the non-traffic-sensitive costs could be recovered in a non-traffic-sensitive manner by imposing a fixed charge per month for each subscriber line at the amount of NTS costs allocated to the interstate jurisdiction. "Every customer, under this approach, would pay a flat (per line) access charge that did not vary with use, plus usage based interstate charges that reflected only usage sensitive facilities."[6] Although such a plan eliminated the concern with bypass and solved the discrimination problem, it required a substantial change in the then-existing pricing policies and in the distribution of the burden of paying for the network. That plan would have increased the costs of light users of long distance service (because they would pay a fixed access fee and would receive few benefits from the reduced long distance charges), while it would reduce the costs of heavy users of the network (because their benefits from the reduced long distance charges would outweigh the fixed cost of the access charge).

The commission designated its original plan for recovering all NTS charges through an equal-usage-based charge as Pure I and the new option of recovering the charges through a fixed charge per subscriber as Pure II. It also described two "mixed" plans that attempted to combine elements of the two pure options in order to soften the impact of the changes that would occur under either one. The commission believed that the mixed strategies "have the advantage that they result in movement toward the more efficient principle of cost allocation on the basis of cost causation" while they "attempt to satisfy the Commission's other objectives as well."[7]

The May 1982 notice sparked an extensive debate both within and outside the commission. Economists inside the commission (primarily in the Office of Plans and Policy) as well as those outside the commission urged that the access charge plan be used as an opportunity to rationalize the industry's pricing practices, improve efficiency, and create opportunities for full utilization of market forces, rather than viewed as a problem to be solved with the least change possible. They supported the Pure II option as a way to bring prices close to actual costs and also argued that the existing revenue flows were unsustainable because of bypass. AT&T, many other telecommunication companies, and major business users of telecommunications also supported the Pure II approach.

Individual state commissions, NARUC, and consumer groups generally opposed the proposal to move prices toward costs because of their concern about rising local rates. They advocated maintenance of the existing revenue flows and argued that the rise in local rates required by cost-based pricing could create hardship for many users and drive marginal users off the network, reducing the value of the network for those who remained. Many FCC staff members were sympathetic to the arguments in favor of preserving the status quo and opposed the radical changes in pricing advocated by the economists.[8]

The entire heated debate took place in a context of great uncertainty and extremely limited information. The existing system of settlements and division of revenue had been administered internally by AT&T in accordance with private contracts and with no public reporting of the money flows and formulas used. The proposed access charges were to be computed by companies that did not yet exist (the BOCs created by the divestiture) in order to meet a revenue requirement determined by cost allocation procedures that had not yet been decided but were concurrently under separate consideration by a Joint Board of federal and state commissioners.

The essential argument concerned how variations in the rules for computing such access charges would affect overall efficiency and the distribution of income among various industry segments and consumer groups, but there was very limited public information on the baseline status quo from which to make such estimates. The arguments raged over the effect of various plans on bypass, efficiency, income distribution, and effects on the total telephone penetration rate, but there were only limited efforts to collect data and quantify those factors. The economists were confident that moving prices closer to marginal cost would result in social improvement regardless of the specific quantitative factors and therefore advocated Pure II. Their opponents were confident that moving prices closer to marginal cost would raise rates for the majority of consumers (because a substantial fraction of long distance calls were made by a small fraction of the users) regardless of the specific quantitative factors and therefore opposed Pure II. Although extensive arguments were made regarding bypass as a reason to support Pure II and subscriber drop-off as a reason to oppose Pure II, they were largely debating points designed to buttress a position adopted on other grounds.

In December 1982 the commission adopted a complex access charge plan that essentially accepted the economic reasoning of the Pure II approach as a long-run goal but adopted a long transition period and many special provisions to take account of particular interests and objections. The complexity of the plan was partly a function of the political compromises necessary to gain support for the plan and partly an intentional feature of the plan in order to obscure the special arrangements made to satisfy particular interests.[9]

The 1982 order observed that the original scope of the proceeding viewed access as a service provided by a local exchange carrier (LEC) to an interexchange carrier (IXC). That service allowed the interexchange carrier to reach local customers, and consequently it was reasonable to think of compensation for the service as a payment from the IXC to the LEC. An alternative conception was to think of the access service as being provided to the customer in order to allow the customer to reach the IXC, with a consequent charge for access to the customer.[10] Although the economic effects of the conceptions are the same, the legal effects may be different because in the first the IXC is part of a partnership with the LEC providing end-to-end service, while in the second the IXC only provides service along its own facilities while the customer receives access from the LECs. The plan adopted was a combination of the two conceptions and included both "carrier's carrier" access charges and "end user" access charges.

At the time of the 1982 order, the interstate NTS revenue requirement for 1984 (the first year of access implementation) was expected to be $8.5 billion, or $85 per year per line for the estimated 100 million access lines. The NTS revenue requirement included $1.4 billion for CPE and $1.6 billion for inside wiring that were expected to be gradually phased out of the rate base.[11] The plan required the imposition of a $4.00 per line per month flat access charge for business lines and a $2.00 per month flat charge for residential lines in the first year. Those charges would recover approximately half of the NTS revenue requirement. The remainder would be collected by a carrier's carrier charge (a rate per minute imposed on interexchange carriers) initially, but switched from carrier's carrier (usage-based) charges to customer access charges (flat rate per line) over a five-year period.

The legal power to impose the charges was based on section 201(a) of the Communications Act, which gave the FCC authority to require physical connections among carriers and to establish the division of revenues. Instead of the normal procedure of carrier-initiated tariffs that are then reviewed by the commission, the access charge tariffs were "prescribed" by the commission in general form through the access charge rules. The rules set up a rigid cost allocation system in which various categories of investment and expense were allocated to particular access elements and then divided by expected units of usage to produce a price per unit. In an effort to avoid discrimination and to create a system of charges that could be monitored by the FCC, the rules largely eliminated the telephone companies' freedom to determine their own price structure for access. Because the access charge plan replaced the AT&T-administered system of transfers with a system of tariffs policed by the FCC, it created a major expansion in the responsibilities of the FCC.

The economic theory behind the plan chosen was the goal of aligning prices to costs. The 1982 plan stated:

The plan is designed to move swiftly and surely from the present reliance on additions to the price of interstate toll minutes as the mechanism for recovery of these costs towards a pricing plan which recognizes that non-traffic sensitive costs covering plant dedicated to individual end users neither increase nor decrease as a result of usage made of that plant. We are taking this important step because we view this new direction as the only means of satisfying our goals of universal service, nondiscrimination, network efficiency, and prevention of uneconomic bypass.

Economics teaches us that, except in certain circumstances involving market failure, prices equal to the cost of producing another increment of a good, i.e., equal to the marginal cost of production, are optimal. Provision of telephone services involves two marginal costs. One varies with the traffic level. The other varies with the number of access lines demanded. For this reason, efficient pricing requires both usage sensitive and non-usage sensitive charges for recovery of access costs.

The costs imposed upon the nation's telecommunications system, and ultimately upon the general public, by our present usage sensitive method of recovering these NTS costs pose a substantial danger to the long term viability of our nation's telephone systems. . . . Prices based upon the true cost characteristics of telephone company plant are necessary both to make a decision on whether use of the alternative technologies is appropriate and to make a decision on whether to substitute telecommunications for other activities.[12]

The imposition of a customer access charge, later designated the "subscriber line charge" (SLC), was effectively an increase in local rates. Each dollar of SLC removed a little over $1 billion of revenue requirement from the usage-based carrier access charges and required individual customers to pay an additional $1.00 per month to the local telephone company independent of the customer's volume of usage. The SLC was opposed by state commissions both because of their longstanding opposition to any action that increased local rates and because it was an intrusion of federal power on traditionally state prerogatives. The economic goal of aligning long distance prices more closely to cost could have been met either by reducing the portion of costs allocated to the interstate jurisdiction or by recovering part of that cost through the SLC. However, reducing the allocation to interstate would have reduced federal control over the local telephone companies. In the extreme case (advocated by some state commissions), the FCC jurisdiction would be completely eliminated and the local telephone companies would be regulated only by state commissions. By maintaining a large allocation of cost to the interstate jurisdiction but recovering part of it through a federally determined SLC, the FCC maintained its authority against the efforts of both state commissions and the DOJ to restrict the scope of federal regulation.

Separations Reform and High-Cost Subsidy

The decision to move toward flat rate recovery of NTS costs accentuated the problem of unequal costs around the country. The costs of the lines required to connect local subscribers to a central office vary widely and are inversely correlated with the density of subscribers. For high-density areas, the central offices are spaced closely and the wires are short; for low-density areas, the connecting wires may be very long, requiring both more wire and various forms of repeater devices to make an adequately strong signal. The separations and settlements system had two different averaging arrangements that contributed to low local rates in high-cost areas: (1) the long distance rates were geographically averaged and the rates charged for access to any long distance call were the same regardless of the location; (2) the general tendency of the sparsely populated areas to have a higher proportion of long distance calls than the densely populated areas meant that a higher percentage of their costs was assigned to the interstate jurisdiction.

A straightforward access system consistent with the general goals of the December 1982 order would have simply allocated the particular interstate percentage of NTS costs in each area to a subscriber line charge (the revenue requirement divided by the number of lines) and then charged a traffic-sensitive charge on a usage basis to recover traffic-sensitive costs. The actual percentage of NTS costs allocated to interstate would be largely irrelevant because it would eventually be recovered on a flat rate basis just as the standard local requirements were. A system of flat rate recovery of NTS charges without pooling would be equivalent to allocating all costs to the intrastate jurisdiction. Such a system would substantially increase the fixed local costs of the high-cost companies. Alternatively, if NTS access costs were recovered on a usage-sensitive basis from each local jurisdiction, then the rate per minute would be much higher in the rural areas than in the urban areas. This difference would create incentives to deaverage long distance prices and charge higher rates between low-density areas than between high-density areas for the same length of call.

Concurrently with the FCC's consideration of various access charge plans, a Joint Board of federal and state commissioners was considering changes in the separations rules for allocating investment and expense to the interstate and intrastate jurisdictions.[13] The separations rules determined the fraction of investment and expense in various categories that must be recovered through interstate access charge rules. The pre-competition Ozark Plan separations rules divided expenses in accordance with usage measurements but applied weighting factors that assigned costs to the interstate jurisdiction at a far higher rate than would be determined through strict proportional usage. The first step in separations reform was to freeze the non-traffic-sensitive allocators for each company (Subscriber Plant Factor or SPF) at the 1981 level ("frozen SPF" or "1981 SPF") so that future changes in relative usage would not change the allocation of NTS costs. The nationwide average of frozen SPF was 25 percent but was as high as 85 percent for some small companies (85 percent of NTS cost recovered from interstate and 15 percent recovered from intrastate), and it was used as the starting point for considering various separations reform plans.

The Joint Board devised a system by which the allocation of NTS costs to the interstate jurisdiction would gradually change from the frozen SPF rate for each company to a flat 25 percent nationwide. They reasoned that because the costs did not vary with traffic, then the division of those costs between interstate and intrastate should not vary with traffic either. However, they also adopted a "high cost factor" that would assign an increasing share of costs to the interstate jurisdiction whenever a company's NTS costs per line exceeded 115 percent of the national average. The factor rose so that companies with costs in excess of 250 percent of the national average assigned all of their additional NTS costs to the interstate jurisdiction. The rates were computed as an additional factor beyond the 25 percent allocator to be added to the interstate revenue requirement and subtracted from the state revenue requirement.

The initial rules allowed companies to assign 25 percent of their costs to interstate if costs were less than 115 percent of the national average, 75 percent of costs between 115 and 160 percent of the national average, 85 percent of costs between 160 and 200 percent of national average, 95 percent of costs between 200 and 250 percent of national average, and 100 percent of costs over 250 percent of the national average. A company with average costs would recover 75 percent of the national average "unseparated loop cost" from the intrastate jurisdiction. A very high cost company would be required to recover a maximum of 106 percent of the national average "unseparated loop cost" from the intrastate jurisdiction, or a maximum of 41 percent higher rates per loop than the average company even though its costs might be several times those of the average company.

The high cost factor meant that high cost companies would assign a high proportion of their NTS costs to the interstate jurisdiction. If that cost were simply recovered through access rates charged by that company, the rates would necessarily be very high. If the rates were recovered through fixed charges per line (subscriber line charges), then the high cost factor would be largely irrelevant because it would simply cause the local subscriber to pay less in "local line charges" and more in "subscriber line charges," with the total bill being the same. If the costs were recovered through usage-based access charges, then the rates per minute for high cost companies would be very high (a large revenue requirement and small number of minutes) relative to average cost companies. The very high usage-based charges would then create incentives for carriers to find alternative methods of reaching the subscribers (bypass) and would create pressures to deaverage long distance rates to more closely align costs with rates in the increasingly competitive long distance market or to refuse service to the high-cost areas.

The plan adopted included a decision to recover the high cost fund amounts by usage-based charges and to have a mandatory pool for those charges in order to equalize them across the country. The Joint Board plan was a compromise among competing conceptions of the long-run goals for the price structure of the industry. Commissioner Marvin Weatherly of Alaska provided a "concurring" statement in which he supported the basic thrust of the action, but objected that the plan gave insufficient attention to the needs of small rural telephone companies such as those in Alaska. He applauded the principle that the federal jurisdiction should accept all NTS costs beyond a particular level, but wanted a more generous sharing formula in which the federal jurisdiction would accept responsibility for all NTS costs in excess of 110 percent of the national average.

Federal Commissioner Anne Jones dissented from the decision because its sharing mechanisms were too generous. She questioned the incentives created by the plan to provide subsidies to the high cost telephone companies rather than to needy subscribers and suggested that the telephone companies might divert their subsidies into other businesses rather than using them to keep local rates low. She suggested that the increasingly competitive telephone business required greater attention to rational prices rather than to the traditional concerns of politically determined equity:

> It is not clear to me that the Joint Board's recommendations can in any event be more than a temporary benefit to either high-cost telephone companies or their regulators. The days are numbered for regulators who believe they can mandate economically irrational behavior in the telephone industry. It is unrealistic to persist in the belief that dynamic telecommunications markets will adjust to a regulator's transition timetable to preserve "equities" among affected market participants. "Equity"-driven policies may be sustainable in a slow growth, static-technology industry. They are simply not viable in a dynamic growth industry such as telecommunications. Consequently, I fear that neither high-cost companies nor their state regulators will find the Joint Board's recommendations a solution to their respective financial and political ills. I am sure consumers will not.[14]

The Weatherly-Jones dispute reflected both the commissioners' respective constituencies and their fundamentally different views of the industry. Weatherly viewed the industry in traditional terms and sought to maintain his views of equity for the rural subscribers: low prices for his constituents paid for by other people who were not his constituents. Jones generalized the bypass argument into a demand for economically rational pricing. Just as the bypass argument questioned whether the LECs retained adequate market power to support the "Pure I" level of usage-based access charges, so the Jones argument questioned the ability to maintain a subsidy scheme in the increasingly competitive and dynamic industry. While Weatherly sought to maintain the status quo distribution of burdens in a new industry structure, Jones sought to use the change in industry structure as an opportunity to sweep out the baggage of the past and install a very different system specifically designed for a competitive industry.

Conclusion

The initial access plan evolved from an effort to solve the problems created by the Execunet decision in the simplest possible way to an effort to rearrange the long-established pricing patterns of the industry. It was well under way prior to the MFJ announcement, but the MFJ provided the incentive to complete the plan faster and to make more substantial changes than originally planned. The MFJ made it more difficult to implement a status quo plan because of the economic changes in the industry structure and because of the incentives it created for former members of the Bell System to work independently in supporting plans consistent with their interests.

Even though the general economic concept of aligning prices more closely to costs was accepted as a guide, numerous political adjustments were made against the recommendations of economists working on the plan. Even in the environment created by the impending divestiture, the FCC attempted to maintain the past practice of slow changes from the status quo and to continue the subsidization of particular companies.

The plan sought to limit the pricing flexibility of the LECs by setting up a rigid system of separations-determined revenue requirements, then allocation of those requirements to specific access elements, and then computation of specific access charges of a specified structure to meet those requirements. The rigid structure was originally conceived to prevent a unified AT&T from discriminating in favor of the affiliated long distance company versus the unaffiliated competitive companies, but it was retained even after the MFJ created structural separation between AT&T and the operating companies. Some of the rigidities were required by the MFJ requirements, but much greater freedom could have been given to the LECs to develop their pricing. The rigid pricing structure was a legacy of thinking about the LECs as pure monopolies and assuming that there was political freedom to allocate costs among particular users without concern for market forces. Although the FCC moved away from that conception in adopting the bypass argument and the SLC (implicitly assuming there was potential competition in access services), it retained the rigid pricing structure for the access elements.

Although the December 1982 plan was based on the Pure II approach, it created a flexible nonideological structure that could be adjusted to meet particular problems or political constraints. By proposing a combination of fixed and usage charges, the mix between them could be altered without changing the fundamental approach. By maintaining a subsidy and averaging scheme, there was room to modify the scheme to meet particular objections.

The FCC became the dominant player in the access charge controversy by asserting authority and taking aggressive action while taking sufficient account of the concerns of other power centers to prevent them from blocking the commission's actions. It was less than a year from the MFJ announcement to the adoption of the access charge rules. The appeals court upheld the FCC's authority to prescribe access charges against NARUC's challenge.[15] The commission backed away from a confrontation with the DOJ by waiving its access rules that ordered companies to structure rates in a manner directly prohibited by the MFJ. As discussed in the following chapter, Congressional pressure induced substantial changes in the 1982 access charge plan without formal legislation. The access charges actually implemented were based on the 1982 plan as modified to avoid being overturned by legislation.

11 / The Implementation of Access Charges

The implementation phase of access charges required translating the general rules and cost allocation requirements of the access charge plan into specific tariffs (detailed contracts setting out terms, conditions, and rates for specific services) that could be defended against stringent attack by parties whose financial viability depended on the level and structure of the charges. The implementation of access charges was a sophisticated exercise in accounting. It included considerable judgment in interpreting the rules and estimating demand and cost, but the numbers had to add up. There was no room for assuming away problematic billions of dollars of difficult-to-understand separations payments. Money could be shifted among jurisdictions and categories, but price cuts in one area had to be compensated either by increases in total efficiency or by price increases in another area in order to keep the companies financially viable. Thus the implementation phase was a reality check on the various forecasts of the earlier period.

The implementation of access charges and associated post-divestiture AT&T tariffs also reopened the competitive controversies of the 1970s. The Justice Department assumed that the divestiture would create a deregulated competitive long distance service market. However, the MFJ itself did not deregulate AT&T. MCI and other AT&T competitors supported the divestiture but opposed efforts to relax the regulatory restrictions on AT&T after the divestiture. The relationship between AT&T and its competitors was the fundamental issue in numerous detailed tariff controversies as AT&T sought freedom to respond to its competitors and the competitors sought continued restrictions on AT&T's pricing patterns.

The access implementation phase created considerable dissatisfaction and turmoil as many parties found that their optimistic assessments of the MFJ could not be sustained. AT&T accepted Baxter's proposal for a clean structural solution rather than a messy regulatory solution, and then after divesting its "natural monopoly" local exchange operations found its remaining "unregulated competitive" operations entangled in a regulatory environment in which every move was challenged by a skeptical FCC Common Carrier Bureau. AT&T also believed that the ENFIA interim tariffs gave an unfair advantage to its competitors and expected the post-divestiture equal rates to improve its competitive position. Instead, it found after the February 1984 revision to the access charge plan (discussed later in this chapter) that its competitors would receive a 55 percent discount on access until equal access was implemented. MCI viewed the divestiture as a great victory and expected to do much better under the new environment. MCI also viewed the ENFIA tariffs as providing an unfair advantage to AT&T and expected the post-divestiture equal rates to improve its competitive position. Instead, it found its access charges increasing while AT&T's decreased, making it more difficult to compete with AT&T.

Many accusations were directed toward the FCC because of its role as the primary agent in implementing access charges. For example, Judge Greene had accepted the Justice Department's view of the world and incorporated into his approval of the MFJ an assumption that local rates would not rise. He had no further authority or responsibility for the development of access charges or their implementation or the relative rates of local and long distance service, but he used an order approving the LATA boundaries (the boundaries for the areas in which divested local exchange companies could provide service without violating the long distance prohibition) to insert a challenge to the FCC's access charge plan:

> There is no legitimate basis for using the reorganization of the Bell System as a means for undermining the universal service objective or as an excuse for raising local rates.
>
> The Court has therefore noted with considerable surprise and some dismay that the Federal Communications Commission, far from using the access charge tool as a means for easing the burdens on the

users of local telephone service, has opted instead, in a major decision issued since the Court's approval of the consent decree, to saddle the local subscribers with the access costs of interexchange carriers. Curiously, although the FCC cites that decree and ostensibly regards its decision as assisting in its implementation, the agency's action runs directly counter to one of the decree's principal assumptions and purposes—that the fostering of competition in the telecommunications field need not and should not be the cause of increases in local telephone rates.

... As a matter of law, the FCC is not bound by the Court's decisions or assumptions in regard to access charges. However, as indicated below, the availability of the access charge in the form used by the Commission is directly tied to the decree in this case. Moreover, it might reasonably be expected that the Commission would not operate at cross purposes with the objectives of the decree in an area where the FCC itself failed for many years to achieve effective regulation in the public interest.[1]

Judge Greene's attack had no legal effect because he had no authority to review the access charge decision. Furthermore, both the DOJ and AT&T supported the FCC's access charge decision. Yet Greene's comment represented the anger of many participants in the process who found that the numbers would not support their assumptions.

Although the public controversies regarding the implementation of access charges concerned disputes among various policy-making bodies (the FCC, state regulators, Congress, Judge Greene), similar controversies took place internally at the FCC as various individuals and offices made different judgments about the policies appropriate to the rapidly changing and highly uncertain telecommunication industry. Extensive disputes raged within the commission staff, with an overriding theme of how to adjust to the new competitive structure while also maintaining the legal requirements inherited from an old structure. The author's notes of one particular meeting in Chairman Mark Fowler's office in early 1984 include the following:

I emphasized that the structure [of a particular tariff at issue at the time] was required by a competitive market after divestiture . . . [Tariff Division Chief] Fritz responded that I was wrong in every way, factually, legally, and otherwise. . . . The meeting became rather hot with frequent interruptions and became difficult to follow. The chairman . . . let the staff argue in a disorganized way. Finally he adjourned the meeting without resolution.

Although the initial implementation of access charges was chaotic and controversial, the rules eventually stabilized and routine procedures were established for the analysis of access charge tariffs. Substantial long distance price cuts softened the opposition to the price restructuring and allowed a political compromise in 1987 to complete the access charge plan. The final plan was delayed and modified by political compromises, but it eventually included the same goals and many of the same features as the original 1982 plan. The long-term plan remained reasonably stable throughout many political controversies in part because of the strong personal commitment to achieving its implementation from Mark Fowler, who remained FCC chairman from the original development of the plan through the 1987 compromise, and his chief assistant, Albert Halprin, who first served as Policy Division chief and then as Common Carrier Bureau chief.

Congressional Influence on Access Charges

Congress had been involved for many years as an ally of the state regulators in their efforts to hold down local telephone rates by shifting an increasing share of the cost of local telephone service onto interstate long distance service through changes in the separations allocators. No legislation had been passed, but the congressional oversight role and the threat of legislation had been effectively used to gain FCC acquiescence in ever larger flows of toll revenue back to the local operating companies. The MFJ agreement of January 1982 revived congressional concerns about maintaining the revenue flows from long distance to local. As discussed in Chapter 9, Baxter defended the agreement before congressional critics as having no impact on local rates. Not all were convinced by Baxter's assurances. Two months after the divestiture agreement, Chairman Timothy Wirth of the House Subcommittee on Telecommunications, Consumer Protection, and Finance introduced a bill to protect local rates from market forces created by the divestiture agreement. The bill quickly won unanimous approval in the subcommittee but was later blocked by AT&T's vigorous opposition to the bill.

The FCC's December 1982 access charge order increased congressional anxiety over the impact of proposed changes on consumers. Several different issues coalesced into general opposition to the implementation of the access charge plan:

1. The proposed Subscriber Line Charge (SLC) was a visible, immediate addition to every customer's telephone bill, with increases of uncertain magnitude to follow, while the long distance rate cuts and efficiency gains were theoretical predictions of what would happen under market forces. It was thus relatively easy to create a "consumer rip-off" issue alleging that this was a plan to help large businesses (either the telephone companies who collected the SLC or the businesses who were intensive long distance users) at the expense of ordinary consumers.
2. There was widespread skepticism about the wisdom of divestiture, and that skepticism turned to anger as the companies filed for huge rate increases that they claimed were necessary for financial viability after divestiture. Although the access charge plan was not directly related to those rate increases, the rate increases associated with the divestiture experiment in economics created doubt about the wisdom of another innovation in the industry supported by economic theory.
3. AT&T's long distance competitors opposed the access charge plan because it left them in a worse competitive position than the ENFIA tariffs did.
4. The state regulators opposed the plan both because of the effective increase in local rates and because it shifted power from the state to the federal jurisdiction.

All the dissatisfied parties sought relief from Congress. Although the concerns of the various complainants were quite different (federal versus state power, access discount for small companies, income distribution concerns), they reinforced each other in attracting congressional efforts to block the implementation of the access plan under the guise of protecting universal service. In July 1983, Republican Senator Packwood and Democratic Congressmen Dingell and Wirth (the respective committee chairmen with telecommunication responsibility) introduced compatible bills to overturn the FCC's access charge plan and held unusual joint Senate-House hearings on the bills.

Both bills explicitly prohibited the FCC's SLC, sought to maintain the status quo revenue flows in the industry after the divestiture, mandated extensive subsidies to high-cost areas paid out of toll revenue, and vested authority to make decisions regarding universal service subsidies in a Joint Board of federal and state commissioners. Both bills prohibited bypass and imposed penalties on any company that attempted to avoid the high access charges that would result from the bills through alternative means of making local connections. Thus the bills provided explicit legal monopoly rights to the local exchange carriers and guaranteed their right to receive a share of long distance toll revenue.

At the Joint Hearings, FCC Chairman Mark Fowler defended the access charge plan against sharp attacks by his fellow Republican, Senator Packwood:

Chairman Packwood: Now in your statement you indicate the Federal Communications Commission acts under a congressional mandate, and you read the directive, "to provide service so far as possible to all the people of the United States," and "it should be a rapid, efficient, nationwide service with adequate facilities at reasonable charges," correct?

Mr. Fowler: Yes, sir.

Chairman Packwood: And indeed, you are a creature of Congress and you are to attempt to administer in this case the telephone laws in accordance with what you think Congress has intended.

Mr. Fowler: With true fidelity, yes, sir. . . .

Chairman Packwood: Now, for years you have followed this policy of subsidizing rural and residential rates with long-distance charges, acting on what you thought was Congress mandate, and Congress never said anything. We seemed reasonably happy with it.

What has given you the impression that Congress has changed its mind as to what we want you to do?

Mr. Fowler: . . . We got into a very real concern about bypass, where you set up alternative systems to bypass the local exchange and thereby escape paying the subsidy . . . we see instance after instance of gigantic systems either being planned for now by businesses or actually under construction, particularly in large major cities, where they are bypassing the local exchange and avoiding having to pay those subsidies. . . .

Chairman Packwood: . . . Did anybody from Congress come and talk to you, however, and say, we want to get rid of this old system we have had where we have subsidized residential and rural rates with long distance? Did Chairman Dingell or Chairman Wirth or Chairman Goldwater or Senator Ford come and say we think the system we have used for a good many years ought to be changed?

Mr. Fowler: No, sir, nobody did one way or the other. But I do believe, and indeed the entire Commission felt, the three Democrats and four Republicans, unanimously believed that had we not acted we ran the risk of seeing the destruction of our great national network, as more and more companies got off the system.

And they are the ones, because of their great use, that have provided the greatest support for that system through the revenues that have been charged to them.[2]

Opposition to the bills by the FCC, AT&T, and the designated heads of the "fetus Bells" that were still legally a part of AT&T slowed the progress of the legislation but did not stop it. In the same month as the joint hearings, the FCC made a number of refinements to the access charge plan in a reconsideration order, but did not change its fundamental features. The July 1983 refinements specified the initial SLC at $6.00 per month for business telephones and $2.00 per month for residence telephones in January 1984, with the residential SLC to rise to cover all interstate NTS costs other than universal service fund costs by 1990. The method of computing the access discount for inferior-quality access received by long distance companies other than AT&T was changed, but the discount remained far less than the small companies considered appropriate. Thus the reconsideration order made no substantial concessions to the concerns behind the legislative efforts.

Congressional concerns were intensified when the companies filed access charge tariffs in October 1983 to become effective with divestiture on January 1, 1984. Both AT&T and the new BOCs attempted to increase their earnings with the proposed new rates. As discussed below, the tariffs and supporting materials were long and complex, but one aggregate fact stood out. Although the SLC would raise about $4 billion in the first year, AT&T's proposed rate cut for long distance services was only $2 billion. The "missing two billion dollars" made it difficult to defend the proposed tariffs as evidence of increased efficiency and improved consumer welfare through competition. The FCC interpreted the problem as one of faulty implementation of its access charge plan and suspended the tariffs for investigation. Congress interpreted the tariffs as further evidence that the plan itself was faulty and renewed efforts to pass legislation to overturn the plan.

In November 1983 the House passed the Dingell-Wirth bill, but the Senate failed to pass either the Packwood bill or a substitute measure calling for a simple delay in the access charge plan. However, the FCC's suspension of the access charge tariffs meant that they did not take effect with the divestiture, and the pre-divestiture procedures were extended temporarily. On January 18, 1984, Senator Bob Dole (Republican from Kansas) sent a letter cosigned by 31 other senators to FCC Chairman Mark Fowler asking that major changes be made in the access charge plan. Senator Dole's lead role and the many other Republican senators who signed the letter made it clear that this was not a partisan battle of the congressional Democrats challenging the Republicans in charge of the FCC. The letter requested four changes in the access charge plan: (1) prohibit telephone companies from imposing flat rate end user charges on residential and single line business customers during 1984; (2) let each small telephone company decide for itself whether to impose end user charges on residential and single line business customers after 1984; (3) cap the flat rate end user charge for all of the residential and single line business customers of larger telephone companies at $4.00 until at least 1990; and (4) substantially reduce the amount of increase in the interconnection charge that must be paid by Other Common Carriers to local telephone companies effective April 3, 1984. The letter contained a gently worded threat that legislation to overturn the access charge plan was likely if the Commission chose not to modify it: "Given the uncertainty and confusion that currently exist within the telecommunications field, it seems to me a particularly inopportune time for Congress to consider major telephone legislation. It may be that members of Congress feel they are in a much better position to resist the temptation to 'do something' about this uncertainty if the commission modifies its 'access charge orders.' "[3]

With the House bill already passed and a third of the Senate signing the Dole letter, the likelihood of legislation was high if the FCC refused to accommodate congressional concerns. On the other hand, the Dole letter offered the FCC a specific set of changes that it could adopt while maintaining its authority and flexibility to pursue long-run goals without having the status quo enshrined in legislation. The day after receiving the letter, the FCC tentatively decided to defer the residential and single line business charges, and then adopted a formal decision on February 3, 1984, making changes in the July 1983 access charge plan consistent with the Senate suggestions.

The February plan deferred the SLC for residential and single line business users until June 1, 1985, and limited the residential and single line business SLC to a maximum of $4.00 per month at least until 1990. The FCC instituted additional proceedings to consider the evidence for bypass and methods to promote universal service. The proposal that SLCs be optional for small companies was folded into the further proceedings. At the conclusion of those proceedings, SLCs remained mandatory but additional assistance was granted to small companies.

A critical part of the February 1984 order was a substantial revision to the computation of the differential between AT&T and its competitors (referred to as the Other Common Carriers or OCCs). The OCCs had gained a great deal of political support for their complaint that the access charge plan imposed a drastic increase in their costs and threatened their viability. The Senate letter requested a cut in the OCC payments. Both the Department of Justice and the National Telecommunications and Information Administration (NTIA) supported making the plan more favorable toward the OCCs. Predictably, the OCCs themselves found the July plan far too favorable toward AT&T, while AT&T found it far too favorable toward the OCCs. After reviewing various attempts to compute a premium value for the superior interconnection arrangements available only to AT&T, NTIA suggested that there was too much uncertainty to make a computation of premium value a viable method of assigning the differential. Instead, NTIA suggested that the existing differential in the ENFIA agreements be taken as a starting point and gradually phased toward equality.

In the February 1984 order, the FCC adopted the Senate's suggestion that the OCC differential be increased, and adopted NTIA's suggestion that the existing ENFIA differential be taken as a starting point. The commission used estimates that the existing ENFIA discount was approximately 70 percent of the implied pre-divestiture AT&T rate. After making various adjustments, the FCC concluded that a 55 percent discount from premium access (applied to *all* elements, not just carrier common line) would approximate three-quarters of the ENFIA discount. It adopted a 55 percent discount factor as a starting point for access charges. Instead of phasing it out on a fixed schedule as planned in the earlier orders, the FCC ordered that the discount would be phased out as equal access became available. When equal access became available, the long distance carrier was required to pay premium rates whether or not it chose to utilize the equal access. Although the computation was to be on a per-minute basis, the order provided that actual payments would be based on an assumed 9,000 minutes per month per line between the OCC and the local company, rather than on actual measurements. This provision simplified measurement problems and also provided an additional discount for any

OCC that could utilize its lines at greater than 9,000 minutes per month.

A further important change in the February order was the decision to impose access charges on the closed end of WATS lines at the switched usage rate rather than at the private line rate. WATS closed ends typically had high usage, and consequently the total switched charges assessed were substantially higher than the private line rate. The change was presented in the February order as a modest technical adjustment to maintain the status quo while a joint board reviewed the separations treatment of WATS access lines, but it had three significant effects:

1. Because AT&T was the only carrier providing WATS, the increase in total switched minutes that occurred when WATS closed end usage was added to other common line usage increased the share of NTS costs paid by AT&T and decreased the share of NTS costs paid by AT&T's competitors. The competitors offered WATS-like service with closed ends that were classified as special access (private lines) rather than WATS access lines and thus did not pay usage charges under the February rules.
2. Because of then-existing rules requiring AT&T to earn the same return on WATS as on MTS, the assessment of switched access costs on the closed end of WATS induced lower MTS rates and higher WATS rates than would have otherwise occurred. This shifted benefits from large business users to small business and residential users.
3. Because WATS lines had heavy usage, they formed a prime target for bypass activities. This increased the credibility of the Commission's assertion that it needed to impose SLCs to reduce bypass. The commission's quantitative model of bypass potential relied heavily on the assessment of switched charges to WATS access lines to show that bypass was a serious threat.[4]

The February 1984 order was more tailored to political concerns and preserved more of the status quo than the previous access charge orders. The previous orders had emphasized economic efficiency as a goal and had sought to overturn substantial portions of the then-existing system in an effort to rapidly bring prices closer to costs. The FCC's initial two access orders created so many dissatisfied groups (OCCs upset about large increases in their costs, state regulators upset about SLCs that would be perceived as local rate increases, consumers worried about sharp increases in telephone rates and skeptical of the entire divestiture process) that a coalition of very diverse interests could be united on the single theme of blocking implementation of the plan. Furthermore, the carriers attempted to use the divestiture to implement longstanding goals of increasing their net earnings, which led them to propose rates that despite the implementation of the SLCs produced only modest long distance price cuts. Thus there were no substantial groups of customers who had an interest in protecting the access charge plan in order to protect their rate cuts. The February order responded to the various concerns in both substance and style. The order hardly mentioned economic efficiency and noted that the SLC should be set to balance universal service concerns and bypass concerns. The commission's commitment to universal service was strongly reaffirmed, and proceedings were begun to ensure that universal service was not harmed by the access charge plan.

Initial Switched Access Charge

The July 1983 order had been scheduled as the commission's final action on access charges prior to implementation. Initial access charge tariff filings were made at the beginning of October 1983 for implementation with the divestiture on January 1, 1984. The initial tariff filings were massive in size and were a complex departure from the status quo in an attempt to implement the MFJ requirements and the commission's access charge plan. The new material included 43,000 pages of tariffs and 160,000 pages of support material.[5] A vast amount of additional material was generated in comments on the tariffs and supporting material by the various interested parties. Despite the volume of material, the filings lacked much of the information requested by the commission. The companies did not have the staff and expertise to prepare proper filings and backup material in the required time. The access rules were complex and represented a wholesale change from previous methods of recovering interstate costs. Furthermore, the Bell-related companies were preoccupied with the final preparations for divestiture.

Because of the divestiture and the new access charge rules, the companies did not have the historical data normally used to justify tariff filings. Tariffs are normally based on a forecast of demand and are cost-justified by historical data. The greater the departure from past practice, the greater would be the uncertainty about the relevant demand and cost estimates. In the case of the initial access tariffs, there was no historical cost or demand for the particular structure proposed. The companies developed cost estimates based on 1982 historical records adjusted for changes into 1984 and adjusted for the effects of the divestiture, details of which were still being arranged while the cost estimates were being prepared. The demand estimates were for "access minutes," a category that did not exist prior to divestiture. The companies had to estimate the likely rate structure of AT&T and its competitors, using the access rates as an input cost, and then derive estimates of access minutes in order to produce tariffs for the intermediate product.

The commission was also unprepared for the burden of reviewing and evaluating the access charge filings. Previous tariff filings had provoked great controversy, but they had been about much more specific problems, and usually resulted in rates that remained in effect for a long period of time. The entire settlements process in which vast sums flowed among companies was largely administered by AT&T without active commission oversight. Under the access charge plan, that process was transformed into tariffs subject to the commission's jurisdiction that were challenged by many interested parties. The initial access charge tariffs created new terms and conditions, rate structures, and actual rates that could not be compared to the existing rates to evaluate reasonableness. Thus the standard practice of focusing only on the change from the status quo and the reasons for that change could not be used because the access charge tariffs were such a radical departure from the status quo.

The commission's inability to fully evaluate the tariffs and prescribe any needed corrections prior to January 1 caused it to suspend the entire set of access tariffs. Thus there were no access tariffs in effect on January 1, 1984. The commission ordered the companies to continue the old settlements and ENFIA system until access charges could be implemented. Judge Greene granted a waiver of the MFJ requirements to allow the Bell companies to comply with the FCC order. While the access tariffs were under suspension, the access charge plan was modified by the February 1984 order in response to congressional concerns. Rather than order an entire new access filing to conform with the modified access plan, the commission chose to work on modifications of the existing filing that could be implemented quickly.

Although many parties were mollified by the February 1984 changes to the access charge plan, AT&T was incensed. Several of the changes came at AT&T's expense. The increased discounts for the OCCs and the decision to imposed switched access charges on WATS closed ends both increased AT&T's share of the total NTS costs and decreased the costs of the OCCs compared to the July 1983 order. The deferral of the residential and single line SLC increased the long distance company access payments and therefore increased the significance of the discount controversy.

Two weeks after the February order was released, AT&T filed an "Emergency Petition for Reconsideration" with the commission in which it asserted that the February access order would cause its earnings at current rate levels (pre-divestiture rates) to drop below 5 percent on interstate investment and below 3 percent on equity. Furthermore, AT&T asserted that it would have no opportunity to recoup its investment even if the commission allowed it to increase rates because the favorable OCC conditions created by the February order would allow them to undercut AT&T's rates. AT&T also filed a petition for review of the FCC's orders with the appeals court, focusing primarily on the commission's lack of substantive reasoning for the increase in the OCC discount.[6] AT&T asserted that the commission "clearly does not enjoy a free hand to choose any rate structure or discount factor it regards as a convenient political compromise. Instead, the Commission must avoid arbitrary and capricious action and base its decisions on reasoned analysis, rationally explaining departures from prior positions . . . [the commission's] automatic resort to AT&T as a kind of piggy bank out of which coins can endlessly be shaken for others is a vestige of history unrelated to the real world."[7]

Despite its inability to fully analyze the thousands of pages of tariffs and quickly resolve the many controversies, the FCC developed a plan to implement the access tariffs along with rate cuts and to defer some of the issues for later consideration. The commission declared that with regard to switched access tariffs, the local exchange carriers had overstated their costs and understated their demand, and that therefore the rates must be reduced. The commission also made adjustments to AT&T's projections and concluded that AT&T's emergency petition contained several errors that caused AT&T to severely underestimate its earnings. It ordered AT&T to reduce its existing MTS and WATS usage rates by 6.1 percent. Thus in May 1984, the switched access charges were implemented with a 6.1 percent reduction in MTS and

WATS prices. Although the commission's shortcuts through the huge maze of supporting material and conflicting arguments stretched its authority and violated normal standards of procedural care, the appeals court did not overturn the basic access implementation. Complex problems with the private line tariffs were deferred, and the initial post-divestiture private line tariffs did not become effective until much later.

Managed Competition for Political Perceptions

The political turmoil of late 1983 and early 1984 slowed the FCC's planned implementation of market-oriented prices, but did not change Chairman Fowler's determination to carry out as much of the original plan as possible. The political opposition to the original plan had made it clear that two conditions would have to be met in order to take further steps in the plan:

1. Long distance rates must be reduced enough to create a substantial constituency in favor of cost-based pricing.
2. The AT&T competitors must remain viable.

The first condition required the FCC to retain tight control over AT&T's rates in order to ensure regular reductions, especially in the most politically sensitive rates. However, pressing AT&T for the maximum reductions also made it more difficult for AT&T's competitors to survive as they moved into a world of equal access and equal payments. The fundamental difficulty was that a key factual premise of the Justice Department's case, that MCI's early success came from costs enough lower than AT&T's to compensate for AT&T's obstructive tactics, was wrong. MCI's pre-divestiture high profits were primarily the result of its advantageous rates for local access.

As AT&T's competitors recognized the dire implications of the 1982 access charge plan for their finances, they pressed both the FCC and Congress for relief. Their previous emphasis on the unreasonably high ENFIA payments turned into an emphasis on how favorable the ENFIA payments were in comparison to AT&T's payments and therefore on the many problems they would encounter after the access charge plan was implemented. Although the competitors received substantial short-term relief in the increased discount provided by the February 1984 revisions, the long-term picture was unchanged. They were required to pay charges identical to those of AT&T in each area that had equal access, and therefore could expect their access charges to rise rapidly as most local companies implemented equal access between 1984 and 1986.

During 1984 MCI's gross revenue increased by 30 percent to almost $2 billion, but access cost increased from 17.2 percent of gross revenue in 1983 to 24.5 percent of revenue in 1984.[8] While MCI's access cost was increasing, AT&T's prices were forced down to show consumer benefit from the access charge plan, and therefore MCI was required to reduce its prices to remain competitive. MCI's pretax profit rate dropped from 18.5 percent of revenue in 1983 to 2.6 percent of revenue in 1984. MCI's drop in profitability, together with the public protestations of the competitors that they might not remain viable under the access charge plan, caused a dramatic drop in investor confidence. By late 1984 MCI stock had plunged to one-quarter of its 1983 high. Sprint and other competitors of AT&T encountered even more difficulties than MCI in adjusting to the post-divestiture environment.

MCI had been a prime supporter of the DOJ case which had ended in the divestiture victory. However, MCI opposed the Justice Department's assumption that divestiture should mean the end of regulation for AT&T. AT&T's competitors were effectively deregulated prior to the divestiture in the Competitive Carrier rulemaking, which limited full regulation to dominant carriers (AT&T) and assumed that non-dominant carriers (MCI and other AT&T competitors) would be indirectly regulated through the competitive pressure of AT&T's price structure. MCI supported continued strict regulation of AT&T in order to limit AT&T's competitive responses to MCI's pricing innovations.

The issues of the degree of regulation of AT&T and the financial viability of the smaller carriers created considerable internal debate within the FCC. Chairman Fowler and the commission as a whole were publicly committed to free market approaches and opposed to the management of a regulated cartel. Yet the long-term commitment to competition could not survive the bankruptcy of both (or possibly of either) of AT&T's two major competitors. Because legal and political constraints eliminated the outright deregulation of AT&T as a viable option, the battle was fought in numerous individual tariff proceedings relating to the freedom AT&T had to restructure its rates to meet competition. The economists in the Office of Plans and Policy (including three people who had worked for the Justice Department on the antitrust case and believed that divestiture radically changed the need for AT&T regulation) generally supported increased freedom for AT&T, while the Common Carrier Bureau generally supported continued tight controls on AT&T's price structure in accordance with tariff standards established prior to the divestiture.

AT&T's goals were clear. It wanted to increase rates for the discounted services offered primarily to residential customers in the evenings and weekends and to decrease rates selectively through targeted discounts to the business segments most susceptible to competition. Although such a strategy was to be expected in a competitive market given the underlying cost structure, it would have had the politically detrimental effect of increasing the relative rates for large numbers of small-scale users and also of reducing the profitability of AT&T's competitors. The commission had already lost once on the access plan to a combination of AT&T competitors and consumer groups and sought to avoid that outcome again by greatly restricting AT&T's freedom. AT&T's overall rates were forced down with decreases in the access charges, but AT&T was given very little freedom to restructure its rates in the early post-divestiture period while the finances of its competitors were precarious.

After Albert Halprin (a key architect of the 1982 access charge plan) returned to the commission as CCB chief in late 1984, access charge changes were managed closely with careful political attention to developing a record to allow further increases in the SLC. The delay in the implementation of the residential and single line business SLC allowed substantial reductions in the long distance price to accompany each increase in the SLC. Because the NTS revenue requirement was declining as CPE and inside wiring costs were gradually removed from regulation while total minutes were growing, the charge per minute paid by long distance carriers to local companies could have been cut even without increases in the SLC. Increases in the SLC accelerated the reductions by contributing part of the revenue requirement, stimulating additional minutes because of the long distance rate cuts to consumers, and reducing the incentives to bypass the switched system.

The first one dollar per month per line of residential and single line business SLC was imposed in June 1985, and the second dollar was imposed in June 1986. The multi-line business rate remained fixed at a maximum of $6.00, while the actual amount averaged about $5.00 because it was also limited to the total of a particular computation of costs that was below $6.00 in some areas. Both increases were accompanied by cuts in long distance rates, and little political controversy accompanied either the 1985 or the 1986 SLC increase.

Completion of the Access Charge Plan

Under the 1984 compromise, the FCC agreed that it would not raise the residential SLC above $2.00 per line per month without a full public proceeding and that it would seek the advice of a Joint Board before increasing the residential SLC. Submission of further SLC increases to a Joint Board meant that the FCC was committed to attempting to satisfy state regulatory concerns about the program. Crucial to the deliberations in late 1986 and early 1987 was the desire of some telephone companies supported by some state commissioners to end the carrier common line pooling process. In particular, Bell Atlantic, supported by New Jersey Commissioner George Barbour, a member of the Joint Board, was anxious to end the pooling process in which it paid significant amounts to other companies because of its low costs. However, if pooling were simply ended without providing a way to keep the prices down for small high-cost companies, geographic rate averaging would be endangered. An increased SLC would reduce the total amount of revenue requirement in the CCL pool and thus make it easier to end pooling.

Because the state commissioners were generally supportive of an end to mandatory pooling along with provisions to keep the CCL of high-cost companies down, the proceedings focused on the minimum SLC necessary to make a depooling plan satisfy the various constraints. In early 1987, a very complex plan was approved by the Joint Board and subsequently by the commission in which the residential and single line SLC would gradually rise from the then-current level of $2.00 to a maximum of $3.50 in April 1989, and in which the mandatory common line pool would be abolished.

The basic concept of the depooling plan was to get the SLC high enough and the residual revenue requirement low enough that the major carriers (including all the BOCs and GTE) would voluntarily withdraw from the pool. The major companies that had benefited from the pool would receive transitional support payments for a time in exchange for leaving the pool. The smaller companies would remain in a much smaller pool. That pool would receive long-term payments from the major carriers sufficient to allow the pool to charge a CCLC rate (the charge paid by interexchange carriers to local exchange carriers to recover the residual NTS revenue requirement) equal to the average CCLC rate of the non-pooling carriers. The CCLC rate charged by the telephone companies remaining in the pool would have been almost three times as high as the national average rather than the same as the national average without the support payments. Although the low-cost telephone companies owned by Ameritech (in the midwest) and Bell Atlantic continued to pay most of the long-term support to the smaller companies, the depooling plan allowed them to eventually eliminate their payments to the high-cost companies owned by Bell South and GTE.[9]

A key aspect of the early 1987 agreement was that the FCC agreed that the plan adopted then would be its final SLC plan and that it would not seek further increases in the SLC in the future. When the phase-in to $3.50 per line per month for residential and single line businesses was completed in April 1989, approximately half of the total interstate common line revenue requirement was recovered through the SLC and half through the CCLC. Thus the FCC abandoned its longstanding goal of eventually recovering all of the interstate NTS charges through fixed charges in order to get support for raising the SLC to $3.50.

With the 1987 agreement, the access charge plan stabilized. The SLC phase-in proceeded on schedule to its final level of $3.50 in April 1989 with only minimal political or public notice. Depooling occurred on schedule in April 1989. The carrier common line charge (the residual revenue source in the access charge plans) was cut in small increments many times as demand increased and the SLC was phased in. It declined from an initial 1984 rate of 5.24 cents per minute at each end to an average (depooled) 1990 rate of 1.00 cent per minute originating and 1.53 cents per minute terminating. Total access charges per conversation minute (including traffic-sensitive charges and carrier common line and counting access charges on both ends of the call) dropped from 17.3 cents per minute in 1984 to 7.8 cents per minute in 1990 at the end of the access charge transition period.

Conclusion

Three distinct issues accounted for the chaos of the initial access implementation period:

1. The political values of the participants differed regarding the overall goals of the process and the weight to be placed on preserving the status quo versus adjusting to market forces. In later stages of the process, this political difference was resolved into a clear distinction between Republican leadership at the FCC favoring market adjustment versus Democratic leadership in Congress favoring more protection for the status quo. In the earlier days the distinction did not divide into party lines, and prominent Republicans such as Senator Packwood supported retention of the status quo. At that time the distinction could be drawn between those who were committed to free market approaches (either as professional economists or because of ideological opposition to government intervention) versus those concerned with practical politics.

2. There was great uncertainty about the effects of any particular policy action. Much of the debate on access charges concerned alternative predictions of what would happen under various scenarios. There was no commonly accepted model or framework for evaluating the effect of taking particular actions. Predictions such as "AT&T competitors will go bankrupt without a larger access discount," "rural areas will be left without service under the FCC's access charge plan," or "bypass will make the maintenance of the status quo impossible" were used as a form of policy argument. The uncertainty in the industry and the frequent opportunistic use of predictions made it impossible to develop commonly accepted forecasts of the effect of various actions.

3. Administrative limitations made it difficult to cope with the vast amounts of new data in unfamiliar form being created at access charge time. The beginning of access charges placed the commission into a role for which it was not prepared. It needed to evaluate and rule on many complex issues supported by large amounts of contested data in a very short period of time. Ordinary administrative requirements, such as the development of staff expertise and appropriate computer and manual procedures for managing the data, were developed gradually over the first few years of the access charge plan. Issues that could be routinely evaluated in later years were either ignored, delayed, or handled in crisis mode at the beginning.

Access implementation was a case in which extreme uncertainty made it impossible to develop a coherent long-range plan. Participants with differing political views also had different expectations of the effects of various policies. It was therefore not possible to develop a long-term compromise plan at the beginning. Instead, the procedure was to experiment with the beginning of the plan and observe the results before undertaking the next step. That process was feasible in this case because the policy was divisible. From the FCC perspective, a $2.00 SLC was not as good as a $4.00 SLC but was better than no SLC at all. Thus the initial concession to congressional pressure to delay the implementation of the SLC and limit it to $2.00 until extensive further proceedings (including state regulatory consultation) were held was superior to having the entire program blocked by legislation.

The FCC's careful management of the initial SLC implementation to ensure large long distance price decreases simultaneous with SLC increases reduced but did not eliminate the opposition to SLCs. Many state regulators and congressional leaders remained opposed to SLCs, but the large price decreases made the advantages of SLCs a benefit worth protecting to many parties. Much of the political anxiety over the access charge plan in 1983 was related to proposed price increases of the local companies unrelated to access charges. Increased depreciation rates and other changes to compensate for errors of the past became effective with the beginning of the access charges even though they were unrelated. At the time of the 1983 congressional hearings, local companies had $7 billion of rate increases pending with state utility commissions. During 1984, almost $4 billion of local rate increases were granted (separate from SLCs), but that figure declined to $300 million in 1986 and went to actual decreases in basic local rates during 1987 and 1988. As measured by the Consumer Price Index, local rates increased at 17.2 percent in 1984, but the rate of increase declined to 3.3 percent by 1987. The Consumer Price Index for interstate toll calls declined each year during the access charge implementation, with a maximum one-year reduction of 12.4 percent in 1987. Thus by 1987, local rates had stabilized and toll rates were declining rapidly, making it possible to negotiate a final adjustment to the access charge rules that continued implementation of the FCC plan.

Part IV / Alternatives to the Divestiture Model

12 / The Dismantling of Structural Separation

The theory of the divestiture required a sharp dividing line between the competitive and monopoly segments of the industry. According to that theory, the local exchange carriers (LECs) should be confined to the provision of monopoly local exchange service and prohibited from participating in the competitive markets of long distance service, manufacturing, or information services. Participants in the competitive markets should be unregulated, unaffiliated with the LECs, and should purchase needed local services from the LECs on a nondiscriminatory basis, with prices for those monopolized inputs controlled by regulation. However, at the time of divestiture the dividing line between competitive and monopoly service was fuzzy rather than sharp. Furthermore, the fuzzy line was shifting over time. Consequently, the boundaries created by the MFJ were challenged by both private companies and other policy-making institutions.

The divestiture itself could not be easily repealed or modified. It was a dramatic structural change implemented at great effort and expense that could not be adjusted easily to changing technology and policy choices. That rigidity was part of its attraction to the Baxter DOJ because it was seen as an alternative to the continuous slow adjustments of the regulatory process. However, the restrictions on the divested Bell Operating Companies (BOCs) that were imposed by the MFJ could be modified. Policy makers outside the DOJ adjusted to the new structure without accepting its logic as their own, and thus the issues remained alive for further consideration. Furthermore, much of the industry had an incentive to oppose the MFJ theory. The BOCs sought freedom to engage in a wide variety of activities. AT&T's competitors sought to continue regulation of AT&T. Eventually, only AT&T and Judge Greene sought to uphold the structure of the decree against the opposition of the BOCs, the DOJ, and the FCC. The decentralized policy process allowed the industry to evolve into a structure very different from that implied by the theory behind the MFJ.

The debates over the wisdom of structural separation have been complex and acrimonious. Beneath the colorful language and apocalyptic claims made by many different parties runs a debate over several fundamental issues:

1. The degree of economies of scope among vertical services in a static sense. Economies of scope can include coordination and standards issues, customer convenience, and cost savings from integrated production. The DOJ originally took the position that economies of scope between allowed and prohibited BOC services were negligible.
2. The opportunities for anticompetitive conduct from vertical integration between the monopoly service and the non-monopoly services. The DOJ antitrust case emphasized that those opportunities and incentives were so substantial that divestiture was necessary to allow the efficient functioning of a competitive market.
3. The effect of vertical restrictions on technological progress. The BOCs emphasized the necessity of offering a wide variety of products in order to maximize technological progress. This is a dynamic version of the economies of scope argument; it asserts that research and development on one product can result in benefits for other products and that the coordination difficulties of bringing new complementary products to market may require management control of the set of complementary products.
4. The effect of integration on U.S. international competitiveness. In the original Reagan administration debate over the wisdom of the then-proposed divestiture, the Commerce Department argued that AT&T's vertical structure and practice of purchasing products from its own affiliates were more desirable than the Justice Department's proposed solution, which would emphasize more opportunities to purchase from foreign companies.

The FCC's Computer II structural separation and the DOJ's divestiture plan both assumed that the opportunities for anticompetitive behavior from the provision of integrated monopoly and competitive services were high, and that the probability of losses from economies of scope, missed technological opportunities, or reductions in international competitiveness were low. Those relative assessments changed over time and caused a reconsideration of the wisdom of maintaining strict structural boundaries. This chapter examines the dismantling of the structural boundary between monopoly local exchange service and competitive information services. Nine years after the original divestiture agreement, the BOCs gained the freedom to provide information services integrated with their local exchange services.

Three different limitations on the mixture of regulated local exchange and information-related services should be distinguished. First, the telephone companies were generally prohibited from providing cable television service. This prohibition was first adopted by the FCC, and subsequently the FCC's rules were enacted into law in 1984. The FCC thus lost the right to modify or repeal the rules. Issues related to the LEC participation in cable television are not discussed in this chapter. Second, the FCC required that "enhanced services" be provided only on an unregulated basis through fully separate subsidiaries as part of the Computer II decision of 1980. At that time the FCC distinguished basic (regulated) service that was "limited to the common carrier offering of transmission capacity for the movement of information" from enhanced service that "combines basic service with computer processing applications that act on the format, content, code, protocol or similar aspects of the subscriber's transmitted information, or provide the subscriber additional, different, or restructured information, or involve subscriber interaction with stored information."[1] Third, as part of the MFJ, the BOCs were prohibited from providing "interexchange telecommunications services or information services" and were not allowed to "manufacture or provide telecommunications products." "Information service" was defined as "the offering of a capability for generating, acquiring, storing, transforming, processing, retrieving, utilizing, or making available information which may be conveyed via telecommunications, except that such service does not include any use of any such capability for the management, control, or operation of a telecommunications system or the management of a telecommunications service."[2]

The MFJ was an additional restriction on the companies, not a replacement for the FCC's Computer II rules. The FCC interpreted its existing rules related to AT&T as applying individually to the various components of the old AT&T after the divestiture. Thus the new

AT&T was required to maintain a separate subsidiary for its enhanced services. The FCC's definition of enhanced service and the MFJ's definition of information service were similar but not identical. It was consequently unclear whether the divested BOCs could provide any enhanced services without violating the MFJ prohibition on the provision of information services, but if they could, they were required to do so under an unregulated, fully separate subsidiary. The close relationship between restrictions on the BOC provision of information services, interpreted by Judge Greene, and restrictions on the BOC provision of enhanced services, administered by the FCC, created many opportunities for conflict between the district court and the FCC. Both claimed primacy and suggested the other should yield to avoid conflict, but neither had clear power to overrule the other.

In terms of the policy model of Chapter 3, the dispute between the FCC and Judge Greene was primarily over different perceptions of the state of the world and of the results of particular policy instruments. Both the FCC and Judge Greene accepted the promotion of technological progress and the prevention of anticompetitive action as goals, though Greene probably put greater weight on the prevention of anticompetitive action than did the FCC. Through a combination of new evidence and changing personnel, the FCC leadership became convinced that structural separation (of either the Computer II or divestiture type) was harmful to technological progress, a change from its view in 1980. The FCC's new view implied that there was a trade-off between minimizing the possibility of anticompetitive action through structural separation and maximizing technological progress. The FCC chose a form of nonstructural separation that it believed provided adequate protection against anticompetitive activities while giving greater freedom to the local telephone companies to introduce new services. Greene remained convinced that structural separation caused no reduction in technological progress and therefore viewed the effort to dismantle structural barriers as harmful (because of reduced protection against anticompetitive activity) with no offsetting benefits.

The public debate recounted in this chapter was essentially a replay of the internal debate within the early Reagan administration about the appropriate policy toward AT&T, but with a different outcome. The FCC took on the role of the Commerce and Defense Departments in emphasizing the potential economies of scope and advantages of integrated operation, while Judge Greene took on the role of the Justice

Department in asserting that economies of scope were minimal and that structural separation was needed to promote effective competition in the industry.

The Third Computer Inquiry

Both the Computer II basic/enhanced distinction and the MFJ local exchange/information services distinction were drawn with reference to the telephone network of the 1970s. That network consisted of communications paths connected to switches. Control signals were telephone numbers passed along the same communications path as the primary communication. Whatever intelligence existed in the network resided in the central office switch. The rigidity of that system was illustrated by the large investments and long time required to implement equal access for competitive long distance carriers. In order to allow presubscription (automatic switching of each customer's call to that customer's preferred long distance carrier without dialing separate access codes for each call), each local switch had to be upgraded with new software ("generics") and in some cases new hardware. In the year of the divestiture agreement there were over 9,000 central offices; of these, 69 percent were electromechanical, 30 percent analog stored program control, and 1 percent digital stored program control.

Over the next decade, the total number of central offices remained approximately constant but the technology mix changed radically to an estimated 9 percent electromechanical, 21 percent analog stored program control, and 70 percent digital stored program control.[3] Advancing computer technology made it desirable to integrate much more computer processing capability (intelligence) into the network. The companies developed plans to separate the intelligence from the pure switching function, and to have a signalling network separate from the voice/data network. The first services for which the separate intelligence was used were pay telephone credit card calls and 800 service. In both cases, it was necessary to look up information in a data base in order to complete the call. For credit card calls, it was necessary to validate the card. For 800 services, it was necessary to translate the 800 number into an ordinary routing number. In both cases, the local office recognized the need for further information, accessed a central data base not included at each local office, and then used information from that data base to complete the call. That sequence was the model for many "intelligent" services in which the customer gains flexibility and variety in calling services by having additional computer processing capability in the telephone network beyond a minimal signalling and switching capability.

The addition of intelligence to the network created a conflict with the strict boundary lines drawn by the MFJ and Computer II rules. In general, intelligence functions could be placed in various places in the network: inside CPE, in the local network, or in the long distance network. A strict application of the MFJ and Computer II concepts would limit the BOCs to a "dumb" network in order to avoid mixing a competitive function (computer processing capability) with the BOC monopoly of physical wires. Yet the intelligent central office was the key to making new services widely available, and there was general agreement that it was undesirable for the anti-monopoly rules to restrict technological progress.

The FCC's initial experience with administering the Computer II rules showed that the clear, bright line the commission had attempted to create between basic and enhanced services did not exist. The first problem originated in attempts to classify packet switching service as either basic or enhanced. Packet switching service was originally implemented by non-telephone companies that added computer checking and routing capability to leased lines in order to provide the service. However, there was nothing fundamentally "enhanced" about packet switching. From the customer's point of view, it was simply a method of accurately transmitting data. So long as the data was received in the same format as it was entered, the service was classified as basic and could be offered by the telephone companies under regulation. However, if the data was received by the telephone company at low speed ("asynchronous protocol") and delivered to the customer at high speed ("x.25 protocol"), this fell under the definition of enhanced service because a protocol conversion had occurred. Although a waiver process was established to give flexibility to the administration of the rules with regard to protocol conversion, the problems resulting from a literal application of the rules caused rethinking of their logic.

A second concern was that the Computer II rules could be prohibiting the integrated provision of services that would not be offered separately. Soon after the Computer II decision, AT&T sought to offer "Custom Calling II" service, which included voice storage without structural separation. Opponents argued that the proposed service met the definition of enhanced service and would be offered on a competitive basis if AT&T were prohibited from colocating voice storage equipment with central offices. The commission accepted the opposition arguments and prohibited the integrated AT&T service, but several years later no comparable service was available.

A third concern was that the rules could be inhibiting general network improvements by restricting the use of computer technology that provided new routing and call capability but at least arguably violated the definitional distinctions of Computer II. This concern arose from controversies over AT&T's introduction of "Advanced 800" service and the recognition that regardless of the final regulatory outcome, the requirement that a new routing plan meet competitive objections and gain approval would slow the introduction of new technology into the network.

After encountering numerous difficulties in interpreting and enforcing the Computer II structural separation between basic and enhanced services, the commission initiated a new inquiry ("Computer III") in 1985 regarding the appropriate boundary between unregulated computer services and regulated communications services. The *Notice* stated:

> The "enhanced services" definition of Computer II, and the deregulation of customer premises equipment, were intended to establish a durable dichotomy between regulated and unregulated activities, to facilitate planning and decision making by the public and by industry. While the treatment of customer premises equipment has served this purpose, the treatment of service offerings has not. At an ever-increasing pace since Computer II was adopted in 1980, we have been called upon to clarify, interpret and apply the "enhanced services" definition to offerings that carriers seek to make to the public on a regulated basis, and to offerings that others seek to make on an unregulated basis. . . .
>
> Carriers have generally not sought to offer data or information "processing" of their subscriber's communications. Rather, they have sought to offer capabilities that seem to improve the ability of users to communicate. Yet the specific definition of "enhanced service" adopted in Computer II brought into question whether such capabilities could be offered on a regulated basis. . . .
>
> Virtually any new call routing feature that AT&T (or a BOC) might propose to introduce can be (and might be) challenged as violative of Computer II. Most of these do not involve manipulation

of information as such, or even protocol conversion. They involve use of stored data in the network by the network to set up users' calls, or delivery of information from the network concerning users' calls. . . . We are asked to bar the introduction of new network capabilities not because of the current proposed users, but because they *might* at some time (if ever) become enhanced services.[4]

As a result of the proceeding, in 1986 the FCC adopted the Computer III nonstructural approach to providing safeguards for companies that were both customers and competitors of the local exchange companies. The Computer III proceeding revived ideas that had originally been devised to limit AT&T's ability to harm competitive providers of private line services prior to the divestiture. At that time the commission had instituted cost allocation rules to separate the cost of AT&T private line services subject to competition from its switched services that were largely monopolized. The FCC had supplemented the cost allocation rules with a partially implemented policy of "building block" tariffs designed to allow competitors to "mix and match" components from AT&T and from their own facilities. AT&T had resisted the building block approach, and it was never fully implemented.

The two primary components of Computer III were Open Network Architecture (ONA) and cost allocation rules. The idea of ONA was to break down the network into a number of building blocks (referred to as Basic Service Elements or BSEs), each of which would be offered separately under tariff at nondiscriminatory rates to all customers. Any customer could choose the necessary building blocks from the local exchange carrier to combine with other services and create the final customer offering. Local exchange carriers could not restrict the BSEs to particular classes of customers and could not tie the availability of one BSE to subscription to another BSE.

Under the Computer III approach, local exchange carriers could provide enhanced services without using separate subsidiaries, but the enhanced service offerings would be unregulated. The unregulated portions of an exchange carrier were required to obtain the necessary local exchange services from the same tariffed BSE offerings made available to nonaffiliated carriers.

The ONA plan was a concept for long-term development of the network rather than a specific set of proposals for immediate implementation. The existing network was not organized in an "open" way, and the FCC did not mandate the massive investments that would have been necessary to restructure the existing network. Rather, the FCC provided incentives for the carriers to make future investment decisions that would open up the network by allowing them to eliminate structural separation between regulated and nonregulated services once ONA was in place.

Because ONA was a long-term program, the FCC also instituted an intermediate program known as Comparably Efficient Interconnection (CEI). The CEI program was similar in concept to ONA, but only required unbundling of specific elements necessary to provide a specific service rather than the more general approach of ONA. Under the CEI program, a carrier could submit a CEI plan for a particular service and after approval could offer that service on an integrated basis with its regulated services. The CEI plans provided a way for the carriers to offer specific services without structural separation in the short term and for both the carriers and the FCC to gain experience with the open connection approach prior to the full implementation of ONA.[5]

An important goal of the Computer III framework was to limit the ability of an integrated firm to transmit competitively useful information to its unregulated affiliates when that information was unavailable to competitors. Unequal access to information can be a barrier to effective competition, but too strict information disclosure requirements could reduce the efficiencies of integrated operation that are central to the rationale of eliminating structural separation. In adopting information disclosure requirements, the FCC attempted to strike a balance between the competing and inconsistent goals of maximizing efficiency by allowing the free flow of information within the firm, on the one hand, and guarding against unfair competition by requiring identical disclosure of information to competitors as to nonregulated affiliates, on the other.

With regard to network disclosure requirements, the FCC required that

> starting at the time that AT&T and the BOCs begin joint planning, research, or development of enhanced services, they will be required, for all new network services or changes to existing network services that affect the interconnection of enhanced services with the network, to notify the enhanced services industry that such a change is planned. Such notification will take place at the time AT&T or any BOC makes a decision to manufacture itself or to procure from an unaf-

filiated entity, any product the design of which affects or relies on the network interface.[6]

With regard to customer proprietary network information (CPNI), the FCC noted that true equality of information would either impose broad restrictions on joint marketing inconsistent with the removal of structural separation, or make CPNI available to all in violation of customer expectations about confidentiality. As an approximation to equality of information, the FCC required AT&T and the BOCs to send an annual notice to multiline customers informing them of their right to prevent access to their CPNI by the enhanced service affiliates of the carriers, and of their right to request that their CPNI be released to competitive carriers. If a customer declined to respond to the notice, then the carrier was entitled to use the CPNI but had no obligation to release the CPNI to competitors. Thus the carriers gained an information advantage over their competitors because of their right to exclusive use of the information when the customer made no election, but the carriers had neither an absolute right to use of the CPNI in their affiliated operations nor the right to refuse to provide the CPNI to competitors when the customer requested such disclosure.

The ONA/CEI approach was a generalization of the equal access requirement of the MFJ. The most controversial part of the definition of "generalized equal access" concerned colocation rights. Because the BOC would be serving its enhanced affiliates directly from its central office, true equality required that it also make central office connections available to all customers. However, mandatory colocation was strongly opposed by the BOCs. Because there was a large number of existing and potential enhanced service providers, mandatory colocation could create problems with the physical availability of office space and security requirements. The FCC declined to require mandatory colocation, but it did adopt safeguards similar to those in the MFJ equal access requirements to reduce the competitive advantages of affiliated colocated enhanced service providers compared to unaffiliated ones.

The initial BOC ONA plans were based on the concepts developed during the access charge proceedings. Offerings were based on a "basic serving arrangement" (BSA) that was similar to ordinary access lines, together with optional "basic service elements" (BSEs) that allowed a user to customize the access line to its particular needs. The BSAs were the existing access services or closely related services such as "trunk-side circuit switched service" or "trunk-side packet switched service." Although some parties vigorously opposed the initial offerings as mere repackagings of existing services and sought much greater unbundling, the FCC allowed the basic approach proposed by the companies to satisfy its requirements for ONA. The strongest opposition was to requiring all services to be provided through BSAs rather than unbundling the transport and switching functions. However, such unbundling would have required colocation in order to allow a customer to take a switching function without transport, and the FCC reaffirmed its earlier decision that colocation would not be required.[7]

Under the Computer III approach, regulated and nonregulated portions of the business could share assets and personnel subject to cost accounting safeguards. In addition to the cost allocation rules for joint activities, there were restrictions on transactions among affiliates in order to ensure that costs were not switched from the nonregulated side into the regulated side of the business. Transfers between affiliates were required to be valued at the current tariff rate or a rate determined from a prevailing price list offered to the public if either rate was available. If neither was available, then assets transferred out of regulation were to be valued at the higher of net book cost or fair market value, while assets transferred from a nonregulated affiliate to a regulated affiliate were required to be valued at the lower of net book cost or fair market value. This asymmetry of treatment was adopted over the protests of telephone companies in order to provide protection from arbitrarily set transfer prices that could be difficult to evaluate and could increase the costs of the regulated business.

The cost allocation principles were adopted as general rules for all carriers, but each carrier was required to submit a detailed cost allocation manual for approval. Each carrier's cost allocation manual contained the detailed application of the rules to that particular carrier's business. After the manuals were approved by the FCC (in general after the carriers made FCC-mandated changes to the originally submitted manuals) and became effective, the carriers were required to provide annual attest audits by outside accounting firms indicating that the carrier's implementation of the rules was consistent with its cost manual. As a final check, FCC auditors reviewed the attest audits as well as conducting some audits on their own.

Although considerable efforts were made to improve both the cost allocation rules and their administration and enforcement, the emphasis on cost allocation was fundamentally a return to the 1970s approach to regulating mixed competitive and monopoly markets that was widely regarded as a failure. The problems with the 1970s efforts had created interest in structural separation as an alternative, but concerns about lost economies of scope under structural separation inspired the FCC to attempt a better version of cost allocation.

The DOJ and the MFJ Information Services Restriction

The FCC's adoption of the initial Computer III order in May 1986 together with its approval of the cost allocation guidelines later that year established the commission's policy of favoring integrated provision of enhanced and basic services and implicitly challenged the continuation of the information services ban in the MFJ. So long as that ban remained in place, the regulatory freedom gained by Computer III was largely illusory. While the Computer III framework provided permission for the integrated provision of basic and enhanced services, it did not impose a requirement that the BOCs provide enhanced services. Thus, even though its policy goals were contradictory to those of the MFJ, the order did not create a direct legal conflict with the MFJ because it was possible for the BOCs to abide by the MFJ without violating the Computer III orders.

As discussed in Chapter 9, the early Reagan administration was divided about the merits of the AT&T antitrust suit, with Assistant Attorney General William Baxter strongly in favor of pursuing the suit and presidential advisor Edwin Meese (along with the Secretaries of Commerce and Defense) opposed to the suit. Although Baxter won that dispute and essentially dictated his settlement terms, he did not remain in office long enough to guard his victory. Baxter's departure and the appointment of Meese as Attorney General prepared the way for a dramatic reversal of the Justice Department's position on the case.

In February 1987, the DOJ filed its report and recommendations regarding the line of business restrictions as part of the triennial review process. The report abandoned the earlier antipathy toward the FCC and the emphasis on the need for strict structural separation between monopoly and competitive sectors. The DOJ recommended the elimination of the information services and manufacturing prohibitions on the BOCs. This radical change in position appears to have been primarily a result of the new top leadership. The economics staff remained convinced that the old position supporting structural separation was correct and objected to the policy reversal, but they were overruled. The DOJ explained its change of position as the result of changing technology in the industry and changed FCC regulations. It now found that the information restrictions were unnecessary and were limiting the introduction of new products:

> Some information services can most efficiently be provided at the level of the switch, *i.e.*, on an integrated basis. These services increasingly are available to large customers that have their own PBX switching systems, and many such services also are provided by foreign and independent telephone companies, which are not subject to the MFJ's restrictions. As a result of the MFJ prohibition and, formerly, the FCC's *Computer II* rules, however, a variety of information services are not available on an equally efficient basis to customers that, as a practical matter, depend on the BOCs' public networks. . . . The fact that a number of services that are unavailable in BOC regions already are offered on an integrated basis by telephone systems in Western Europe and Japan, and by independent telephone companies in this country, also supports the concern that BOC customers are being deprived of useful services. . . . While we cannot be certain about the existence or magnitude of the foregone efficiencies that result from the information services prohibition, we have no reason to dispute the virtually unanimous conclusions of PBX providers and users, non-BOC telephone companies and the expert agency charged with regulation of interstate telecommunications.[8]

In the 1987 report, the DOJ portrayed the FCC's Computer III regulations as the appropriate framework for distinguishing regulated communications services and unregulated enhanced/information services, and sought to avoid Judge Greene's detailed regulation of the boundary lines through waivers and interpretations:

> The FCC thus has established detailed standards and procedures for review and enforcement of CEI, ONA and accounting plans submitted by the BOCs. Moreover, its rules fully comport with the equal access standard and related competitive principles of the decree that the Court and the Department would have to attempt to apply if they were to process information services waivers on a case-by-case basis. The FCC, with its technical expertise, superior resources, and notice

and comment procedures, however, seems to us to be better suited than the Department and the Court to applying these standards to the relevant competitive issues in the current information services environment. . . .

The FCC is better equipped than the Department and the Court to make the cost-benefit decisions involving complex technical and economic questions, heavily influenced by a variety of federal and state regulatory policies, that now are required in the information services area. Not only is the FCC likely to do at least as good a job in the short run in a case-by-case process under its CEI requirements, but it has the capacity to do a substantially better job in the long run by inducing reconfiguration of the BOCs' local networks under its ONA standards.[9]

Judge Greene and the Information Services Restriction

At the time of the divestiture agreement, Judge Greene accepted the Baxter perspective on the case and on the benefits of structural boundaries between monopoly and competitive services. He continued to maintain that perspective even after the FCC and the DOJ changed positions. Greene retained jurisdiction of the consent decree for interpretations and modifications. Although in many cases such a role is minimal and limited to formally approving agreements made by the parties, Greene viewed his role more broadly as upholding the public interest in telecommunications.

At the time the agreement between AT&T and the DOJ was presented, Greene initiated hearings to determine whether the decree was in the public interest.[10] After several months he proposed modifications to the decree. The parties were given the choice of accepting his modifications or resuming the litigation after Greene rejected the settlement. The Greene modifications blurred the lines the DOJ had attempted to draw between competitive and monopoly services by allowing the divested BOCs to provide some competitive services and providing a waiver procedure. Baxter and other DOJ leaders disagreed with Greene's modifications, but accepted them rather than resuming the litigation. Several years later, Baxter described Greene's modifications as the source of his continuing role in telecommunication policy:

[The Greene modifications to the decree] indicated a state-of-mind on the part of the Judge that he was receptive to an endless succession of petitions—a kind of "Mother, may I?" game that was going to go on for a very long time. It was precisely the exhibition of that attitude on his part that sentenced us to having two regulators rather than one for a long period of time. Certainly, it was my notion that there would be a clean cut on the entry of the decree. The problem would be remanded to the FCC which had jurisdiction, and the Court would more or less step out of the picture. That is the way it should have worked, and I continue to be disappointed that it did not.[11]

Greene disagreed with Baxter's assertion and commented with regard to the above quote:

Professor Baxter is wrong in suggesting the continuing campaign of the Regional Companies to escape the line-of-business restrictions came about because the changes I required in the decree departed from the so-called quarantine theory. In my judgment, it is naive to think that the companies would not have made the same effort, just as vigorously and just as often, if what Professor Baxter calls a more "elegant" theory had been adopted.[12]

Regardless of which participant was correct about the source of the petitions, there was a continuous effort by the divested BOCs to gain relief from the restrictions imposed on their activities by the decree.

In a 1986 ruling, Greene reiterated his view of the case and of the importance of restricting the BOCs to monopoly local exchange service:

The history of the government's struggles with AT&T indicated to those who negotiated and approved the current consent decree that, when the local companies were divested to continue on their own the provision of the local monopoly telecommunications services, they had to be prohibited from engaging also in competitive long distance and information services. Accordingly, a specific prohibition to that effect—one of the few decree provisions directly applicable to the local companies—was incorporated in the decree.

The logic of such a provision was as obvious as its incorporation in the decree was crucial. Without it, the result of the break-up would have been to exchange one nationwide monopoly with the incentive and ability to exploit monopoly power and injure competition for several smaller monopolies with the identical incentives and abilities. ... the Regional Companies, or some of them, indicate by their public statements, their advertisements, and their rush to diversification, combined with their relative lack of interest in basic telephone service itself, that an ascent into the ranks of conglomerate America rates far higher on their list of priorities than the provision of the best and least costly local telephone service to the American public. . . . These companies inherited billions of dollars in tangible and intangible assets at the time of divestiture because the Court and others concluded that these assets would be used in the public interest, that is, in the provision of excellent yet low-cost telephone service to American consumers, and that this objective would be accomplished without the re-creation of the dangers to fair competition that existed before. This Court firmly intends to enforce the decree in light of that purpose.[13]

Greene's belief in the importance of structural separation together with an expansive view of his role in evaluating any changes to the decree caused him to reject the BOC and DOJ requests for removing the information services restriction. Sterling and Kasle reported:

> In June 1987, a clearly angry Judge Greene held a three-day hearing on the Huber report [the study accompanying the DOJ recommendations] and the modified Justice Department recommendations. He was outraged at the turn of events and, like others, stunned that the Justice Department, which had fought the case so vigorously, was now suggesting that the restrictions of the MFJ were ill-advised and should be discarded. AT&T, for its part, urged the judge to keep many of the restrictions in place, arguing that divestiture had fulfilled its purpose. The operating companies agreed with the Justice Department, their former adversary, and suggested that circumstances in telecommunications had changed so dramatically—so many new companies, so many new markets—and the realities of competition were so compelling that they could not operate with their corporate hands tied.[14]

In September 1987 Judge Greene issued a 223-page order analyzing and rejecting the positions of the DOJ, the FCC, and the BOCs. He accentuated his policy disagreement with the FCC and challenged the effectiveness of the Computer III framework, which the DOJ found an effective substitute for service restrictions. He reiterated the criticisms of FCC regulation from the trial period and asserted that the FCC had since that time been following a deregulatory philosophy and therefore was unlikely to be a better regulator. Greene even threatened sanctions against the FCC and others who challenged his interpretations:

Claims to the contrary—that the restrictions were justified or intended to apply only immediately after divestiture, *see, e.g.*, Southwestern Bell Comments at 2; FCC Comments at 4—are so devoid of legal and factual support that, were it not for the fact that there appears to be no practical way to sort out a few statements out of many, and the further fact that several assertions by others are likewise close to or below the acceptable line, sanctions under Rule 11, Fed. R. Civ. P., would have been imposed.[15]

Along with detailed analyses of the faults of particular FCC regulations, Greene challenged the reliance of the Justice Department on the FCC when the FCC was pursuing a deregulatory course:

> Between the 1950s and the early 1970s, the FCC was committed, as was the nation generally, to vigorous regulation of a variety of business enterprises, especially those with public utility characteristics. Much of that has changed. The FCC and individual members of the Commission have repeatedly expressed themselves in favor of wide deregulation. The Court of course does not express any judgment on the wisdom of that policy; that is beyond its jurisdiction. However, a regulatory body that is committed in principle to as little regulation as possible can hardly be cited at the same time in support of the proposition that it will probably regulate more vigorously and more effectively than its predecessors which wanted to engage in tight regulation and operated in a general governmental environment that regarded strict regulation as a positive goal.[16]

Greene vigorously rejected the DOJ and BOC requests for removal of the restrictions:

> Since exhortations, regulations, and orders requiring a cessation of the Bell System's activities had proved fruitless, the remedy adopted in the decree, as simple as the problem itself, had but two basic aspects: first, the divestiture from AT&T of its local monopoly affiliates . . . and second, an order prohibiting the new owners of the local bottlenecks—the Regional Companies—from engaging in the competitive long distance, manufacturing, and information services markets. . . .
>
> It is the attempted destruction of that careful design that the motions now before the Court are all about. Almost before the ink was dry on the decree, the Regional Companies began to seek the removal of its restrictions. These efforts have had some success, in that they have tended to cause the public to forget that these companies,

when still part of the Bell System, participated widely in anticompetitive activities, and that, were they to be freed of the restrictions, they could be expected to resume anticompetitive practices in short order, to the detriment of both competitors and consumers. . . .

Once before, in 1956, an antitrust suit against the Bell System was aborted precipitously by a Department of Justice decision, and that step laid the groundwork for many years of turmoil and travail in the industry, the courts, the regulatory commissions, and the Congress. That history must not be repeated. This Court cannot and will not lend its authority to so self-defeating an enterprise. It is therefore denying all the requests for the removal of the core restrictions of the decree.[17]

Although Greene denied the DOJ/BOC/FCC request to eliminate the information services restriction, he expressed concern about the slow development of information services in the United States relative to other countries (particularly the French Minitel system), and softened the information restrictions so that the BOCs could provide "gateway" services. Under that structure, the BOCs were not allowed to provide the actual information but could structure a communications service that included previously prohibited elements to simplify access to database services. Greene also eliminated the general prohibition on the BOCs' participation in non-telecommunication services.

The dispute between Greene and other policy makers escalated in November 1987 when the Commerce Department's NTIA under the leadership of Alfred Sikes (who later succeeded Patrick as FCC chairman) filed a Petition for Declaratory Ruling asking the FCC to rule that "the provision of information services by the Bell operating companies is in the public interest" in order to "terminate controversy and eliminate needless uncertainties caused by a recent Federal district court ruling." Continuing the 1982 Commerce Department opposition to the case, the 1987 petition asked the FCC to make a formal legal challenge to Greene's authority in order to maintain U.S. competitiveness in global markets:

> The communications systems operated by the Bell operating companies constitute a major national resource. Capital assets exceed $140 billion; human resources include some half a million highly trained, talented, and motivated employees. The full potential contribution of information services to the economy and national welfare cannot be achieved without allowing these assets and resources to be

mobilized. We can, in short, no longer afford to acquiesce in consent decree-based regulation which has at its core a policy of unproductively warehousing half the nation's telecommunications sector.

Permitting the Bell operating companies to use their own and others' networks to offer information services to American industry, small businesses, and the public at large would make a significant positive contribution toward ensuring U.S. competitiveness in global markets. That, in fact, was the consensus opinion reached by the Commission, the Justice Department, and the Department of Commerce, and advanced earlier this year to the court reviewing the AT&T consent decree.

Conversely, precluding Bell company participation in the information services sector, or hobbling that involvement with an unnecessary district court-mandated regime, places important communications policy goals at unacceptable risk. . . .

The Commission has the statutory authority to find that, under the Communications Act, the provision of information services by the Bell operating companies is in the public interest, and that the determination made by the district court prohibiting such entry would be contrary to the public interest mandate of the Communications Act. The Commission's public interest determination should take precedence over a conflicting view by the district court.[18]

Although the FCC staff was sympathetic toward the concerns expressed in the NTIA petition, it was unwilling to recommend that the commission embark on a direct legal challenge to Judge Greene. The petition could have been granted in a trivial way by simply reiterating the findings of Computer III that the commission found provision of enhanced/information services in the public interest. Such a finding would not provoke direct conflict with the MFJ because it did not require the companies to provide the services. In order to grant the substance of the petition, it would have been necessary to issue an order requiring the companies to provide a service prohibited by the MFJ restrictions and then allow the appeals court (which had authority to review both Judge Greene's rulings and FCC rulings) to sort out the conflict. The FCC attorneys were less confident than the NTIA attorneys that the commission would prevail in such a situation.

The commission had earlier backed away from a direct confrontation in a situation where its legal position was stronger than in the information services problem. A portion of the rate structure prescribed by the access charge rules directly conflicted with an MFJ access provision. During 1983, AT&T requested a waiver of the commission's rules so that it could follow the MFJ requirement. The commission staff initially drafted a denial of the waiver and ordered the companies to prepare tariffs in accordance with the commission's rules and contrary to the MFJ requirement. AT&T's vigorous protests and agreement to accept a rate cut through an action not directly related to the access charge structure caused the commission to grant the waiver. In that case, the commission was in a strong legal position because tariffs and tariff rate structures were clearly under its authority, and it had adopted the rules after full notice and comment procedures. It was unlikely that the appeals court would allow that process to be overruled by a private agreement between AT&T and the DOJ. However, the NTIA petition presented a more difficult issue because the commission had not previously found that the companies must provide information services. Granting the substance of the NTIA petition would have required reworking the framework of Computer III in a way that was obviously designed to create a conflict, with a significant risk that the commission would lose. Consequently, no action was taken on the petition.

The controversy was continued the next month (December 1987) when Greene issued a further order construing the meaning of the prohibition on "manufacturing." AT&T and others had complained to the DOJ that the BOCs were engaging in prohibited services by performing design work for new products. The DOJ took no action on the complaints because of uncertainty over whether the prohibition on manufacturing included prohibitions on design or only on actual product fabrication, and because of its developing position that the decree restrictions were inappropriate and should be removed at the triennial review. AT&T then filed a formal request with the court for an interpretation of the word "manufacture." Greene took the opportunity of that interpretation order to attack both the DOJ and the FCC for their efforts to loosen the decree restrictions:

> It is appropriate . . . to consider the failure of the Department of Justice to take enforcement action for well over two years after receipt of requests therefor. During that period, the Department came to accept the view that the definition of the term "manufacture" presents a difficult issue, and that the best course of action therefore was to halt enforcement until the Department's triennial report was

due in court in the spring of 1987. . . . In short, the complaints regarding the Department's failure to act are well taken . . . the Department did not await waiver or triennial review proceedings and the Court's decisions in connection therewith, but made its own decision on the competitive situation outside the framework established by the decree.

The Chairman of the Federal Communications Commission recently took the unusual, if not unprecedented, step for the head of a regulatory agency, of exhorting those whom the agency regulates to refuse to comply with orders duly issued by this Court, stating that he was "quite frankly, surprised by the apparent acquiescence of some of the Bell Operating Companies in the ongoing administration of the [decree in this case]." Address of Hon. Dennis R. Patrick, October 13, 1987. The only acquiescence that occurs between the Court and the Regional Companies is that the companies carry out the Court's judgments and orders directed to them, as they must under law. Incitement to noncompliance, if successful, could thus have serious consequences.

In the same address, the FCC Chairman also questioned the legitimacy of the Court's jurisdiction, presumably again for the benefit of those whom the Commission regulates, characterizing as a willingness "to supplant the role of Congress" the Court's enforcement of the decree in this case . . . such thoughtless statements by a high official of government are unfortunate. . . . However, there should also be no doubt that this Court will carry out its constitutional and statutory responsibility to protect and enforce the decree in this case, as in other cases, against violation, obstruction, or interference by anyone, public or private, as federal judges have done throughout history. [citations provided to the history of civil rights enforcement][19]

Although the FCC chose not to provoke a direct legal conflict with Greene, the DOJ and the BOCs appealed Greene's order that continued the information restrictions. In 1990, the appeals court found that Greene had erred in substituting his own judgment for that of the parties to the case (the BOCs and the DOJ) and had used the wrong legal standard for evaluating the information service request. The court remanded the case to Greene for further proceedings with instructions that left Greene little choice but to grant the DOJ and BOC request to lift the restriction. In the remand proceedings, Greene emphasized that he remained adamantly opposed to the removal of the restrictions:

In the first place, the contention that it will take the Regional Companies to provide better information services to the American public can only be described as preposterous.... Moreover, the Court considers the claim that the Regional Companies' entry into information services would usher in an era of sophisticated information services available to all as so much hype. Experience suggests that once these companies have achieved the removal of the information services restriction, ample reasons will be found and cited why the more expensive promises could not be fulfilled.

In the opinion of this Court, informed by over twelve years of experience with evidence in the telecommunications field, the most probable consequences of such entry by the Regional Companies into the sensitive information services market will be the elimination of competition from that market and the concentration of the sources of information of the American people in just a few dominant, collaborative conglomerates, with the captive local telephone monopolies as their base. Such a development would be inimical to the objective of a competitive market, the purposes of the antitrust laws, and the economic well-being of the American people.[20]

After reiterating his belief in the importance of the information services restrictions and his disdain for the DOJ and BOC analyses supporting the removal of those restrictions, Greene reluctantly lifted the restrictions as the only way to comply with the directives of the appeals court:

For the reasons stated in Parts I through VI above, were the Court free to exercise its own judgment, it would conclude without hesitation that removal of the information services restriction is incompatible with the decree and the public interest. However, as will now be explained, the Court is not free to exercise its own judgment. Indeed, it has concluded that several rulings of the Court of Appeals in its 1990 opinion . . . leave it no choice but to remove the restriction. . . .

It is the Court's judgment that in view of the requirements imposed by the Court of Appeals which are summarized above, it could not responsibly and with proper deference to that court rule that the information services restriction must be retained. Accordingly, the Court is ordering simultaneously herewith that the restriction shall be removed.[21]

Judge Greene's reluctant decision to lift the information restrictions of the MFJ, together with the FCC's implementation of the Computer

III nonstructural framework as a substitute for the Computer II structural separation, gave the BOCs freedom to expand into information services in competition with other companies. Of course, the decision to lift the ban did not mean that the concerns of Greene or the Justice Department staff who supported retention of the ban were unfounded. Information on the effect of the information services restriction on either the protection of competition or the promotion of technological progress continued to be very scarce. Knowledgeable economists continued to argue both for and against the restriction, with neither side able to convince the other of the correctness of its position. That division of opinion regarding the information services restriction contrasted with the near unanimity of economists over the wisdom of eliminating legal barriers to entry in CPE and long distance competition and of matching prices more closely to cost in the access charge proceeding. In both of those cases, generally accepted economic theory could suffice to reach a recommendation even when empirical data was very limited. In the information services case, neither the economic theory nor the available data were decisive, and various individuals came to different conclusions as they examined the ambiguous evidence.

Conclusion

The long fight over the information service restrictions was in part a reflection of the fact that the MFJ itself had a narrow base of support among the relevant policy agencies. Baxter's ability to dictate the terms of the settlement had prevented a full examination of the merits of the restriction at the time of the divestiture agreement. The Commerce Department, the FCC, and the state regulatory commissions had all opposed imposing severe restrictions at divestiture time. The appointment of Meese, an early opponent of divestiture, as Attorney General facilitated the DOJ's change of position on the wisdom of information service restrictions. Greene remained committed to the restrictions but lost the power to maintain them against the unified recommendation of the DOJ and the BOCs. Clearly, Greene would have retained the restrictions if he could, and he would have had the power to retain them if the DOJ had continued to support them even if the FCC, Commerce, and other power centers opposed them. Thus the critical act in the 1991 removal of the restrictions was the 1987 DOJ decision to support lifting the restrictions.

The FCC's decision to allow the integrated provision of enhanced services with local exchange service originated in the difficulties of determining the dividing line between those classes of service and in fears of limiting technological advance. The increasing integration of computer technology into all phases of communication during the 1980s made any distinction between computer and communications service appear artificial. Telephone companies routinely provided "information services" integrated into their ordinary operations through directory service, credit call validation, and 800 service. There was no clear distinction between that type of information service (classified as basic because they were aspects of providing traditional telephone service) and newer services such as voice storage that were classified as enhanced because they provided nontraditional services to the consumers. The FCC was concerned that a continuation of its strict Computer II structural separation policy could cause "basic" to simply mean "old technology" because the danger of crossing the boundary line into "enhanced" would limit new telephone services.

The FCC's decision to move forward with Computer III nonstructural boundaries despite the existence of the MFJ limitations was a crucial feature of the eventual elimination of the restrictions. The FCC's action eliminated its own structural restrictions and provided a basis for the DOJ to argue that changed conditions made the continuation of the MFJ restrictions inappropriate. It was far easier to defend a DOJ concurrence with the FCC than simply a change of position. The formal structure of the DOJ argument was that the new FCC regulations were a substantial improvement over the FCC regulations in effect at the time of the trial, and that therefore the MFJ restrictions were no longer needed. Although Judge Greene and other observers disputed the sincerity of that argument, it had enough force for the appeals court to consider it within the exercise of reasonable DOJ discretion.

While the FCC, the DOJ, industry participants, and Greene argued the merits of the information services restriction, aided by numerous attorneys and economic consultants, the actual event that triggered the removal was the appeals court ruling regarding the method of construing the MFJ. The appeals court ruling was not formally an evaluation of the evidence presented and a finding that the restrictions should be removed. Rather, it was an analysis of the proper standards for evaluating the evidence that instructed Greene to give greater deference to the judgment of the DOJ and less weight to his own evaluation of the merits of the case. Thus the appeals court did not order the restrictions removed but remanded the case to Greene for further proceedings in accordance with the specified standards.

While the formal structure of the appeals ruling was the procedural point of how to evaluate evidence presented in the administration of a consent decree, the effect (and probably the intent) of the ruling was to remove the restrictions. This case was similar to the 1978 *Execunet* case in which the appeals court made a decisive procedural ruling that most parties interpreted as an intentional substantive policy intervention. Each agency must express its policy preferences in the language appropriate to its authority, and the most natural language for appeals court interventions is a challenge to the procedural correctness of the court or agency decision they wish to reverse. Even after the remand proceedings, Greene was clearly unconvinced by the evidence presented (including affidavits supporting the removal of the restrictions from the economists Jerry Hausman, Franklin Fisher, Dennis Carlton, George Stigler, and Alfred Kahn) but removed the restrictions after evaluating the evidence according to the standards set by the appeals court.

Although the lifting of restrictions occurred specifically as a result of the appeals court ruling on the interpretation of the decree, the result was caused by and consistent with the perspective of a majority of U.S. telecommunication policy makers. During the 1980s there was a widespread shift of concern from problems of controlling monopoly power (the focus of the restrictions) to problems of enhancing productivity and international competitiveness. By 1991, Greene was the only significant power in telecommunication policy that still supported the information services restriction, though there were many other individuals and companies still looking for a political sponsor for continuing restrictions. Greene's strong views and position extended the restriction beyond the time the FCC and DOJ agreed that it should be removed, but could not continue it indefinitely. It is likely that in the absence of appeals court action, some other method would have been found to eliminate the restriction. On the other hand, if the other policy-making institutions had been divided about the wisdom of retaining the restriction, it is likely that Greene would have retained the power to impose his views as a reasonable exercise of judgment interpreting conflicting evidence.

The removal of the MFJ information services restriction and the implementation of the FCC's Computer III framework eliminated the "MFJ model" of structural separation between competitive and monopoly services. Local telephone companies were encouraged to enter enhanced and information services in competition with other companies. The DOJ's antipathy toward ineffective FCC regulations of the 1970s and advocacy of a structural solution were replaced by praise for a modified form of the 1970s approaches in the Open Network Architecture and cost allocation rules of the Computer III framework. With the Justice Department's change of position and the limitations on Greene's authority, there was no sufficiently powerful entity that supported the structural separation model to defend it against its many critics.

13 / Competition in Local Service

The rigid boundaries envisioned by the theory of the MFJ required the local exchange companies (LECs) to be monopolies in their geographic areas and to be limited to those monopoly services. The previous chapter discussed how that structure was revised through changes in technology and policy that allowed the LECs to add services other than monopoly local exchange services. This chapter examines the development of partial competition within the local exchange, which had the effect of reducing the monopoly power of the LECs in the services treated as a natural monopoly in the MFJ theory.

During the access controversy after the MFJ agreement, the FCC put considerable emphasis on the possibility of limited competition in the local exchange ("bypass") as a reason to restructure the price system. Many policy makers put little confidence in the bypass argument. Judge Greene and some congressional leaders argued that the then-existing price structure of high long distance and low local exchange prices should be maintained through the imposition of high usage-based access charges. They argued that bypass was not very likely, and that in any case it could be prohibited. The "Universal Service Preservation Act of 1983," which was passed by the House and received strong support but was not passed by the Senate, contained severe restrictions on bypass. The Senate version included the provision: "Whoever, with the intent to deprive any exchange company of any revenue to which it is otherwise entitled in connection with access charges, transmits telecommunications in a manner so as to avoid accessing a local exchange for the purpose of avoiding the payment of such charges shall be fined not more than $100,000."[1]

The legislation guaranteeing legal support for local monopoly did not pass, and the FCC declined to take the advice that it should solve the bypass threat to access charges through rules rather than through changing price incentives. Thus the FCC declined to turn the observed economic fact that there was very little competition in the local exchange into the legal policy that competition was prohibited. Just as at the beginning of long distance competition, the FCC did not adopt a formal policy on the preferred structure of the market but allowed its policy to develop over time in reaction to particular events and controversies.

The FCC's access charge plan defined two basic kinds of access, switched and "special." Switched access provided connections between an interexchange carrier's Point of Presence (POP) and the local carrier's switch. It was the standard method for originating and terminating long distance calls. Switched access was charged at a rate per minute, with both the structure and level of charges closely regulated by the FCC. Special access was local private line service designed to provide the connecting links between a customer's premises and the interexchange carrier for interstate private line circuits. Special access was charged at a rate per month per facility independent of the number of minutes carried by the facility. Carriers had considerably more freedom in choosing the structure of special access rates than in choosing the structure of switched access rates.

Although special access was designed for origination and termination of interstate private line circuits, it could also be used for the origination and termination of switched calls from customers with a high volume of traffic. Special access provided a direct connection between the customer and the POP, and the LEC would not know whether the special access circuit was connected to a private line system or to the interexchange carrier's switch. The fixed monthly fee for special access meant that customers with a large volume of traffic would find a special access connection cheaper than switched access connection. The availability of special access put an upper limit on the prices that could be charged to high-volume customers for switched access. The use of special access as a substitute for switched access was considered a form of bypass even though both services were provided by the local carrier because special access avoided the subsidy loadings included in the switched access charges.

So long as the LECs had a monopoly in the local exchange, the arbitrage between special and switched access provided an incentive to keep special access rates high. Similarly, potential arbitrage between various classes of special access rates limited LEC freedom in setting rates for very high capacity lines. For example, a low rate for high-speed digital service provided over optical fiber lines would have created an incentive for customers with multiple low-speed lines to switch to the high-speed service.

The greatest opportunity for competition in the local exchange came in high-speed lines. Either microwave systems or optical fiber lines could be built by individual users or competitors of the local exchange company to provide high-speed communication among a limited set of points. Competition in high-speed special access was analogous to the original competition in private microwave systems: it could only be used by a limited number of large users but still upset the monopoly-based rate structure. Limited competition for high-volume users also created pressures for interconnection with the LEC networks to bring the benefits to smaller users just as it did in the long distance microwave case.

The development of competition in the local exchange is still in an early stage. The competitive revenues are tiny in comparison to the LEC revenues. However, the competitors have already created changes in the LEC practices and gained interconnection rights with the LEC networks. Thus the MFJ-defined LATA boundaries are no longer the demarcation point between monopoly and competitive services. The local exchange itself is a mixture of competitive and monopoly services, with no stable dividing line. Policy makers once again have had to establish policies for communication firms with pockets of monopoly but no clear dividing line between competition and monopoly, just as before the divestiture.

Network Issues with Local Competition

As in most previous issues of competition, the network nature of telecommunication causes interconnection arrangements to be the crucial competitive issue in local competition. The two critical questions in determining the feasibility of local competition, as in other forms of competition, are the following:

1. Is interconnection required, or is it purely a business decision for the parties involved?
2. Is a specific compensation arrangement (interconnection fee) prescribed, or is the compensation fully open to negotiation among the parties?

Earlier competition controversies led to a general right to interconnection for each competitive service, but with two distinct models followed regarding the prices of interconnection. In the terminal equipment case, interconnection was required at a zero price. That is, any consumer with equipment conforming to specified publicly available standards could be connected to the network with no fee charged for the type of service provided by the interconnected equipment. The time in which customers were charged for a protective connecting device supplied by the Bell System was a time in which the price for that device could be considered a charge for interconnection. As developed in detail during that controversy, such a charge reduces competition in the devices that connect and, if set high enough, could eliminate competition altogether. The development of standards for interconnection together with the Computer II rules that deregulated terminal equipment allowed interconnection at a zero price. It would have been possible to charge a connection fee for each piece of terminal equipment attached to the network (though detection and enforcement would have been problematic) in order to generate subsidies for other aspects of the network. It was a policy choice to eliminate the revenue flows that had previously come from extension telephones and other high-priced terminal equipment, not an inevitable result of competition in terminal equipment.

The original MCI Execunet service was an attempt by MCI to apply the terminal equipment model to the interconnection of local and long distance service. MCI simply wanted to procure local service at the established tariff rate and to connect that service to MCI's facilities, as would have been clearly allowed for connecting a private communications system (such as a system of extension telephones connected through a PBX) to the local network. As a result of the complex and drawn-out access controversy, the decision was reached to impose a specific and substantial connection charge on long distance service and not to allow free interconnection as with terminal equipment. The access rules and tariffs are formally charges for the service of local origination and termination of long distance calls, but the subsidies built into the charges are effectively an interconnection fee charged to long distance networks that connect with local networks. That fee is charged on a per-minute basis. The December 1982 FCC access charge plan envisioned that the interconnection fee would be primarily a transitional measure to avoid rapid changes in rate levels as the Subscriber Line Charges were gradually increased. The proposed Universal Telephone Service Act of 1983 envisioned a high permanent interconnection fee that would provide large amounts of revenue to subsidize local exchange service. The political compromise resulted in a modest long-term interconnection charge paid by long distance networks to local networks.

In both the terminal equipment and the long distance cases, interconnection rules were determined for communication crossing a particular defined boundary (from public right of way to the customer premises for terminal equipment, interstate communication for federal access charges, intrastate interLATA communication for state access charges). The emerging local competition will still require interconnection, but at present there are no well-defined boundaries. Thus the problem of developing appropriate policies for interconnection is more complex than in the previous cases because the policies must apply to a wide variety of cases.

In the most general case, the competitive issues created by local network competition are analogous to the competitive issues of product standardization. Standardization and network interconnection both increase the value of the product to consumers. Both can play an important part in competitive strategy. Free interconnection is analogous to the case of a public industry-wide product standard, while interconnection fees are analogous to licensing fees paid to achieve compatibility with proprietary technology. There is a considerable formal economic literature on network and standardization issues.[2] However, the results depend upon specific features of the model construction that do not closely match the issues in communications, and it is therefore difficult to draw directly applicable conclusions from the general theoretical models.

Local Competition and Interconnection

Local exchange competition began with private line services, just as it did for long distance competition. Two distinct events at about the same time greatly increased the opportunities for local private line competition:

1. The divestiture and access charge plan increased incentives for using local competitors by allowing large-volume users to avoid high switched access charges through a direct private line connection between the customer premises and the interexchange carrier POP (bypass). Such private lines provided by companies other than the local exchange carriers were interconnected with the IXC to provide switched long distance service but were not interconnected with the LEC and paid none of the subsidy charges that were incorporated into switched access charges.

2. The cost reductions in optical fiber technology that made it the least expensive method of transmitting high-volume communication reduced the barriers to entry into local exchange service. The new technology reduced the advantages the established companies gained from their massive investment in older facilities because both incumbents and new entrants had to build new optical fiber facilities to provide high-speed accurate digital communications.

As the technological advantages of optical fiber became clear, a number of companies including Teleport Communications and Metropolitan Fiber Systems began constructing competitive optical fiber facilities in the densest areas of the largest cities. The facilities were used to provide local private line service between major businesses and the interexchange carrier POPs for connection to either switched or private line long distance systems. They were also used for local connections between sites with high-volume short-distance communications traffic, such as a computer center in a separate building from many users of the data. Because the downtown areas of major cities such as New York and Chicago contain customers with extremely dense communications requirements, the new competitors were able to compete for a substantial amount of business over networks that were very limited in extent.

The entrants were particularly effective competitors for very high speed digital communications (DS-3 level or 45 megabits per second) that could not be carried over the older telephone company copper wire plant. The telephone companies sometimes had to install newly constructed optical fiber cable to meet a customer's request for DS-3 service because they did not have ubiquitous facilities capable of that level of service. The telephone companies were hampered in their ability to respond to the competitors by the access plan's requirement that rates be averaged throughout a "study area" (the area of a state served by a single telephone company). That requirement meant that special access rates were the same in downtown Chicago as in small Illinois towns, and the local exchange carriers could not target price reductions to the dense areas served by the competitive companies.

The competitive optical fiber companies expanded rapidly from a combined total of 133 route miles in 1987 (7,770 fiber miles because of the large number of fibers included on a single route) to 782 route miles in 1989 to 2,071 route miles by the end of 1991. At that time 23 Competitive Access Providers (CAPs) reported a total of investment of $82.6 million and a total customer base of 5,891 locations. Although the total deployment and investment represented only a tiny fraction of the optical fiber of the combined local exchange companies at that time (150,000 route miles), the CAPs provided some competition in the center of many of the nation's largest cities.[3]

Even though the CAP networks were physically intrastate, the initial services they offered were classified as jurisdictionally interstate. They provided local connections from customer premises to the interexchange carrier POPs for connection to interstate networks. Thus they competed with the FCC-regulated jurisdictionally interstate special access services of the local exchange carriers. The interstate access services provided by the CAPs were exempt from state regulation, but the CAPs also provided services that were not a part of interstate service and thus were subject to state jurisdiction. Both the CAPs and the LECs provided local private line circuits that could be classified as jurisdictionally interstate or intrastate depending only on what service they were connected to. There was consequently no sharp dividing line between the services subject to the respective jurisdictions, and the companies were able to seek regulatory support in the jurisdiction that appeared most favorable to their interests.

As the CAP networks developed, they sought interconnection with the LECs in order to provide service to customers with requirements beyond the ability of the CAP to provide alone. In contrast with the policies regarding long distance competition, the entrants received greater initial assistance from state regulatory commissions than from the FCC. Although some state commissions maintained their longstanding skepticism regarding competition, regulators in New York and Illinois supported the CAP positions, opening the crucial New York City and Chicago markets to interconnected local competition and providing a model for later federal action. In a series of orders between 1989 and 1992, the New York Public Service Commission required New York Telephone to provide interconnection and physical colocation to Teleport and other CAPs.[4]

In the federal jurisdiction, Metropolitan Fiber Systems filed a Petition for Rulemaking in late 1989 asking the FCC to develop rules for the interconnection of CAPs with LECs. In 1991 the FCC issued a Notice of Proposed Rulemaking in which it proposed adopting interconnection requirements. In September 1992, the commission adopted a crucial order setting out specific requirements for the interconnection of private line circuits, and in August 1993 it adopted similar rules for the interconnection of switched circuits.[5]

The fundamental policy decision that interconnection of competitive local access providers with established telephone companies is desirable was fully predictable from the precedent set by many similar controversies. All through the various controversies over terminal equipment competition, long distance private line competition, and long distance switched competition, the FCC and the courts had continually proclaimed the rights of competitors to interconnect with incumbents. Although the FCC had attempted to reduce the incentives for bypass through the Subscriber Line Charge, it had never found that bypass was illegal or that the access market should be reserved as a monopoly to the LECs. Insofar as the CAPs were legitimate competitors, they were entitled to interconnection based on the general principle that all competitors were entitled to interconnection with incumbent carriers.

Although the general policy that interconnection was desirable was never in doubt, the details of the arrangements that determined how significant the interconnection privilege would be were controversial. The crucial issues were the following:

1. Whether physical colocation would be required.
2. Whether the telephone companies could charge a contribution fee for interconnection or only the actual cost of providing interconnection facilities.
3. Whether the LECs would gain freedom to make competitive price responses.

The LECs argued that the choice between physical colocation and virtual colocation (pricing and technical arrangements that provide similar capabilities to colocation without actually having competitive equipment on the central office premises) should properly vary with the details of particular situations and that they should have the choice of how to satisfy interconnection requests. The CAPs along with large users and enhanced service providers argued for a legal right to physical colocation except in cases where a LEC could demonstrate that the colocation was impossible. In a rare exception to the normally dominating powers of the chairman, the FCC adopted a physical colocation requirement over the objections of Chairman Alfred Sikes.[6]

The LECs maintained that they should be entitled to charge an interconnection fee that included both the actual cost of interconnection and a substantial contribution charge. Although the subsidy structure was built into switched access charges and therefore was not directly affected by the private line interconnection, the LECs argued that they should impose a contribution charge on private line interconnections to cover costs associated with geographic averaging, cross-subsidies built into the cost allocation rules that were used to determine the total revenue requirements for particular access categories, cost of plant needed to meet carrier of last resort obligations, and cost of stranded investment because of competition. The LECs proposed to compute a contribution charge for interconnection based on total special access revenues minus the LEC's incremental cost of providing the services. In other words, the CAPs could only compete if their total cost was below the LEC's computation of the LEC incremental cost even if that computation was far below the price charged for the service. A contribution charge computed that way would be so high that the interconnection privilege would be irrelevant.

The CAPs and most parties other than the LECs argued that no contribution charge should be allowed or that, if allowed, it should be only to recover specifically identified support flows. The CAPs particularly objected to the LECs' proposal of imposing an interconnection contribution charge designed to recover their overhead costs. The commission accepted the concept of a contribution charge for interconnection, but determined that it should only be for specified subsidy flows:

We believe that all market participants should contribute to regulatorily mandated support flows reflected in the LECs' rates for services subject to competition. We are not permitting the implementation of a contribution charge absent further Commission action, however. Instead, we are proposing to eliminate the only support flow that appears to warrant a contribution charge based on the current record. We will, however, permit the LECs to seek approval of a contribution charge based on other support flows.

At the outset, we reject the method for developing a contribution charge proposed by many of the LECs and Dr. Kahn, who advocate allowing the LECs to recover a contribution amount generally equivalent to their special access and interconnection revenues minus their incremental cost of providing these services. This approach would force interconnectors to bear a significant portion of LEC overheads and would tend to result in an unduly high contribution element, unreasonably discouraging the use of expanded interconnection.[7]

The method for computing interconnection fees was crucial to the significance of the interconnection rights. Had the FCC adopted the methodology proposed by the LECs, the interconnection fees would have been so high that the fees would have constituted an interconnection prohibition. On the other hand, had the FCC adopted cost-based interconnection fees for both switched and special access, the interconnection decision would have eliminated the established subsidy flows. The subsidy flows embedded in the access system remained feasible even with initial non-interconnected CAP competition because the CAPs could only provide bypass service to very large customers. If the CAPs were able to interconnect their networks with the switched LEC networks at minimal fees, then the CAPs could gather low-density traffic from many small customers over the LEC network and pass it to the interexchange carriers over the CAP network, eliminating the ability of the LECs to impose high access fees.

The CAP request for interconnection with the switched LEC network was analogous to MCI's original development of the Execunet service. Had MCI been allowed to connect its switches to the local exchange at the then-existing local business rates, it would have eventually eliminated the long distance to local service revenue flow. The creation of the legal category of "interstate access service" with a higher price than physically identical local service allowed the continuation of the subsidy flows at the beginning of long distance competition. A similar solution was developed with regard to CAP interconnection with LECs in order to maintain the subsidy flows. When a CAP interconnected with the switched services of a LEC, the LEC was allowed to impose a charge above the actual cost of inter-connection that was based on the charge that was imposed on interex-change carriers that connected directly with the LEC switched services.[8] The switched interconnection charge allowed the continua-tion of the subsidy flows established through the access charge plan even after competitive access providers gained interconnection rights.

With regard to rate flexibility, the LECs argued that special access competition and interconnection should be accompanied by freedom to make competitive pricing responses including individually nego-tiated rates, rates that differ by location, and increased freedom in choosing appropriate rate levels for high-capacity private lines. The CAPs and interexchange carriers argued that existing constraints on LEC pricing freedom should be maintained until competition is more established. The commission declined to give the LECs full pricing flexibility, but it did adopt the approach used in Illinois to allow competitive responses. Illinois regulators had previously al-lowed Illinois Bell to set three separate rates based on the density zones of downtown Chicago, the remaining Chicago area, and the remainder of the state. The FCC allowed the LECs to define three density zones within their areas of service and to set separate rates in each zone, relieving them of the obligation to use averaged rates across an entire state service area. The order required the density zones to be defined in a plan submitted to the commission so that they could not be easily changed to conform to changing service areas of the competitors.

Although many issues remain to be settled in the further consider-ation and implementation stages of providing interconnected local competition, the interconnection orders set out a general approach that is likely to remain stable. The critical elements of the approach are as follows:

1. A competitor's right to interconnection and central office colocation.
2. Connection charges based on the actual cost of providing connection service plus a contribution element limited to specifically defined and approved subsidies to other services.
3. Limited LEC flexibility in responding to competition by using sep-arate rates in separate density zones.

A strict application of the FCC's decision to maintain existing subsidies through interconnection charges would lead to the conclusion that local competition either will have no effect or will lead to specific price reductions without changing the overall pricing pattern. However, two factors suggest that local competition and interconnection may create substantial changes in the existing price patterns. First, the existing subsidies are not fully known and might not be approved by public policy if they were known. The 1993 situation with regard to local interconnection is analogous to the controversies in determining access charges for long distance competition. In the early days of long distance competition, various individuals in the industry and government held very different views of what the subsidy patterns actually were and whether they should be maintained. Similarly, it will take considerable time to establish the pattern of subsidies in the current price structure and to determine which subsidies should be preserved.

Second, local competition and interconnection will increase the opportunities for arbitrage between services that include subsidies and those that do not. There is no sharp distinction between special and switched access. Rapid advances in fiber optic technology have greatly reduced the cost of high-capacity communications. The existence of inexpensive high-capacity communication channels from multiple suppliers together with expensive switched services that include subsidy loadings will create incentives to bypass the switched access services that include the subsidy loadings. Just as it was possible for MCI to use its private line interconnection rights to develop a close substitute for switched long distance service, it is likely that the new competitors will find ways to use their rights to receive inexpensive services that do not include subsidies in order to develop good substitutes for expensive services that continue to include subsidy payments.

Conclusion

Local competition is still in the early stages, but it is growing rapidly and appears likely to continue its development. The greatest competitive area so far is the market segment for high-capacity local private lines in densely populated areas of major cities. The competitors have been successful in that market segment even without interconnection. By 1992, the CAPS were providing 40 percent of the DS-3 (45 megabit) circuits in New York and in the Bell Atlantic service area.[9] The combination of interconnection, growth in existing competitive optical fiber networks, and the development of additional local service technologies is likely to greatly expand local competition.

In 1993 effective local competition was limited to customers with a demand for high capacity between two points near the center of major cities. There was no effective alternative to the local telephone company for low-density communication among a large number of different locations. However, several factors suggest much greater local competition in the medium-term future. The extensive development of data communications outside of telephone company control (local area networks and wide area networks) has provided a foundation for greater telephone competition. The transformation of cellular telephone service from analog to digital will reduce the frequency congestion in cellular service and increase the opportunities for its use. The development of Personal Communications Services (radio-based communication similar to existing cellular service but with smaller cells and higher frequencies) is expected to provide a partial substitute for wire-based communication. Planned enhancements of cable television facilities will give them more capability to substitute for telephone lines.

With the development of local competition, the MFJ model of the industry (separate markets for competitive long distance service and natural monopoly local service) no longer resembles the actual industry structure. There is no serious possibility of applying the MFJ solution of structural separation between competitive and monopoly segments of the industry because that boundary is shifting with changes in technology and competitive decisions. However, the continued existence of a great deal of LEC market power together with the network nature of this industry that makes interconnection conditions so crucial means that total deregulation is not a likely solution either. Thus it is likely that there will be a continuation of the regulated competition that the MFJ attempted to eliminate.

Although the basic policies for interconnected local competition have been established, it is likely that there will be a long and controversial phase of refining those policies and clarifying their implementation. The details of the interconnection arrangements will make a substantial difference in the competitive conditions in the industry. As in the access debates, there is a conflict between the goal of maintaining status quo benefits for various groups after competition and the goal of using competition to force prices toward the cost of service.

Local competition does not eliminate the possibility of maintaining subsidies in the industry. The access charge plan for long distance carriers was based on extracting the subsidy payments from the remaining monopoly power in the local exchange. However, the network nature of the industry makes it possible to extract subsidy payments for some segments even without monopoly power in any single segment. When there is a high degree of competition, the monopoly power is in the interconnection terms and conditions rather than in any particular segment of the industry.[10] Thus it is not necessary that existing residence versus business pricing plans, or local versus long distance price structures, be revised as competition becomes more prevalent in local services. However, subsidy flows create arbitrage pressures, and the greater the subsidy flows attempted under competition (the greater the interconnection charges), the stronger will be the incentives to find ways around those subsidy flows.

14 / Price Caps and Regulatory Boundaries

In the past chapters, there has been little emphasis on the actual mechanics of regulation. The rate base rate of return method was developed early in regulatory history and applied quite generally to all regulated industries, whether federal or state. In essence, the goal was to limit companies to a fair rate of return determined by the general economy. That basic method was so well accepted by regulators and so frequently affirmed in the courts as consistent with the legal requirements of "just and reasonable" rates that little consideration was given to major changes in the overall approach to regulation.

Although simple in concept, the rate base rate of return method requires extensive controls over a company. The accounting system must be specified and the depreciation rates prescribed in order to make the profit figures reasonable. Otherwise, the monopolist can escape the control of regulation by accounting changes that hide the true profits. The entire process occurs in a formal way through public rulemaking and administrative determinations. Regulators do not have the freedom to merely set prices as they see fit, but must set up a defensible system of formal rules and procedures that lead to the appropriate prices.

The complexities and importance of the particular procedures used for regulation are a function of the uncertainty in the industry and the need for formal procedures to guard against arbitrary action. There are no generally known correct prices in an industry in the abstract. Thus there must be specified standards in order to check whether prices are reasonable and to evaluate changes in the prices.

The rate base rate of return method was developed for monopoly public utilities. The accounting rules and allowed rate of return determine a total revenue requirement, which is then recovered from the sum of revenues of the particular services provided. In the FCC context, the prices are set to bring together revenue and total cost on the basis of forecasts of expected quantities and costs in the future. There is normally considerable freedom in the actual structure of prices (business versus residential, and so forth) that will produce the necessary total revenue. The price structure is not determined by the rate of return process but by the preferences of the firm and the political considerations of the regulators, including simple continuation of the status quo structure of prices. At the FCC, the evaluation of individual tariffs for reasonableness and the evaluation of total rate of return conformance were two separate steps in the old unified AT&T rate structure. After the divestiture, the steps continued as separate for AT&T, but the rigid access charge structure attempted to bring the evaluation of individual access charge rates into the rate of return context. The access charge structure provided a detailed cost allocation methodology as well as a price structure so that access charges were reduced to evaluation of the projected cost and demand rather than evaluation of the proposed rate structure.

Deficiencies in the incentives created by the rate of return method have been well known and often discussed in the economics and regulatory literature. Two particular problems were the following:

1. The incentive to overbuild capital because that increases the allowed total profit (gold-plating or Averch-Johnson effect).
2. The incentive to increase accounting costs rather than to make efforts to maintain costs at the minimum possible.

Regulatory controls exist to limit both effects, but they are not fully effective. The Communications Act and other regulatory statutes include provisions requiring advance approval of major construction projects so that firms are limited in their ability to construct unnecessary facilities. It is possible to disallow costs that were unnecessarily expended. However, in general the regulatory ability to ensure that companies produce efficiently is extremely limited. The regulators do not know enough about the details of the business to evaluate individual decisions and lack the legal authority to second-guess compensation schedules and other major items.

Despite the well-known problems with rate of return regulation, it was considered generally satisfactory so long as it was applied to pure monopolies. The beginning of competition on the edges of telecommunication began to create severe strains in the regulatory approach. Rate of return was designed to equate *total* revenue to *total* cost, not to equate revenue for any particular service to the cost of that service. When private microwave was authorized and AT&T responded with the Telpak tariff, which provided drastic discounts to large-scale private line users, attention was focused on the relationship between the cost of an individual service and the rates for that service. AT&T's 85 percent discount on bundles of 240 lines (cutting the price of a 100-mile system of 240 lines from $75,600 per month to $11,700 per month) in response to the private microwave authorization (with no change in technology or other obvious cost factors) indicated that AT&T either was charging an outrageously high price prior to the authorization or was pricing below cost after the authorization.

The Telpak case together with later controversies over private line rate structure changes in response to initial competition led to interminable and inconclusive efforts to determine the actual costs of individual services. The goal was to adapt the rate of return system to the pricing of individual services rather than only to the sum of all services. Ideally, such a procedure would bring prices closer to cost and limit the ability of AT&T to engage in predatory pricing. Yet the various monopoly and competitive services were provided over a single physical network using many of the same personnel, and therefore there were no unambiguously defined individual service costs. Instead, there were a variety of possible reasonable answers to the service cost question depending upon which cost allocation system was used.

The efforts to develop service-based costs during the 1960s and 1970s were widely recognized as a failure both within and outside the FCC. The inability to determine individual service costs meant that FCC regulation of individual service prices was ineffective because the commission's primary authority for denying a particular price structure was an inappropriate relationship to cost. Carriers had a legal right to file tariffs of their own choosing, and they went into effect automatically unless the commission found them "unjust and unreasonable." Thus without service-specific costs to use as a guideline for whether a tariff was just and reasonable, the commission was generally ineffective in evaluating AT&T's competitive responses. AT&T's competitive response was generally to reduce prices in services offered by competitors and to increase prices in services for which it retained a monopoly while maintaining the same total revenue in conformance to its overall rate of return constraint. The FCC often criticized these responses but allowed them to go into effect because it lacked the information and legal authority to order an alternative rate structure.

The FCC's inability to adapt the rate of return system to an effective evaluation of individual service prices was a major factor in the Justice Department's determination to require structural separation between monopoly and competitive services. With structural separation, there would be no ability to shift revenue requirement from competitive to monopoly services. According to the DOJ theory, the competitive services would be unregulated while the monopoly service provided by a separate entity would be regulated but without competitors. Thus the structural separation solution would continue rate of return regulation where it was most suited (determining overall revenue requirements for firms only engaged in monopoly services) and would eliminate the efforts to adapt it to the much more difficult task of controlling the rate structure for the unified provision of services subject to both monopoly and competition.

Unfortunately, the DOJ structural solution was also unsatisfactory. As discussed in the last two chapters, the BOCs, which were supposed to remain regulated natural monopolists, expanded their offerings into more competitive services and also had their core local services attacked by new competitors. Furthermore, AT&T retained a large share of the interstate long distance market and faced varying degrees of competition in its many different service offerings. Even after the divestiture, AT&T's competitors accused it of underpricing services in which there was greater competition and overpricing services in which there was less competition. The fundamental issue was the same as in the pre-divestiture controversies: how can rate of return regulation be used to judge shifts of revenue requirement from more competitive to less competitive markets in the absence of individual service costs?

One approach to that problem was the ONA and cost allocation system developed for the BOCs as an alternative to structural separation. That system revived the efforts to develop cost allocation rules, but with a much narrower focus than the earlier approaches. The assumption was that a small part of the BOC equipment would be used jointly for regulated and unregulated services, and it would be possible to construct rules that protected the regulated ratepayer for that small amount of jointly used equipment. The focus of the Computer III cost allocation rules was on ensuring that the regulated services as a whole paid no more because of the BOC participation in unregulated services. Thus several characteristics simplified the problem:

1. The system was concerned only with dividing total cost into two sections—regulated and unregulated—and not on determining the greater detail required for individual service costs.
2. The unregulated services using joint equipment and personnel were expected to be a very small portion of the total regulated services. Because the BOC always had the option of supplying unregulated services with dedicated personnel and equipment and thus avoiding the cost allocation rules, it was considered appropriate to structure the cost allocation rules to give the benefit of uncertainty to the regulated services. Thus the rules were not fully symmetric but were designed to ensure that the regulated services did not pay too much.
3. The cost allocation rules were designed only to protect the regulated rate payer from paying too much, not to protect the unregulated services from being charged at too low a price. Thus the rules did not directly apply to the predatory pricing controversies of the earlier period. Those controversies were primarily concerned with whether the more competitive regulated services were priced too low. In the ONA context, that question was irrelevant because the more competitive services were unregulated ones for which no prices were being regulated. The commission considered any pricing issues in those unregulated services to be issues for ordinary antitrust consideration and not ones to be examined by regulation.

The AT&T tariff controversies in the post-divestiture period were more closely related to the failed efforts of the 1970s to develop service-based pricing than to the Computer III cost allocation rules. AT&T had not been deregulated after the divestiture. The FCC lacked both the desire to fully deregulate AT&T and the legal authority to do so, and Congress showed no interest in passing new legislation to deregulate AT&T. Consequently, AT&T's activities remained subject to the full regulatory structure that was established prior to the divestiture. Each AT&T effort to introduce new services or pricing plans in response to its competitors was met by objections from the competitors with arguments similar to those offered prior to the divestiture: AT&T was using its remaining market power in some market segments to raise prices there while reducing prices by an unreasonable amount in competitive segments in order to maintain a constant overall revenue requirement.

As a result of the controversies of the 1970s, the FCC had approved an Interim Cost Allocation Manual (ICAM) for AT&T that provided rules for allocating cost among three categories: private line, WATS, and MTS switched services. When the ICAM was being developed, the primary competitive issues were in private line. By the postdivestiture period, the controversies were much more narrowly focused, such as the ability of AT&T to offer targeted discounts to particular customer sets that were the focus of competitive activity. The ICAM categories were of little benefit in settling those disputes. Furthermore, the fully distributed cost methodology employed in the ICAM would have put severe limitations on AT&T's pricing freedom if it had been extended to more detailed service categories because it took no account of the marginal cost pricing policies that were almost universally accepted among economists. There was also consideration given to applying the Computer III cost allocation rules to AT&T's services in order to distinguish the costs of more competitive from those of less competitive services, but many potential problems with that approach caused it to be abandoned.

An alternative to further refinement of the cost allocation scheme was to develop a modified form of regulation that was less dependent upon observed accounting cost. Then the cost allocation rules would decline in importance. Legal constraints prevented moving totally away from observed cost because the basic legal standards for judging prices as reasonable and avoiding challenges that the allowed prices amounted to unconstitutional confiscation of property were based on cost tests. However, there was enough flexibility in the legal standards to develop alternatives that reduced reliance on observed costs. During the late 1980s the FCC and many state regulatory commissions developed alternatives to the traditional rate of return regulatory methods that were known as price caps, social contracts, or more generally as incentive regulation. Although the details differed among the plans, the unifying feature was direct limits on the output prices rather than indirect limits through a rate of return process.

Most of the rhetoric in favor of incentive regulation plans was concerned with the flaws of traditional regulation in a monopoly environment, particularly the problem of weak incentives for efficient production created by the "cost plus" nature of rate of return regulation. However, another important aspect of the incentive regulation plans was that they de-emphasized observed accounting costs and therefore were less sensitive to changes in cost allocation rules than the traditional rate of return regulation. Incentive regulation could therefore more easily be used to regulate the mixture of competitive and monopoly services that characterized post-divestiture common carriers than could the rate of return methods.

The First Plan: Bridge to Deregulation

During 1986 a number of economists (including the author) within the FCC's Office of Plans and Policy (OPP) were becoming increasingly concerned that the commission's methods of regulating AT&T were poorly matched to the actual competition existing in the long distance market. The equal access process was rapidly giving AT&T's competitors connections that were equal in quality to that received by AT&T; the competitors were expanding their range of services and their physical networks; and AT&T's market share was dropping. Yet the competitors remained largely free of regulation through the commission's "forbearance" policy (non-dominant carriers are subject to the commission's jurisdiction, but the commission will forbear from exerting that jurisdiction except to resolve complaints), while AT&T's regulation remained essentially the same as before the divestiture. Because political and legal constraints prevented serious consideration of full deregulation, the OPP economists began considering various ways to provide greater freedom to AT&T while remaining within the existing legal structure. The goal was to find a bridge between the then-existing full rate of return regulation and the total elimination of regulation. The assumption was that competitive pressures would continue to grow in the industry and that deregulation would be feasible eventually, but that a more flexible method of regulation was needed for the interim period.

The OPP economists reached a consensus that an appropriate bridge for AT&T would be to replace rate of return with a limitation on the rate of change of an index of AT&T's prices. Such a limit would eliminate the commission's traditional concern with the details of AT&T's business, including accounting methods and construction plans. If the limit were based on expected changes under rate of return regulation, then it would provide the same consumer protection as the existing methods did while providing incentives for AT&T to focus on efficiency more than on regulatory arrangements. Furthermore, if market pressures should require AT&T to price below the allowable limits, it would be a clear indication that regulation was no longer needed. The price limit regulations could be continued in form but become irrelevant in practice if market forces caused AT&T to price below the price limit.

At the time the idea was formulated, neither Chairman Mark Fowler nor CCB Chief Albert Halprin favored pursuing the concept. However, Commissioner Dennis Patrick was quite interested in it and encouraged the OPP efforts as well as giving a speech proposing a serious examination of the "price cap" form of regulation. In early 1987, the commission issued two OPP working papers examining the price cap concept. The economists John Haring and Evan Kwerel analyzed the state of competition in interstate long distance communication and found that the market was changing from monopolistic to competitive. They then proposed a price cap form of regulation for AT&T's "core" services in order to control remaining market power while competition continued to evolve.

The Haring-Kwerel paper proposed long-run deregulation with transitional protection against the exercise of market power through two mechanisms:

1. Continuation of the policy of geographic rate averaging to avoid exercise of market power in geographic areas with limited competition.
2. Limitations on the rate at which prices could be raised for a set of "core" services that faced limited competition.

Haring and Kwerel described their preferred price cap option as follows:

> The essence of this approach is to replace the current system of rate-of-return regulation with a price ceiling on a small set of core offerings. Core services would be defined so that for any service over which AT&T has significant market power, that service would either be within the core or there would be a close substitute for the service among the regulated core services. AT&T would be required to offer the core services at a uniform price throughout the country. These core services might include MTS and WATS or perhaps only MTS. . . .

The price cap on core services would initially be set at the current level. A formula would then be established for changes in the cap. For example, the cap might be indexed to reflect changes in the purchasing power of money as well as the rate of long-term productivity growth in the telecommunications industry. The cap should also be adjusted to allow for changes in access charges. AT&T would be free to set the price of services outside the core offerings any way it chose subject to continuation of the current nationwide averaging requirements. It would also be free to offer any new services without FCC approval.[1]

The companion paper by OPP attorney Kathleen Levitz (who had been the common carrier legal assistant for Commissioner Dennis Patrick) provided a legal analysis of the Haring-Kwerel price cap proposal and concluded that such a plan would meet the requirements of the Communications Act. Levitz analyzed the case law regarding standards for "just and reasonable" rates and concluded:

> Neither the Communications Act, its legislative history, nor legal precedent requires the continued use of rate-of-return regulation to control the earnings of AT&T or to assure its customers just and reasonable rates. Under current circumstances, the Haring-Kwerel proposal appears to offer a less onerous means of assuring just and reasonable rates for all service users.[2]

Levitz emphasized that the proposal was an alternative form of regulation that continued the requirements of the Communications Act in a new form, rather than deregulation:

> It is important to emphasize that the Haring-Kwerel proposal does not alter or suspend AT&T's obligation to file tariffs pursuant to Section 203 of the Communications Act, 47 U.S.C. Section 203(a). Nor does it eliminate AT&T's obligation to avoid unreasonable discriminations or preferences in its rate levels and structures. . . . Moreover, while it would suspend any obligation to file economic cost support for any proposed rate changes within the zone of reasonableness defined for core services, or for any filing for non-core services, the proposal does not foreclose interested parties from filing petitions to suspend or reject AT&T's tariff revisions, or from invoking the Commission's complaint process.[3]

The Revised Plan: Better Regulation

The Haring-Kwerel and Levitz papers were released near the time of the transfer of the FCC chairmanship from Mark Fowler to Dennis

Patrick, effective April 1987. Patrick drew heavily on OPP for the senior leadership of his administration, appointing OPP chief Peter Pitsch as his chief of staff and OPP staff members John Haring as OPP chief, Lex Felker as Mass Media Bureau chief, and the author (at that time having left OPP to serve as chief of the Accounting and Audits Division in the Common Carrier Bureau) as Common Carrier Bureau chief. In discussions among Patrick and his advisors prior to his formal assumption of the chairmanship, it was decided that deregulation of long distance communications was desirable but politically and legally infeasible. Consequently, Patrick instructed the author to develop a price cap proposal for AT&T as a top priority. In order to speed the process, Levitz was temporarily assigned from OPP to CCB to write the Notice of Proposed Rule Making outside of established CCB procedures.

The first critical decision was whether to formulate the price cap plan as an intermediate step between traditional regulation and deregulation or to formulate it as a better method of long-term regulation. The OPP discussions had focused on the problems of regulating AT&T while competition was maturing and had assumed that the long-run solution for that market was deregulation. In that context, the plan could be formulated without close attention to long-term effects because the long term would be determined by the market.

A price cap plan is more sensitive to long-term effects than a rate of return plan because it is not continually adjusted to observed costs. The errors in a price cap plan tend to be cumulative over time. The basic approach is to begin with existing prices and then determine an index of allowable price changes based on what is expected to be feasible. If the index of allowable changes is set with a small systematic error (say 1 percentage point either above or below the level that would have been set with perfect knowledge), the error in price is 1 percent in the first year, 5 percent in the fifth year, and 11 percent in the tenth year. Thus even a small error in the index can lead to large errors in price after many years of compounding. If observed profits are used to correct the error, that moves the system back toward rate of return regulation. If the plan was formulated as an intermediate step toward deregulation, then the long-term potential errors would be irrelevant. If it was designed for long-term regulation, then some error-correcting mechanism had to be built in.

The problem of formulation was closely related to the scope of the proposal. An intermediate-step formulation focused the scope on AT&T while the LEC access charges would continue under rate of return regulation. If price caps were considered better than rate of return regulation in general, then the new method should be applied to all services under FCC regulation. At the time, Britain had created a price cap system for British Telecom (with monopoly elements comparable to U.S. local carriers), and many states were evaluating various forms of "social contract" regulation as a move away from strict rate of return regulation for the portion of LEC costs subject to their jurisdiction. Thus there was precedent for developing a price cap system for monopoly services. However, the minimal competitive forces in LEC access charges, the wide variety of LECs, and the cost allocation and subsidies involved in determining jurisdiction and revenue flows made the development of a price cap plan for LECs far more difficult than for AT&T. It was consequently clear that a comprehensive plan for both AT&T and the LECs would require much more detailed specification as well as much more attention to objections than a deregulatory plan for AT&T alone.

The question of formulation was important for the public definition of the benefits to be gained from price caps. The plan was not a request of the industry or of political leaders outside the commission. It was an economists' solution to the particular problems observed with the existing regulatory process. If such a solution could be implemented with little public notice, it could be done with attention only to the technical problems of making it work. However, the price cap proposal was sure to attract attention and opposition and therefore needed an easily explained and understood rationale that could be used to generate public support. It was difficult to summarize the problems of regulatory boundaries in a simple way, but everyone could understand the goal of lower prices. The emphasis chosen was improved incentives for efficiency and lower prices. The inefficiency associated with "cost-plus regulation" was emphasized, and the price cap plan was portrayed as a "win-win proposal" in which both AT&T and the consumer could be better off through improved efficiency.

An initially unnoticed side effect of the efficiency emphasis was that it increased the difficulty of developing an initial price cap plan for AT&T alone. Insofar as AT&T already faced competition in many of its services, it already had incentives for efficiency even though it was subject to rate of return regulation. AT&T could not be confident of obtaining all of the revenue allowed under rate of return because of competitive limits on raising its prices. However, the LECs had much more monopoly power and therefore could be expected to have greater incentives for inefficiency than AT&T under rate of return regulation. Thus insofar as the plan was designed to improve efficiency incentives, there was more reason to apply it to the LECs than to AT&T.

If the plan had been formulated as a solution to boundary problems in a mixed competitive and monopoly market or as an intermediate step between regulation and deregulation, it would have been difficult to apply it later to the LECs. The goal at the beginning of the Patrick administration was to develop a fast-track plan for AT&T and then to consider applying the proposal to the LECs. In order to preserve the option of applying it to the LECs, it was important not to make any critical part of the proposal dependent upon competition to solve the long-term issues. The skeptical reaction to the bypass arguments of the access charge controversies had convinced many who were closely involved in the process that it would be impossible to make a public case that competition in the local exchange required changes in regulation. Thus an emphasis on competition would tend to either limit the application of the price cap system over a long period of time or require a later reformulation of the rationale.

As the price cap NPRM was prepared for FCC action in the summer of 1987, the LECs began a strong campaign to be included in the initial notice. They viewed the price cap proposal as a way of relaxing regulatory controls and therefore as beneficial to them. They also considered themselves in competition with AT&T (despite the MFJ boundaries that attempted to provide a strong separation between AT&T and the LECs) and therefore saw any additional freedom granted to AT&T without being granted to them as a competitive threat. At Commissioner Dawson's request, the LECs were added into the initial NPRM. Although the price cap NPRM that was approved unanimously by the commission in August 1987 followed the general outline of the OPP papers, it placed much greater emphasis on efficiency and administrative convenience as the rationale for price caps than on competition. While the Haring-Kwerel paper had devoted a great deal of attention to evaluating the increasing level of competition in the long distance market, the NPRM hardly mentioned competition or deregulation and provided the following rationale for price caps:

The price cap model promises many benefits to consumers. Because it would permit the carrier to retain at least some of the profits arising from increased efficiency or creativity, this method of regulating would encourage greater efficiency and innovation than exists now, especially in less competitive markets. This approach would substantially decrease incentives to shift costs from more to less competitive service offerings. The rules governing the periodic revision of the caps could reduce, if not eliminate, any perverse incentives to inflate rate bases. Carriers would no longer be able to exploit factors within their control to increase their earnings at ratepayers' expense. . . . This model could also prove to be simpler to administer than our current cost-of-service approach.[4]

The NPRM applied the proceeding to both AT&T and the LECs, but suggested that price caps would be implemented more quickly for AT&T because of administrative difficulties:

We tentatively conclude that a price cap approach to regulating rates promises many benefits to consumers which outweigh the disadvantages it may possess. . . . Implementation of this form of regulation for the LECs, however, raises administrative issues that appear to be more complex than those for AT&T. . . . There are now approximately 1400 LECs. . . . With such rich diversity in the capital structure and legal nature of the LECs as well as in the manner in which they determine the rates they charge for their interstate services and receive compensation for those services, a price cap approach to regulating their interstate basic service rates that accounted for or reflected that diversity would likely take longer to develop and would be more difficult to implement than would a price cap approach developed for only a single interexchange carrier.

Thus we tentatively conclude that we would implement a price cap approach to regulating the rates for AT&T's interstate and international basic services before we did so for the LECs.[5]

Two separate decisions during the summer of 1987 ensured that the price cap proposal would not be quickly adopted:

1. The decision to add the LECs and therefore to deal with all the complex problems that caused.
2. The decision to abolish the "fairness doctrine," a substantively unrelated issue dealt with at the same August 1987 meeting as the price cap NPRM. The fairness doctrine was a politically charged issue of broadcasting rules in which Congress had passed a law encompassing

past FCC rules in order to prevent them from being changed. President Reagan vetoed the law, and then the Patrick FCC abolished the rules. That controversy caused a rift between the Patrick FCC and the Democratic leadership of the congressional oversight committees, which resulted in skeptical challenges to the price cap reforms.

The decision to apply price caps to the LECs as well as to AT&T required a great deal of administrative effort in order to review all of the rules and procedures that would be affected by such a change, and the development of detailed alternatives. There was considerable skepticism among the CCB staff as to whether it was desirable or feasible to make a wholesale change in the form of regulation, but that staff was the only source with sufficient expertise to develop the necessary details for how a LEC price cap plan could be implemented within the existing regulatory structure. The routine organization for developing a major initiative was the CCB's Policy Division, but that division was occupied with Computer III and other matters and the division chief requested that the project not be assigned to his division. The administrative requirements were increased by numerous skeptical congressional inquiries that required detailed responses.

In order to carry out the project, a Price Caps Task Force was established outside of regular administrative channels, reporting directly to the bureau chief. Michael Wack, the senior legal assistant to the bureau chief, took charge of the task force and convinced several of the most skilled attorneys in the CCB to join the effort. John Kwoka, a professor of economics at George Washington University, agreed to assist the task force with economics issues as a supplement to the FCC's staff economists. Considerable efforts were made to "socialize" the project throughout the bureau to eliminate the perception that this was a radical OPP idea that would soon die, and to emphasize that Chairman Patrick was fully committed to finding a way to make it work.

The August 1987 proceeding generated comments from more than 80 parties as well as congressional and public interest and numerous presentations to FCC staff. AT&T emphasized the market forces constraining its actions and the need for regulatory freedom, while the LECs emphasized the need to obtain price caps at the same time as AT&T. The comments raised numerous detailed issues, especially with regard to the LECs, that made it impossible to develop a comprehensive simple plan. The most contentious issues were the productivity offset factor and the constraints to be placed on the pricing of individual services. The generic price cap system could range from extremely confining to effective deregulation depending on how those parameters were determined.

The productivity offset factor played the same role as the rate of return in a rate of return regulation system. Although judgment was required in setting an allowed rate of return, there was extensive precedent for how that process should occur and the kinds of relevant benchmarks that limited the range of reasonable values. Under price caps, the productivity offset factor was designed to reflect the potential rate of productivity improvement of the regulated company above that of the economy as a whole. While economists had studied productivity methods extensively, there were no legal precedents that determined acceptable methods.

There was good evidence that the productivity improvement rate had been between 2 and 3 percent per year for the Bell System as a whole over a long period prior to the divestiture. However, there was less evidence for the post-divestiture period and considerable uncertainty in interpreting the evidence available. For example, measured rates of productivity improvement in the post-divestiture period varied widely among the BOCs. If those measured rates were interpreted as representative of the potential productivity of individual companies, then it would be necessary to set individual productivity targets for each company. However, if those rates were interpreted as random variations around a common mean rate of productivity, then unreasonable rates would soon result from applying the measured post-divestiture productivity factors to individual companies.

The productivity problem for AT&T and the BOCs was complicated by the numerous accounting adjustments necessary to measure productivity in the post-divestiture period. As the access charge plan was implemented, there were numerous changes in the rates and costs of both AT&T and the LECs caused by regulatory activity. Those factors were large in relationship to the desired measurement of changes in cost that were not caused by regulatory activity. By the official FCC computation, AT&T's post-divestiture measured productivity was 2.48 percent per year, but reaching that number required numerous adjustments to account for ten separate regulatory events between 1984 and 1988 that reduced AT&T's costs by changes in access charges and in tax and pension rules. The total impact on AT&T's cost from changes in laws and regulations amounted to $8.4 billion over the four-year period compared to AT&T's average direct cost of $17.1 billion during that period. Because the adjustments were so large in relationship to the residual productivity effect, variations in the method of computing the adjustments could lead to significant differences in measured productivity. However, problems with measuring AT&T productivity were of less importance than problems with measuring LEC productivity because of the existence of competition.

The original proposal had not specified what limits, if any, would be placed on individual service prices. The various companies each provided a large number of different services. The least restrictive form of price caps would be to impose a single price index on all of the services provided by a particular company. Under that arrangement, decreases in the price of one service and increases in the price of another service would be averaged together to compare the average price change with the allowable average price change for the entire company. That approach would provide no regulatory protection to individual service prices and would allow a company with different degrees of competition in its various services to raise prices in the more monopolized services so long as it reduced prices in the more competitive services. The most restrictive approach would apply the price cap to each service individually. Under that approach, no service price could rise more than the allowable price index because no averaging would occur with other prices that were reduced.

The decision was to establish a set of "baskets" and "bands" as an intermediate form between the two possibilities. Political feasibility of the proposal demanded that consumers of individual services (such as discounted off-peak long distance calls used by many residential customers) receive similar protection as in the past. AT&T's services were divided into three baskets, with each basket separately subject to the price index computation. The first basket included the most politically sensitive ordinary switched long distance services (the "grandma basket"). The second basket included 800 service (In-WATS) in which AT&T retained some market power because of limitations on the ability of other carriers to use the necessary data bases. The third basket contained the services used primarily by the larger business customers and most subject to competition (the "bye-bye basket") and included the services that would have been outside the core in the original core/noncore distinction. It was assumed that competition would force prices below the allowable limit in the third basket, but that at least for a time the limit would be a binding constraint in the first two baskets. Within each basket, prices were averaged but with limitations on the amount by which any particular service price could be changed in a single year.

Political Issues in the AT&T Price Cap Plan

Soon after the first NPRM was issued, Commissioner Dawson left the commission to become Deputy Secretary of Transportation. Fowler's and Dawson's resignations left the commission with one Republican (Chairman Dennis Patrick) and two Democrats (Commissioners James Quello and Patricia Dennis). President Reagan's nominees of two Republican commissioners to replace Fowler and Dawson were not acted on by the Senate, leaving the commission with three members until President Bush's nominees were confirmed in August 1989. Thus at the completion of eight years of a Republican president, the commission had a majority of Democrats. Although Patrick continued to dominate the commission through careful exercise of the chairman's powers, it was more necessary to satisfy outside interests than it would have been with no vacancies in order to continue to operate. Because three commissioners were required for a quorum and there were only three commissioners, any one of them could exercise a veto simply by refusing to vote on an item. A vote against an item could be overruled by the other two voting in favor of it, but a refusal to participate left the commission without a quorum and therefore unable to conduct business.

Both the House and the Senate were controlled by the Democrats, and therefore the chairmen of the oversight committees were Democrats. The political structure of the commission increased the power of the oversight committees relative to their normal relationship with the commission. FCC initiatives are normally started by the chairman's office, and the price cap plan in particular was considered Patrick's personal project. In addition to the normal oversight committee powers of persuasion, the Democratic congressional leaders had the opportunity to block commission action simply by convincing a Democratic commissioner to withhold action on an item. The political issues were accentuated by the scheduled action during a presidential election year and by the Democratic leaders' displeasure with Patrick over the abolition of the Fairness Doctrine.

Congressional skepticism about the possible move to a price cap plan was expressed from the beginning of the Patrick administration, even before the first NPRM was approved. Both John Dingell, Chairman of the House Committee on Energy and Commerce, and Edward Markey, Chairman of the House Subcommittee on Telecommunications and Finance, requested information about the possibility of a price cap plan in the early summer of 1987. After the initial NPRM, Markey convened an oversight hearing on price caps and followed that with a December 1987 letter from both Dingell and Markey expressing opposition to the plan. After the pleading cycle closed for the initial NPRM (with 5,000 pages filed), Patrick submitted an additional extensive report to Dingell and Markey responding to their concerns and questions. They responded with a joint statement (February 2, 1988) emphasizing that the FCC should not take final action on the proposal without further opportunity for comment.

Several of the FCC attorneys also recommended a further NPRM because of concerns that the initial NPRM was too general to provide sufficient notice of the complex plan being developed. Patrick abandoned the original plan to proceed directly from the August 1987 NPRM to a final order and instructed the CCB to revise the order that was being drafted at that time into the form of a further NPRM. He notified Dingell and Markey that he would issue a further NPRM prior to final action.

After the May 1988 FNPRM, the House subcommittee held another oversight hearing on price caps in July, and the Senate oversight committee held a hearing in August. At both hearings, the Democrats expressed a variety of concerns about the proposal (focusing in particular on insufficient protection for the night and weekend discounts used by residential consumers) while the Republicans expressed varying degrees of support. As the price cap plan neared final action, the congressional opposition was made more explicit. In September 1988, Markey and Dingell sent a letter to Patrick that stated:

> As you are well aware from our previous correspondence and the record of three Telecommunications and Finance Subcommittee hearings, we continue to oppose any profit deregulation or price cap model that fails to address appropriately and concretely the numerous procedural and substantive concerns raised by Members of the Com-

mittee, segments of the telecommunications industry and the general public. To date, the Federal Communications Commission has failed to provide an adequate record to support the theoretical underpinnings or the specific plans proposed in the Commission's price cap model. . . .

At three Subcommittee hearings earlier this year, we were presented with testimony from a wide range of witnesses who articulated serious flaws in the plan. . . .

The fundamental nature of the charges raised against the Commission's price cap plan, and our own review, have convinced us that the price cap proposal in its present form remains deeply flawed. . . . We, and the clear majority of our colleagues on the Committee, believe that you have not made the case for this proposal and you must not take final action at this time. . . .

We would expect that the Commission's handling of the price cap docket will reflect the substantive and procedural concerns expressed in its public record, at this year's Congressional hearings and in this letter. If the Commission proceeds otherwise, we stand prepared to make price caps the first item of common carrier policy we address next year.[6]

On the same day, Senator Daniel Inouye, chairman of the Senate Communications Subcommittee, also sent a letter opposing immediate action on price caps, but with specific requests rather than generalized opposition:

After discussions with my fellow Senators on both sides of the aisle, with representatives of the telephone industry, and with consumer representatives, I have concluded that the FCC's "price cap" proposal has such severe problems that it would not serve the public interest for the Commission to move forward now to reach a final decision. The Commission should instead (1) rework its current proposal to address problems with its theory, evidence and specific provisions, (2) produce a computer model that will show the effects of the proposal and the alternatives on rates for specific services, and (3) permit full comment on both its reworked proposal and the computer model. A hasty decision on such an important and controversial proposal would only harm the chances for long term regulatory reform in this area . . .

A consensus on a proposal as controversial as this may be impossible to reach. Nevertheless, there is no reason that a serious effort could not be made to resolve some of the major differences between the parties in this proceeding before moving ahead on this plan.[7]

The Markey/Dingell challenge to price caps was continued in November of that year when Markey's staff completed a legal analysis of the price cap proposal that concluded that the FCC lacked the authority to implement it:

> The Federal Communications Commission (FCC) does not have the legal authority to abandon cost-based regulation and replace it with the price cap model proposed in the FCC's Further Notice of Proposed Rulemaking (FNPRM). Section 201 (b) of the Communications Act of 1934, which mandates "just and reasonable" rates, requires the FCC to ensure that carriers realize a reasonable return on their investments and that rates charged to the public be in line with their costs. While Congress did not explicitly define "just and reasonable" in the Communications Act, this report demonstrates that Congress clearly intended the Commission to ensure that charges for telecommunications services are based directly on their costs. This conclusion is supported by an unbroken line of FCC decisions which have consistently held that the "just and reasonable" standard requires cost-based regulation.[8]

The Markey committee's legal analysis presented a narrower interpretation of the FCC's authority to choose appropriate rate-making concepts than did the FCC's own legal analysis. Both sides agreed that the required "just and reasonable" rates must be related to cost, but differed on the interpretation of the relevant cases. The FCC asserted that profit regulation based on observed historical cost was one option among several for judging the reasonableness of the rates. The efficiency-enhancing properties of the price cap proposal were based on revealing a carrier's true underlying cost with best managerial efforts rather than regulating on the basis of accounting cost according to the regulatory rules. The Markey staff's legal analysis was not an issue on which negotiation and compromise were possible. Rather than challenging a particular feature of the price cap plan, it challenged the entire legal authority for any version of incentive regulation and asserted that only rate of return regulation was legally sufficient.

From an economic point of view, the dispute was over information-revealing mechanisms. The information economics literature assumes that individuals or firms provide information in a self-interested manner. In other words, they lie when it is in their interests to do so. That literature provides a variety of methods to induce individuals to provide accurate information by making their private incentives compatible with telling the truth. From that perspective, the system of price caps is one method of inducing firms to provide accurate information about the minimum costs of providing service. It is therefore based on cost, but on the unknown (to the regulator) minimum cost of providing service rather than on the reported accounting cost, which may not be an accurate indicator of the true minimum cost. However, if one believes that the reported accounting cost is a true measure of the minimum cost of providing service (as was implicit in the Dingell/Markey opposition to price caps), then the use of price caps allows a departure of price from cost that is prohibited by rate of return regulation. The FCC perspective was that incentives should be created for the firms to act in the way desired by regulators, while the Markey/Dingell perspective was that incentive problems could be dealt with through more intensive regulatory scrutiny of the firms, including more audits and disallowances of improper expenditures.

After another 5,000 pages of material were filed in response to the FNPRM in a pleading cycle that ended in September 1988, intensive work was begun on drafting a final order with the goal of commission approval in January 1989 for implementation April 1, 1989, at the same time as other revisions necessary for the final phase-in of the access charge plan. On January 13, 1989, Dingell and Markey sent another joint letter emphasizing their opposition to the plan:

> We are writing to reiterate our opposition to the Federal Communications Commission's profit deregulation proposal, known as price caps (CC Docket 87-313). The FCC's record in this proceeding has failed to address substantive concerns raised by Members of Congress and the public, and the Commission has not adequately responded to our correspondence of September 28, 1988.
> We must restate our position that speculative analysis and theoretical benefits are not acceptable when addressing an issue of this magnitude. . . . We expect a response to our concerns about the price cap proposal before the Commission acts.[9]

The Dingell/Markey letter was followed by a private meeting between Patrick and Markey along with separate meetings among various congressional and FCC staff members at which the intensity of opposition to the scheduled vote was emphasized. Patrick then decided that although the probability of blocking legislation was low, he could not be certain of the votes at the FCC to proceed without greater efforts to satisfy the opposition. Consequently, the vote was delayed for two months to allow more time for satisfying congressional concerns.

Six days after the January 13 Markey/Dingell letter, Patrick transmitted a detailed response to both the House and Senate leadership. After further negotiation, he reluctantly agreed to make public the major part of the draft order and to allow congressional hearings and comment on it. The procedural response of delaying the vote and making public the draft order led to considerable progress in reducing the congressional opposition. Further progress was made after a private meeting between David Leach, staff member to John Dingell, and Patrick. Leach emphasized that Dingell was not opposed to the entire concept and that it might be possible to satisfy Dingell with minor adjustments, a considerably more conciliatory position than had been taken by Markey and his staff representative, Jerry Salemme, who had expressed opposition to the entire project. Because Dingell was chairman of the full committee that included Markey's subcommittee, satisfying Dingell would be reasonable assurance that Markey could not block the action.

After further discussions between Leach and the author as well as several other FCC and congressional staff members, a series of cosmetic adjustments to the plan were developed that were accepted as adequate to stop the active opposition of Dingell. The adjustments primarily consisted of making explicit commitments that were implicit but not obvious in the structure of the plan. For example, the opportunity for AT&T to raise rates for services used primarily by residential customers while reducing the rates of services used primarily by business customers had been criticized by opponents of the plan. The structure of the baskets and bands allowed the rates for any one service to be raised by 5 percent relative to the price cap index in a particular year so long as the average price of services in the basket remained under the price cap index. However, it was impossible to raise all services used by residences by the maximum 5 percent and still meet the basket average requirements.

With the then-existing mix of AT&T demand, the proposed structure would limit the residential rate increase to 1 percent relative to the basket. In the FCC-congressional staff discussions, the FCC staff agreed to put that result into the rules rather than leaving it as an implication of the other features of the plan and AT&T's then-current mix of demand. Furthermore, the FCC staff agreed to portray the result as a guarantee that residential consumers would have prices *declining* at least 2 percent per year in real terms rather than stating that residential consumers could face no more than a 1 percent *increase* in prices relative to the price cap basket. Because the basket price index was required to decrease by 3 percent per year, the statements are economically equivalent. However, a guarantee of declining prices is politically more attractive than a limit on how fast prices can increase.

After general agreement had been reached with Dingell's staff regarding consumer issues, a final congressional challenge to the plan came from Republicans concerned about the absence of price floors for AT&T. One of the original goals of the plan had been to limit regulation to ceilings and provide freedom to reduce prices without regulatory approval. However, several of AT&T's competitors objected to the price reduction freedom, and their scenarios of predatory pricing found a sympathetic ear among several congressmen led by Republican Tom Tauke, normally a strong supporter of Patrick's initiatives at the FCC. Tauke and his colleagues asked Patrick to add limits on downward flexibility to guard against predatory pricing.

After receiving conflicting staff advice, Patrick ordered relatively weak pricing floors that required AT&T to show that its prices covered average variable cost for any service for which price was reduced more than 5 percent in a year relative to the basket index. The average variable cost test was one interpretation of the antitrust standard for guarding against predatory pricing. Insofar as it required no more than the antitrust laws, the floor was nonbinding, but by placing the burden on AT&T to justify large price decreases it provided opportunities for competitors to object to those decreases and possibly delay or eliminate them.

After the various congressional adjustments were made, the final AT&T plan was approved unanimously by the commission on March 16, 1989. In sharp contrast to his earlier opposition, Dingell issued a press release expressing qualified approval of the action:

> The Commission's decision today represents a substantial improvement over the "Price Cap" plan that was the subject of a Telecommunications Subcommittee hearing on February 28th. It is clear that FCC Chairman Patrick took the Subcommittee's concerns back to the Commission and has made substantive improvements in the consumer protections contained in the proposal. I am pleased the Commission responded to the concerns of Chairman Markey and others in this fashion.[10]

The changes required by the congressional leaders helped make the news coverage of the action generally positive. The requirement to quantify consumer savings and divide it into business and residential portions led to price reductions being highlighted in press coverage. The *Washington Post* story on the action was headlined "FCC approves long-distance rate reductions" and began by stating: "Residential long-distance rates will fall by at least 2 percent a year after inflation under a new regulatory system approved yesterday by the Federal Communications Commission, officials there said." The *Washington Times* began its story on the action with "The Federal Communications Commission yesterday rewrote the rules for regulating AT&T's long-distance rates, creating a system officials say will save customers $900 million in the next four years." The Associated Press story began: "The Federal Communications Commission today abolished regulations by which American Telephone & Telegraph Co. sets long-distance rates, replacing them with a formula designed to save consumers $900 million over four years."

The various political concerns made the AT&T plan far more complex and a less radical regulatory revision than the original goals had intended. The simple concept of a price index limit for services not subject to extensive competition was finally described with a 500-page order containing 1,875 footnotes. The attempted major reform caused a full reexamination of many issues that had already been dealt with informally. For example, the attempt to write in the level of pricing freedom for AT&T that had been existing administrative practice in CCB tariff rulings became highly controversial as various parties made their case for restrictive rules. The expansion of the scope of the item brought parties into the process that were excluded in the narrow context of individual tariff rulings. It was difficult to create an effective challenge to a bureau chief's tariff ruling either at the full commission level or in Congress because the issues required considerable knowledge of the particular situation. When the implicit policies were codified, it was easier to challenge them and to create "worst-case" scenarios of what could happen that would attract political attention. Thus some of the rules of the price cap regime were tighter than the then-existing practice.

Although the final system was a complex compromise between the original deregulatory goals and the regulation-oriented critics of the plan, it did free a substantial part of AT&T's regulated business from routine regulatory scrutiny. AT&T's cost allocation requirements were abolished and its degree of freedom in individual pricing cases was clearly defined rather than being dependent on administrative discretion at each point. The actual implementation of the price caps plan was straightforward, with little controversy over the construction of the various price indices and the allowable movements within the price cap plan. As expected, the initial prices of the residential/small business basket and the 800 services basket were at the maximum allowable (indicating that the price cap was an effective constraint), while the prices for the services primarily used by large businesses were below the limit, indicating that constraint was not effective. In 1991 the price cap requirements for services in Basket 3 were removed and those services were effectively deregulated.[11]

After the AT&T price cap implementation on July 1, 1989, further regulatory controversies largely focused on the structure of AT&T's prices rather than the level. AT&T sought frequent restructuring of its prices in order to meet special competitive situations and also sought freedom to offer individualized prices for bundles of services to large businesses. Neither area was covered by the price cap plan and both efforts were opposed by AT&T's competitors, causing the FCC to continue dealing with AT&T tariff disputes.

The LEC Price Cap Plan

Throughout the consideration of the price cap plan, there was conflict between AT&T and the LECs regarding the plan. AT&T was the largest customer of the LECs for their interstate access services and also a potential competitor. The LECs were particularly concerned about the increased bypass incentives that AT&T could gain under the price cap plan. The bypass argument depended on a view of AT&T as being primarily controlled by regulation rather than by competition. Under rate of return regulation, payments to the LECs for access services were part of AT&T's cost and were included in the computations for allowable rates. If AT&T found a less expensive alternative to LEC access services (bypass), its cost was reduced and then it must reduce its prices, leaving its profit the same as before the bypass. However, under price caps, AT&T's price limits were indexed to a measure that included the LEC access charges. If AT&T could find a cheaper alternative to LEC access charges, it could increase its profits because the cheaper alternative did not affect its allowed prices. In other words, the LECs opposed price caps for AT&T because they believed that the efficiency argument for price caps was correct and would cause AT&T to seek lower-cost alternatives to their interstate access services.

Neither AT&T nor the LECs proposed price caps, but once the FCC suggested it, each thought it would be appropriate for itself but not for the other. After the decision to include the LECs in the plan at the initial NPRM stage, Patrick insisted to both AT&T and the LECs that they must support price caps for the entire industry and not just for themselves. The LECs were anxious to remain on the same schedule as AT&T in order to guard against having AT&T receive price caps and then no further action being taken to include them. However, the technical problems of creating a price cap plan for the LECs were far more complex than for AT&T. Furthermore, the LECs were diverse, with many different interests, and therefore had to undertake extensive negotiations among themselves to reach a position on the many specific details rather than having a single company that could appoint a representative to negotiate with the FCC staff.

By late in the AT&T process it became clear that it was not feasible to adopt a final order for the LECs with the then-existing record. Patrick decided to issue a final order for AT&T at the same time as an additional NPRM for the LECs, allowing AT&T to implement price caps prior to the LECs. Although that decision was necessary in order to avoid delaying the AT&T implementation, it made the LEC leadership suspicious that they would never get price caps. In an effort to prevent the LECs from opposing implementation for AT&T, Patrick assured them of his strong personal support for implementing a LEC price cap plan. However, soon after the AT&T price cap order was adopted, Patrick announced his intention to resign, leaving inadequate time to adopt a LEC price cap plan under his chairmanship.

In late 1989, the commission's top leadership changed completely. Dennis Patrick and Patricia Dennis resigned, leaving only James Quello as a veteran member of the commission. President Bush appointed four new commissioners (three Republicans and one Democrat) with Alfred Sikes as chairman to bring the commission to its full complement of five. Three of the four new commissioners were familiar with and generally supportive of the commission's price cap initiative from their prior service: Sikes as head of the Commerce

Department's NTIA, Sherrie Marshall as head of the commission's Congressional Affairs office under Patrick, and Andrew Barrett as a member of the Illinois Commerce Commission. Sikes and the new commissioners chose new top staff officers, including the appointment of Richard Firestone (the general counsel at NTIA under Sikes) as CCB chief.

Despite the wholesale change in top leadership, including the departure from the commission of the primary proponents of price caps, the price cap initiative continued with relatively little change. The price cap task force under the leadership of senior attorney Mary Brown continued to analyze the comments and develop solutions to the many technical difficulties of creating a price cap plan for the LECs. The most difficult problems included developing an appropriate treatment for the common line portion of the LEC access charges and devising an appropriate correction formula for cumulative errors in the price cap formulas. The complexity of the LEC plan as well as the desire of the new leadership to fully examine the issues caused the commission to issue an additional NPRM for comment on modifications to the last Patrick plan in March 1990. The commission then adopted a final LEC plan in September 1990.

The common line portion of the access charges was not a service produced in any ordinary sense. It was a charge per minute to interexchange carriers for switched access that resulted from a series of cost allocations designed to maintain regulatory determined revenue flows from the interexchange carriers to the local exchange carriers. Thus computing expected "productivity" for that element required considerable care. The most straightforward computation of the price index for that element in a way consistent with other parts of the price cap plan would have been extremely generous to the LECs. Extensive disputes over the appropriate common line formula occurred, with a sharp division of opinion between the LECs and the interexchange carriers (the customers for the service). The issue was settled with a complex compromise known as the "balanced 50/50" formula that essentially found a median point between the LEC proposals and the IXC proposals.

The problem of cumulative errors arose from the expectation that LEC price caps would be a binding constraint for many years, in contrast to the expectation that competition would eventually force AT&T's price below the allowed cap. It was accentuated by widely varying estimates of post-divestiture observed productivity among different LECs. Furthermore, the computed average post-divestiture productivity was very sensitive to the starting date used. The 1984 data showed a drop in productivity that could be interpreted either as a real decline or as errors in the data because of the many accounting changes that accompanied the divestiture. The computed average productivity and trends varied significantly depending on whether 1984 was included or excluded. All of these reasons made the choice of a LEC productivity factor subject to considerable error. Under a pure price cap plan (no adjustment based on observed profits), an error in the productivity target would increase cumulatively over time, leading to either very high profits or confiscatory prices.

Under the final Patrick LEC plan, the LECs would have been subject to a correction factor known as an "automatic stabilizer." The automatic stabilizer consisted of a wide range of rates of return in which the price cap formula would be the binding constraint with provisions to adjust the formula if the observed rate of return reached either the upper or the lower band of the zone. Under the Sikes and Firestone leadership, the same idea was adopted but the zone within which rate of return could fluctuate without adjustments to the price cap formula was narrowed. The combination of rate of return zones and price caps produces a hybrid of the two approaches, with the width of the zone determining which approach determines the effective constraint. A very wide zone of allowable rates of return puts primary emphasis on the price cap (because it is unlikely that the rate of return will reach the boundaries), while a narrow zone puts primary emphasis on rate of return because once rate of return reaches the boundary of the zone, the rate of return is the binding constraint.

The LEC price cap plan set an expected 3.3 percent per year productivity factor (compared to the 3 percent factor chosen for the AT&T plan). With a 3.3 percent productivity target, LECs were allowed to retain all earnings up to one percentage point above the prescribed rate of return and half of all earnings for the next four percentage points above the rate of return. If the price caps caused actual earnings to fall below the prescribed rate of return by less than 1 percent, there was no adjustment, but if by more than 1 percent then there was an adjustment to avoid illegal confiscatory regulation. At that time the prescribed rate of return was 11.25 percent. Thus a LEC operating under price caps would ignore rate of return so long as actual earnings were between 10.25 and 12.25 percent and would gain half the benefit of earnings over 12.25 percent if actual earnings were between 12.25 and 16.25 percent. Earnings above 16.25 percent would be returned to the consumers. The company would be allowed to price above the price index limits if actual earnings using those limits were below 10.25 percent.

The LECs were also given the option of electing a productivity factor of 4.3 percent. Under that option, the LEC would be required to reduce prices an additional 1 percent each year compared to the standard plan, but would also gain the right to retain higher earnings. Thus in return for accepting a higher productivity target, the LEC could retain all earnings below 13.25 percent and half of the earnings between 13.25 and 17.25 percent.[12]

The final LEC price cap plan was essentially a loose form of rate of return. The relatively narrow earnings zones implied that accounting rules, cost allocation rules, and the prescribed rate of return would continue to be major factors in LEC planning. However, the capital-intensive nature of the local telephone business means that two percentage points of earnings on the entire rate base is a very significant factor in overall company profitability. Thus there is a strong incentive to attempt to generate enough productivity to raise the rate of return into the higher allowed range rather than to use the minimum return as an opportunity to price above the allowed cap.

The initial implementation of a conservative plan that was only a modest departure from rate of return fell short of the original goal of eliminating rate of return problems through price caps. However, a modest modification of the status quo is the expected action when information is very limited. The commission probably would have encountered both legal and political difficulties in justifying a long-term commitment to a particular productivity number without a rate of return backup given the inconclusive data available on potential productivity. A more substantial change from rate of return methods will be possible in the future if the initial experience with the hybrid plan is satisfactory.

Conclusion

Price cap development at the FCC began as a simple idea to provide a short-term bridge to deregulation for AT&T. It was originally developed as an alternative to rate of return for a carrier that could not be deregulated but was subject to considerable competition. The AT&T plan remained quite distinct from rate of return but evolved into a complex set of regulations because of the political necessity to meet a wide variety of objections with protections for particular groups. The LEC plan was more complex than the AT&T plan, which caused its development to extend over two administrations at the FCC. The final plan was a hybrid of rate of return concepts and price cap concepts because the limited information on potential future productivity made it impossible to develop a fully defensible pure price cap plan.

A pure price cap plan eliminates the dependence of regulated prices on observed accounting cost. A hybrid plan such as the one adopted for the LECs reduces that dependence but does not eliminate it. Thus the implementation of price cap plans provides a possibility for reducing or eliminating the importance of controversies over cost allocation for companies that produce a mixture of monopoly and competitive services. As discussed in Chapters 11 and 12, the LECs have been allowed to expand out of local exchange services into competitive services while other firms have provided limited competition within the local exchange. Thus the future importance of price caps is likely to be in facilitating the continuing regulation of mixtures of competition and monopoly for which rate of return is ill suited. The system of price caps is the latest entry in the continuing search to find a satisfactory method of managing the combination of competitive and monopoly elements in the telecommunication industry.

15 / Conclusion

This book has viewed public policy in telecommunication as the result of a large number of decisions made by different individuals. Each policy maker has specific limited ability to change the existing state of public policy. A choice to change certain rules automatically implies a choice by that policy maker to allow other rules to remain in place. The decisions are made at different points in time and in different agencies, with no necessary coordination among them. Decisions are generally incorporated into rules or court decisions that remain in effect until explicitly repealed. The state of policy at any one time has the characteristics of a public capital good that was created through the investments of individual decisions in the past.

Policy makers have "ethical preferences" for the state of society, as well as ordinary personal preferences for the state of society as it affects them individually. The ethical preferences are not necessarily uniform, but there is considerable agreement on the goals of policy because of wide acceptance of particular principles. If the policy makers correctly perceive the state of the world and the relationship of the potential policy instruments to outcomes given that state of the world, then the decentralized process results in a weighted average of the ethical preferences of the participants.

The results of particular rules are dependent upon the state of the world, but there is no automatic mechanism to adjust the rules to changing states of the world. Rules designed to produce a particular outcome in the current state of the world remain in effect when the state of the world changes and therefore produce a different outcome than was originally expected. The state of the world is imperfectly perceived by policy makers through noisy signals that indicate the state of the world. Different policy makers may draw different conclusions regarding the state of the world from observing the same noisy signals, and consequently they may adopt different policies even if they are seeking the same goals.

The decentralized policy process takes place in a fog of great uncertainty over the state of the world and the effect of any particular policy instrument on desired outcomes. Policy evolves over time in response to changes in ethical preferences (general goals) among the active policy makers, in response to changing perceptions of the state of the world, and in response to learning about the effects of past policy actions. The resultant policy at any one point in time is a weighted average of both the goals and the perceptions of the policy makers. It is a conservative process weighted toward the average perspective of the individuals involved in the process over a long period of time.

The Evolution of Telecommunication Policy

In the 1950s, the telephone industry was managed as a single entity through the dominance of AT&T. Even though there were many independent telephone companies serving primarily rural areas, they were dependent upon AT&T for interconnection with other companies and for revenue-sharing arrangements. AT&T established the standards for the telephone industry and managed the network as an internal matter with little concern for market forces in individual parts of the industry.

Public policy toward the industry was based on controlling local rates through political persuasion and rate of return regulation. The Communications Act of 1934 and similar language in many state regulatory statutes provided the legal basis for regulating the industry. Regulators limited the total revenue that could be received by the telephone companies and influenced the specific rate structures. Because a wide variety of rate structures were sustainable in the regulated monopoly environment, rate structures were determined through a combination of managerial discretion and political influence, with little concern for the costs of providing particular services. State and federal regulators disagreed over the relative shares of the total cost burden that should be borne for their respective jurisdictions, but neither state nor federal leaders questioned the basic monopoly nature of the industry and the desirability of managing the network through internal rather than market forces.

Network services were provided over both wire and radio (microwave) facilities. Microwave frequencies were also licensed for a limited class of private communication, such as communication along pipelines and railroads. Private facilities were considered completely separate from the public network and were not interconnected. The network externality had long been recognized as an important characteristic of the telephone network and had led to interconnection of the independent telephone companies with AT&T through the Kingsbury Commitment of 1913. However, interconnection requirements applied only to common carrier systems, not to interconnection between the public network and either private equipment or private communication systems. That isolation of private systems from the public system was imposed by AT&T but generally accepted by policy makers as a necessary element of preserving the quality of the public network.

The network externality played a crucial role in all of the competitive controversies. Because individual pieces of equipment or communication systems were of limited value in isolation, interconnection requirements (including technical conditions, locations of interconnection, and charges for interconnection) received extensive attention. Interconection terms and conditions affected both AT&T's ability to manage the network and its ability to maintain historical pricing patterns. So long as AT&T maintained control of interconnection terms and conditions, it could exclude competition.

The consensus of the 1950s contained a conflict between the accepted monopoly control of the public network and the accepted goal of allowing consumers full freedom to satisfy their own needs. The initial resolution of those two potentially conflicting goals was to allow consumers to provide their own services so long as they did not require interconnection with the public network. The first two crucial steps toward a competitive market arose in the context of the fuzzy boundary between those two goals. The Hush-A-Phone controversy involved interconnection according to AT&T's definition, but not in a way that had any possibility of harm to the network. The passive device performed essentially the same function as using a hand around the receiver to shield out noise. Although the FCC was willing to call that interconnection and allow AT&T to prohibit the device, the appeals court was not. The appeals court ruled that because no harm to the network could be caused by the device, the AT&T prohibition was an unreasonable interference in the customer's right to make use of the telephone. Although the decision had little immediate effect, it provided a legal structure for challenging AT&T's restrictive policies in later years.

The "Above 890" decision authorizing private microwave systems was also made in the context of protecting customers' rights to privately beneficial systems. The focus of the proceeding was on the factual question of the availability of adequate frequencies for both common carrier and private systems. Customers such as pipelines or railroads that had their own right of way did not need regulatory permission to construct private wire-based systems for their own use. Customers without right of way could only construct private systems with radio-based technologies, which required a license. It was accepted policy that top priority for spectrum should go to common carriers for use in the public network, but that considerable freedom should be granted to individuals to use spectrum in privately beneficial ways when there was adequate availability. The factual determination that there was adequate spectrum available for both common carrier and private use therefore led to the conclusion that private microwave systems should be authorized. The decision did not authorize commercial systems (capacity for sale to others) and therefore was not considered a policy of initiating competition. However, by providing the opportunity for individual companies to supply their own internal communications needs, the decision created a competitive check on a portion of AT&T's price structure. AT&T's Telpak pricing response (drastically cutting the rates for high-volume private line service) provided clear information that private line rates for some services were far above cost, and therefore increased the incentives for attempted entry in competition with AT&T.

The Carterfone and MCI decisions a decade later were based in part on the precedents established in the Hush-A-Phone and Above 890 decisions. However, the Carterfone and MCI decisions explicitly created limited classes of competition with AT&T rather than attempting only to protect customers' private rights. Both decisions were related to changing technology, particularly the growing intersection between computer and communications technology. The changing state of the world caused FCC leaders (especially Common Carrier Bureau chief

Strassburg) to rethink their previous acceptance of strict boundaries between the public network and private systems. With time-sharing computer systems that utilized telephone connections, there was no longer a clear and obvious boundary between the computer and communications industries.

A rigid interpretation of the non-interconnection doctrine would have required either that AT&T own the computers or that a separate computer communications network be established. Because neither of those alternatives was attractive, the FCC relaxed the interconnection restrictions by reviving and reinterpreting the Hush-A-Phone principles. The FCC's decision that the strict non-interconnection tariff was illegal, together with continued fears about the technical viability of a free interconnection policy, led to interconnection of customer-supplied terminal equipment through protective connecting arrangements. Under that approach, AT&T allowed interconnection while maintaining control of network signalling and imposing a protective barrier between the public network and customer equipment. Although that was an unstable solution, it met the need at the time for a method to attach some equipment to the network without risking degradation as a result of the then-unknown issues of managing a network without unified control of signalling along that network.

The initial MCI decision was also related to the desire to provide consumers with specialized services that were not available over AT&T's public network. MCI's initial application proposed specialized services different from those offered by AT&T, not simply competition for available classes of service. The application was approved as an experiment in limited competition to provide new services and stimulate AT&T to be more responsive to the specialized needs of its competitors. The application also suggested an opportunity to bring some of the benefits of private networks to smaller users by sharing a microwave system. The initial decision left many questions unanswered, and treated the application as proposing too small a system to have any effect on the basic policies toward the regulated monopoly.

During much of the 1970s, policy makers struggled with the unstable situation created by the initiation of both terminal and long distance competition. Although both forms of competition were started to provide specialized new services, the competitors quickly expanded into direct competition with services provided by the established monopoly. All forms of terminal equipment gradually became subject to competition. The specialized services of MCI were expanded into full competition with AT&T's private line services and then into partially switched (foreign exchange) services. Each step was challenged by AT&T and generally opposed by the state regulators, but federal support for the competitors together with their own efforts at fitting additional services into particular legal definitions gradually increased the scope of competition.

The most significant expansion of competition came about through a combination of MCI's innovative approach to packaging its previously available components and court protection of its procedural rights. MCI's Execunet service was created by combining previously authorized service components into a package that was competitive with AT&T's switched long distance service, contrary to the boundary that the FCC had established between competitive private line service and monopoly switched service. Although the FCC ruled that the service was illegal because it was beyond the scope of MCI's authorized services, the appeals court disagreed and overturned the FCC decision. While the FCC had sought to protect the then-existing revenue-sharing mechanisms by prohibiting competition in the services that provided the revenue, the court decision authorizing competition in switched services forced an examination of what subsidies should be retained and how to best provide them in a competitive environment.

The confused situation in the late 1970s provided an incentive for several different parties to attempt to develop a comprehensive policy for managing the mixture of competition and monopoly in telecommunication. The FCC created structural boundaries between terminal equipment and network services through the Computer II decision of 1980 and began working on an access charge plan to adjust the revenue-sharing arrangements to the advent of competition in long distance service. Various congressional leaders sponsored bills to rewrite the Communications Act of 1934 and provide a new framework for telecommunication policy, but Congress failed to pass any of them. The Department of Justice increased its efforts to prepare the AT&T antitrust case for trial and seek a structural boundary between the competitive and monopoly portions of the industry.

The DOJ approached the industry from an antitrust perspective that looked for barriers to competition, rather than from the regulatory perspective that accepted the possibility that protecting revenue flows in a monopoly setting could be more important than developing competition. The DOJ divestiture goal was developed in response to frustration with the observed slow regulatory process. The Justice Department was not satisfied with either the state or the federal regulatory process and viewed as anticompetitive many of the actions that the state regulators supported and the FCC ineffectually discouraged. The DOJ had both a different understanding of the industry and different goals than either the FCC or state regulators.

The concept of the divestiture was similar to the concept behind the deregulation of terminal equipment: shrink the scope of regulation to natural monopoly services and require interconnection of the monopoly services with all competitors on an equal basis. However, the large revenue flows from long distance to local would have been greatly reduced or eliminated if competitive long distance companies had simply been allowed to connect with local companies and pay established tariff rates for services received. Through a long series of controversial and complex actions, a system of access charges was developed to continue paying a substantial portion of local service expense out of long distance toll revenue, with a particularly high fraction of rural companies' expenses defrayed from toll revenue.

The structural boundaries created by the divestiture and access charge system eroded over the years following the divestiture. Although the divestiture theory implied that the remaining (competitive) AT&T should be deregulated, AT&T continued under regulation and therefore continued the regulated competition that the divestiture was designed to stop. Advancing technology blurred the lines created at the time of divestiture as intelligence was spread throughout the network. The BOCs sought permission to enter competitive communications businesses integrated with their local exchange service and gained that freedom after a long dispute. Technological advances in fiber optical communication allowed new competitors to provide limited local services in major city centers.

By the early 1990s, competition was widespread in the industry and developing technologies appeared to provide potential competition in existing monopolized areas. Yet the competitive policy problems were still not solved. The network nature of the industry made interconnection rights and prices a crucial determinant of competitive opportunities. Leaving interconnection conditions to private negotiation would allow the incumbent firms to exclude entrants. Consequently, government officials continued to search for appropriate policies toward firms participating in a combination of monopolized and competitive markets.

Fact Perceptions Incorporated into Policy

Crucial telecommunication policy decisions have been made by various parties on the basis of their differing perceptions of the relevant facts, or the "state of the world." Even when goals are identical, different perceptions of the facts lead to different policy actions. As a result of the decentralized process, inconsistent sets of factual premises have been incorporated into telecommunication policy as each power center acted on its own beliefs about the state of the world. Fact questions that have been particularly important to the development of telecommunication policy have included the following:

1. Whether it is feasible to rely on a decentralized network composed of many different pieces supplied by different parties, or whether unified control is necessary.
2. The extent of subsidies paid to local service by optional terminal equipment and long distance service under the separations and settlements process prior to divestiture
3. The degree of economies of scope among various services provided by the industry.
4. The efficiency of a rate of return regulated monopoly.

The question of whether it was necessary to have managerial control and responsibility for managing the public network, including long-term planning, setting standards, technological upgrades, network signalling, and fault isolation, or whether the network would work adequately as interconnected networks of separately managed systems, was a factual question on which regulators initially had very little information. The parties with the most information on the subject (including AT&T, the independent telephone companies, and the government-operated telephone companies in most other countries) all agreed that hierarchical planning and control of the telephone network were necessary to efficient operation. Although most regulators initially accepted the assertions of the telephone companies that complete managerial control was necessary, early experience with terminal equipment interconnection provided evidence that network quality did not necessarily decline with interconnection and led many to discount the AT&T arguments as self-serving attempts to prevent competition. Policies based on the assumption that unified control of the network was necessary were gradually replaced with policies that assumed the network would function reliably without central control.

The second issue is concerned with the fact question of what subsidies existed in the pre-divestiture environment, not with the value question of whether the subsidies were desirable. Different views on the extent of subsidies paid by terminal and long distance competitors have generated variant policy prescriptions. State and federal regulators along with AT&T and the independent telephone companies considered the subsidy flow as clearly established and a central part of the interpretation of initial competitive activity. Protecting the subsidy flow was the reason for state regulatory opposition to early terminal equipment competition. It was also behind the federal reluctance to authorize competition in switched long distance service during the late 1970s despite a general policy in favor of increasing competition. The sharp distinction made between protecting the rights of competitors to offer all versions of private line service (including interconnection rights for foreign exchange service) and the prohibition on offering switched service was based on the perceived difference in subsidies among the services. The FCC along with AT&T and the state regulators considered it well established that the separations and settlements system transferred a large proportion of total toll revenue back to the local exchange companies, especially the rural companies, while the private line services were much less subject to the subsidy tax. Individual regulators were not necessarily confident about the particular amounts of toll transfer, or how those amounts translated into effective costs per minute, but they were convinced that subsidy flow was a major issue that would not be easily maintained in a competitive market.

The *Execunet* appeals court did not take a formal position on the existence of subsidies. The decision to overrule the FCC's prohibition on long distance competition was structured as a protection of MCI's procedural rights. Formally, the FCC retained the option either to limit further competition by not authorizing additional facilities, or to devise a system to maintain the existing subsidy flows. However, it appears likely that the court implicitly questioned the significance of the subsidy argument as a reason for prohibiting competition. Insofar as the subsidies were the real issue, the court believed that there were less radical means of dealing with the problem than through a ban on competition.

The DOJ and MCI believed that the subsidies did not really exist. They treated AT&T's efforts to recover part of the subsidies through the ENFIA tariff as anticompetitive, and consequently saw no justification for the FCC's reluctance to authorize switched long distance competition. The factual question of what subsidies existed affected both the evaluation of AT&T's actions and the development of a remedial policy. Given the DOJ/MCI assumption that no subsidies existed, then the ENFIA tariff represented an anticompetitive attempt by AT&T to use its market power in local exchange to reduce competition in long distance services by charging unreasonable fees for interconnection. MCI's ability to grow and make a profit in that environment was evidence of its much greater efficiency than AT&T. The policy solution was therefore a "level playing field" in which the separated local exchange companies treated all companies alike. Given the factual assertion of no subsidies, there was no reason to expect that solution to cause local price increases. The general argument of the DOJ was that the advent of competition would produce such great gains in efficiency that long distance prices would decline without any changes in the local price structure.

As the FCC developed the access charge plan during 1982 and 1983, it became clear that massive subsidies had been flowing from long distance to local service. The FCC/state regulator/AT&T view on that question was generally correct and the DOJ/MCI view wrong. Just as with terminal equipment, experience showed a previously held factual basis for a policy to be in error. However, it was much more difficult to adjust policy for the new information in the case of access charges than in the case of terminal equipment. As it became clear that the "harm to the network" argument was erroneous, terminal equipment interconnection was gradually liberalized and eventually the equipment was deregulated. However, in the case of subsidies, the antitrust policy based on the assumption that no subsidies existed was incorporated into the case and then the divestiture agreement.

Although the subsidy flows were a matter of accounting for various transfers and thus consisted of seemingly objective and available information, the complexity of the process and the extent to which it consisted of internal transfers among subsidiaries of AT&T allowed individual policy makers to hold substantially different views on the significance of the subsidies. The many interrelationships among the Bell companies made it possible to assume that there were offsetting revenue flows to those defined by the separations and settlements process. William Baxter took the position that the separations payments were offset by the license fees paid from the Bell companies to AT&T and by the excessive prices paid by Bell for Western Electric equipment.

The subsidy controversy was an example of the effect of bounded rationality on the policy process. Detailed information on the question was available to both regulators and the DOJ. Although limited information was available publicly, the regulators had audit authority to review internal records and the antitrust authorities had discovery authority, giving both full access to records of the payments and settlements. Yet the complexity of the information made it infeasible for all participants to fully read and understand it. Only after the extensive access proceedings focused attention on the extent of the payments was it generally accepted that the ENFIA payments provided MCI a substantial discount relative to the implicit AT&T payments. Once the extent of the prior payments became widely known, extensive attention was focused on the question of how to manage subsidy payments in the post-divestiture environment. Congress, the FCC, and the state regulators provided different answers to that question based on their respective goals, but largely working from the same baseline numbers. In the earlier period there was no consensus on what the relevant numbers were, and therefore the DOJ and the FCC proposed separate answers based on different views of the state of the world.

The third critical factual question was the degree of economies of scope among various services provided by the industry. This question had some relationship to the question of the need for hierarchical management, but it was not the same issue. That question focused on the problems that would occur if individual companies attached products to the network, while the economies-of-scope question was concerned with the relative benefits of producing individual services in separate companies versus producing them in the same company.

The economies-of-scope question was first raised in a limited form during the Computer II consideration and then in a more general way during the AT&T trial. The Computer II decision required separate subsidiaries for the provision of terminal equipment and enhanced services. The strong separation provisions were based on the premise that there were no economies of scope among the services in the separate subsidiary and the basic telephone services. The DOJ trial carried the question much further. The DOJ case for divestiture was based on the assumption that the industry could be divided into separate sectors without loss of efficiency. AT&T's defense asserted that the industry could not be so divided. The opposition to the DOJ divestiture plan by the Department of Defense and the Department of Commerce assumed that there were substantial economies of scope in a unified network. Economies of scope could occur in a technical sense (greater efficiency in the production of multiple services in a unified way), in a consumer sense (simpler procurement from a single source, as well as simpler fault detection), and in a technological progress sense (greater ability to develop new products and to provide an innovative network).

As the FCC gained experience with the consumer confusion and limitations on new products created by its Computer II rules, it concluded that economies of scope were greater than it had originally believed. That determination caused the FCC to revise its own rules (creating the Computer III nonstructural framework to replace the Computer II structural separation rules) and to actively work against the restrictions on the Bell Operating Companies created by the MFJ. The DOJ staff members who had originally supported the divestiture did not change their position, but the DOJ officially changed its position through a change of personnel. When Edwin Meese (who had opposed the DOJ divestiture proposal prior to AT&T's acceptance of the agreement) was appointed Attorney General, he facilitated the DOJ's official adoption of a new policy that implied an acceptance of the existence of economies of scope. The Meese DOJ advocated the relaxation of the MFJ restrictions so that the BOCs could expand into previously prohibited lines of business. Judge Greene never accepted the existence of economies of scope, but he was forced to eliminate the information services restrictions after the appeals court ruled that he must give great weight to the DOJ recommendation.

The extent of economies of scope is still not fully resolved. Clearly, AT&T's assertion that economies of scope were so great that the network could not function in a divested mode were wrong. After some initial confusion and great efforts on the part of AT&T to develop a workable divestiture plan, the resulting eight companies have all been financially successful and the network has continued to provide good service with improving productivity. However, the question of what new services could have been developed with a more unified network cannot be fully answered. The general consensus in favor of structural separation at the beginning of the 1980s has shifted toward much more concern about possible losses from restrictions. However, that concern may be due in part to the public relations efforts of the BOCs rather than to truly new information. There was little information on the degree of economies of scope at the time the divestiture agreement was reached, and there remains little information on the question at present.

Differing perceptions of the degree of economies of scope remain an important source of inconsistent policy actions. Differing views on economies of scope will almost certainly continue to play a major role in considering such telecommunication policy issues as the remaining BOC MFJ restrictions, the participation of the telephone companies in cable television and participation of cable companies in telephone service, and the eligibility for licenses for mobile telephone services. It appears unlikely that the factual question of the degree of economies of scope will be answered in a definitive way that commands full acceptance. Thus policies will continue to be made by various groups on the basis of contradictory assessments of the degree of economies of scope in the industry.

The fourth factual question for which varying answers have been incorporated into telecommunication policy was the efficiency of a rate of return regulated monopoly. Rate of return regulation can control the reported profit rate of the firm, but cannot control all of its actions. Insofar as a regulated firm is just as efficient as a competitive firm, there is little advantage in competition. During most of the period considered in this book, state regulators have generally assumed that rate-of-return-regulated firms are efficient. They perceived few efficiency benefits from introducing competition and were therefore opposed to competition because of the possibility of harm to other goals. Beginning in the late 1980s, many state regulators developed a more negative view of the efficiency of rate of return regulation and adopted various forms of incentive regulation to improve incentives for efficiency.

The FCC initially assumed that the network was best managed by AT&T and implicitly assumed that it was reasonably efficient. As competitors entered and personnel changed, the negative critique of rate of return regulation in the academic literature gained credence. The

FCC's active support of competition was in part related to the assumption that the telephone companies would become more efficient with a competitive benchmark. The FCC also used the inefficiency of rate of return regulation as a key component of its switch to price cap regulation in the late 1980s. Price caps, and incentive regulation in general, were based on the assumption that rate-of-return-regulated firms fail to attain full efficiency.

The Justice Department believed that regulated monopoly was extremely inefficient. It attributed the high observed prices for long distance service to the inefficiency of regulated monopoly rather than to subsidy payments from long distance to local service, and consequently expected great efficiency gains from additional competitive opportunities. The assumption that regulated monopoly was extremely inefficient allowed the DOJ to focus on reducing regulation to the maximum extent possible. It accepted the view that the FCC was a positively bad influence on the industry, not merely that it had not provided maximum efficiency. In the Justice Department's view, the FCC had been captured by the dominant firm and helped it erect barriers to entry to maintain its market position. The DOJ attempted to minimize the role of regulation in order to avoid the inefficiency created by regulation.

Policy Goals

Several goals of telecommunication policy have been widely accepted by the various individuals and institutions that have been influential in the development of policy. Throughout the policy evolution there has been a consensus that universal service must be preserved. There have been disagreements over whether particular policy measures (such as the Subscriber Line Charge) would threaten universal service, but no substantial disagreement over the proposition that policy should ensure universal service. Consequently, it has been easy to gain support for the proposition that some subsidies to rural and high-cost areas are appropriate. No institution has taken a position in favor of any policy that could reasonably be considered to be a threat to universal service.

There has also been a consensus that a reliable network is imperative. The disagreements over the need for hierarchical management versus market determined combinations of networks were related to the factual question of which arrangement best promoted a reliable network, not to the value question of how important the goal of network reliability should be. From terminal equipment to divestiture to the development of price caps, each policy that affected potential network reliability has provided assurances that it will enhance network reliability rather than retard it. It is unlikely that any policy that proposed explicit network degradation in exchange for some other worthy goal would be given serious consideration.

There has likewise been a consensus that network efficiency and opportunities for technological progress are important goals for policy. As with the other consensus goals, there have been many disputes over whether particular proposed policies would help or harm network efficiency or technological progress, but no dispute over whether those are desirable goals.

While several goals have been widely shared by telecommunication policy makers, differing views on the importance of allocative efficiency or cost-based pricing have been incorporated into policy. The benefits of marginal cost pricing for total allocative efficiency are a celebrated theme of economic analysis. Many economists assume that allocative efficiency is a universally accepted goal. However, in the telecommunication policy process, allocative efficiency has been controversial because of its interrelationship with other goals. There was no effort by regulators to force individual service prices toward their marginal cost prior to the advent of competition. In some cases, opposition to competition was premised on the belief that competition would force prices to marginal cost and that that result was undesirable. State regulators have often sought to provide some telecommunication services at prices explicitly different from cost, such as pricing basic local service below cost and various optional services above cost.

Federal regulators initially gave little weight to allocative efficiency, but subsequently incorporated allocative efficiency into their goals in the 1980s. The effort to establish the Subscriber Line Charge and bring prices closer to costs was in part based on an attempt to achieve allocative efficiency. In the process of defending the SLC against its many critics, the argument for cost-based pricing was bolstered with other arguments (such as the bypass threat to the sustainability of high access charges) because many of the critics did not accept allocative efficiency as a policy goal.

The Justice Department considered allocative efficiency an important goal and sought to bring prices closer to cost through the competitive process. It saw little value in maintaining the existing system of subsidies in the industry, if they existed at all. Congressional leaders who supported bills to ban bypass and limit the operation of the FCC's access charge plan did not see allocative efficiency as an important goal.

The support for allocative efficiency was closely related to support for various income distribution schemes. Forcing prices to marginal cost provided one particular version of sharing the total burden of paying for the network. In general, those who believed strongly in allocative efficiency as a goal considered the cost-based sharing system an adequately fair distribution of the total burden. Those who preferred a politically determined allocation of the cost burden saw the efforts to establish cost-based pricing (and often the competitive movement in general) as counterproductive. The issue of cost-based versus politically determined prices was focused most clearly during the access charge debate, but it also arose in many other issues during the movement toward competition.

The final access charge plan was a political compromise that incorporated a partial movement toward cost-based pricing with continuing protection of some of the past subsidy flows. The beginning of local competition renewed debate over the wisdom of cost-based pricing versus maintaining particular revenue flows through non-cost-based pricing. Those questions are not yet fully resolved. The value question of how much revenue flow should be explicitly protected by the political process, and the accompanying factual question of how feasible it is to accomplish any desired protection through a particular policy action, are likely to continue as crucial components of telecommunication policy well into the future.

Notes

1. Introduction

1. Henry Geller, "Reforming the Federal Telecommunications Policy Process," in Paula R. Newberg, ed., *New Directions in Telecommunications Policy* (Durham: Duke University Press, 1989), vol. 1, p. 315.
2. U.S. Department of Commerce, National Telecommunications and Information Administration, *NTIA Telecom 2000: Charting the Course for a New Century*, NTIA Special Publication 88–21 (Washington, D.C.: U.S. Government Printing Office, 1988), pp. 165–167.
3. Martha Derthick and Paul Quirk, *The Politics of Deregulation* (Washington, D.C.: The Brookings Institution, 1985).
4. James Q. Wilson, *Bureaucracy: What Government Agencies Do and Why They Do It* (New York: Basic Books, 1989), p. 326.
5. Alfred Chandler, *The Visible Hand: The Managerial Revolution in American Business* (Cambridge, Mass.: Harvard University Press, 1977).
6. James March and Johan Olsen, *Rediscovering Institutions: The Organizational Basis of Politics* (New York: The Free Press, 1989), pp. 7, 8.
7. Charles Lindblom and David Cohen, *Usable Knowledge: Social Science and Social Problem Solving* (New Haven: Yale University Press, 1979), p. 91.
8. March and Olsen, *Rediscovering Institutions*, pp. 11, 12.

2. Perspectives on the Policy Process

1. A comprehensive survey of the economic approaches to regulation can be found in the articles by Roger Noll, Ronald Braeutigam, David Baron, and Paul Joskow and Nancy Rose in Richard Schmalensee and Robert Willig, eds., *Handbook of Industrial Organization* (Amsterdam: North-Holland, 1989), vol. 2, pp. 1253–1506.
2. The interpretation of Blackstone and Bentham used here follows Richard

303

Posner, *The Economics of Justice* (Cambridge, Mass.: Harvard University Press, 1981), chap. 2.

3. Jeremy Bentham, *A Fragment on Government*, ed. J. H. Burns and H. L. A. Hart (Cambridge: Cambridge University Press, 1988).

4. Posner, *The Economics of Justice*, pp. 45, 46.

5. Ibid., pp. 39, 40.

6. F. A. von Hayek, "The Pretence of Knowledge," Nobel Memorial Lecture, December 11, 1974, reprinted in *American Economic Review* 79 (December 1989): 1–7 at 7.

7. Thomas McCraw, *Prophets of Regulation: Charles Francis Adams, Louis D. Brandeis, James M. Landis, Alfred E. Kahn* (Cambridge, Mass.: Harvard University Press, 1984), p. 184.

8. The lectures were published as James Landis, *The Administrative Process* (New Haven: Yale University Press, 1966).

9. Ibid., p. 8.

10. Ibid., p. 10.

11. Ibid., pp. 11, 12.

12. Ibid., pp. 23, 24.

13. Kurt R. Leube, "George J. Stigler: A Biographical Introduction," in Kurt R. Leube and Thomas G. Moore, eds., *The Essence of Stigler* (Stanford, Calif.: Hoover Institution Press, 1986).

14. George J. Stigler, *Memoirs of an Unregulated Economist* (New York: Basic Books, 1988).

15. George Stigler, "The Theory of Economic Regulation," *Bell Journal of Economics and Management Science* 2 (Spring 1971): 3–21, reprinted in George Stigler, *The Citizen and the State: Essays on Regulation* (Chicago: University of Chicago Press, 1975), chap. 8.

16. Stigler, *Citizen and the State*, p. 132.

17. Ibid., p. 167.

18. F. M. Scherer, *Industrial Market Structure and Economic Performance* (Chicago: Rand McNally, 1970), p. 537.

19. John R. Meyer et al., *The Economics of Competition in the Transportation Industries* (Cambridge, Mass.: Harvard University Press, 1959); Richard Caves, *Air Transport and Its Regulators* (Cambridge, Mass.: Harvard University Press, 1962).

20. A review of the literature is contained in David Baron, "Design of Regulatory Mechanisms and Institutions," in Schmalensee and Willig, eds., *Handbook of Industrial Organization*, vol. 2, pp. 1347–1447; see also J. J. Laffont, *The Economics of Uncertainty and Information*, trans. J. Bonin and H. Bonin (Cambridge, Mass.: MIT Press, 1989).

21. Baron, "Design of Regulatory Mechanisms and Institutions," pp. 1363–1376.

22. David M. Kreps, *A Course in Microeconomic Theory* (Princeton, N.J.: Princeton University Press, 1990), p. 611.
23. Oliver E. Williamson, *Markets and Hierarchies: Analysis and Antitrust Implications* (New York: The Free Press, 1975); Williamson, *The Economic Institutions of Capitalism* (New York: The Free Press, 1985).
24. Williamson, *Economic Institutions of Capitalism*, p. 387.
25. K. J. Arrow, *Social Choice and Individual Values*, 2nd ed. (New York: Wiley, 1963); Amartya K. Sen, *Collective Choice and Social Welfare* (Amsterdam: North-Holland, 1970).
26. J. C. Harsanyi, "Cardinal Welfare, Individualistic Ethics, and Interpersonal Comparisons of Utility," *Journal of Political Economy* 63 (1955). A commentary and analysis of Harsanyi are contained in Sen, *Collective Choice and Social Welfare*, pp. 141–146.
27. James Buchanan and Gordon Tullock, *The Calculus of Consent: Logical Foundations of Constitutional Democracy* (Ann Arbor: University of Michigan Press, 1962), pp. 92, 93.
28. John Rawls, *A Theory of Justice* (Cambridge, Mass.: Harvard University Press, 1971).
29. Amitai Etzioni, *The Moral Dimension: Toward a New Economics* (New York: The Free Press, 1988).
30. Ronald Dworkin, *Taking Rights Seriously* (Cambridge, Mass.: Harvard University Press, 1977), p. 22.
31. *Riggs v. Palmer*, 115 N.Y. 506, 22 N.E. 188 (1889) at 189, 190; quoted in ibid., p. 23.

3. A Model of the Decentralized Policy Process

1. Samuel H. Beer, *To Make a Nation: The Rediscovery of American Federalism* (Cambridge, Mass.: Harvard University Press, 1993), p. 23.
2. Michael Polanyi, "The Republic of Science: Its Political and Economic Theory," in Marjorie Grene, ed., *Knowing and Being: Essays by Michael Polanyi* (Chicago: University of Chicago Press, 1969), p. 69.
3. Ibid., pp. 51, 52.
4. Ibid., p. 53.
5. Ibid., pp. 54, 55.
6. Ibid., p. 71.
7. 47 *Code of Federal Regulations* 69.205(c).
8. Davis Bobrow and John Dryzek, *Policy Analysis by Design* (Pittsburgh: University of Pittsburgh Press, 1987), p. 92.

4. Institutions of Telecommunication Policy

1. *Communications Act of 1934*, Section 1, codified at 47 *United States Code* 151.

2. 47 *United States Code* 154(i).
3. 47 *United States Code* 201–220.
4. *Administrative Procedure Act of 1946*, revised and codified at 5 *United States Code* 500–576.
5. 47 *United States Code* 155.
6. Fred Henck and Bernard Strassburg, *A Slippery Slope: The Long Road to the Breakup of AT&T* (New York: Greenwood Press, 1988), p. 20.
7. 47 *Code of Federal Regulations* 0.91 and 0.291.
8. 47 *Code of Federal Regulations* 0.21.
9. This book examines the development of telecommunication policy primarily from a federal perspective. For an analysis of some of the same issues from a state perspective, see Paul Teske, *After Divestiture: The Political Economy of State Telecommunications Regulation* (Albany: State University of New York Press, 1990).
10. See Joel D. Aberbach, *Keeping a Watchful Eye: The Politics of Congressional Oversight* (Washington, D.C.: Brookings, 1990); Christopher H. Foreman, Jr., *Signals from the Hill: Congressional Oversight and the Challenge of Social Regulation* (New Haven: Yale University Press, 1988).

5. Economic Characteristics of the Telecommunication Industry

1. A detailed account of the history summarized here is contained in Gerald Brock, *The Telecommunications Industry: The Dynamics of Market Structure* (Cambridge, Mass.: Harvard University Press, 1981).
2. Studies of the externality aspect of telephone demand appeared in a series of articles in the *Bell Journal of Economics*, including R. Artle and C. Averous, "The Telephone System as a Public Good: Static and Dynamic Aspects," 4 (Spring 1973): 89–100; L. Squire, "Some Aspects of Optimal Pricing for Telecommunications," 4 (Autumn 1973): 515–525; J. Rohlfs, "A Theory of Interdependent Demand for a Communications Service," 5 (Spring 1974): 16–37; and S. C. Littlechild, "Two-Part Tariffs and Consumption Externalities," 6 (Autumn 1975): 661–670.
3. Bureau of the Census, *Historical Statistics of the United States: Colonial Times to 1970* (Washington, D.C.: U.S. Government Printing Office, 1975), vol. 2, Series R-2, p. 784.
4. Theodore Vail speech, "Lest We Forget," undated, AT&T files.
5. *Historical Statistics of the United States*, Series R 71–74, p. 790, and R 13–16, p. 784.
6. James W. Sichter, "Profits, Politics, and Capital Formation: The Economics of the Traditional Telephone Industry," Harvard Program on Information Resources Policy, 1987, p. 8. Parts of the United States, particularly in Alaska, remain unassigned to any telephone company.

7. *Smith v. Illinois Bell Tel. Co.*, 282 *U.S.* 133 (1930).
8. Quoted in Fred Henck and Bernard Strassburg, *A Slippery Slope: The Long Road to the Breakup of AT&T* (New York: Greenwood Press, 1988), p. 44.
9. C. E. Wilson to H. Brownell, Jr., July 10, 1953, reprinted in *Hearings before the Antitrust Subcommittee*, House of Representatives, 85th Cong. (March 25–May 22, 1958), 2029–2031.
10. In general, the addition of the $(n + 1)$th person to a network of n people adds $2n$ new communication paths.

6. Competition in Terminal Equipment

1. Fred Henck and Bernard Strassburg, *A Slippery Slope: The Long Road to the Breakup of AT&T* (New York: Greenwood Press, 1988), chap. 3.
2. Ibid., p. 35.
3. Ibid., pp. 38, 39.
4. *Hush-A-Phone Corporation v. U.S. and FCC*, 238 *F.2d* 266 at 269 (1956), emphasis added.
5. *Federal Communications Commission Reports* 22 (1957), 114, with referenced report beginning on p. 112; future references will be cited in the form 22 *FCC* 112 at 114 (1957), in which the numbers refer to the volume number, beginning page of report, referenced page, and year, respectively. Later years have new volume numbers in the "second series," cited as *FCC 2d*.
6. Quoted in 13 *FCC 2d* 420 at 437 (1968).
7. Ibid.
8. Peter Temin with Louis Galambos, *The Fall of the Bell System* (Cambridge: Cambridge University Press, 1987), pp. 44, 45.
9. Henck and Strassburg, *A Slippery Slope*, p. 130.
10. Ibid., p. 131.
11. Ibid., p. 132, 133.
12. John deButts, "An Unusual Obligation," speech to NARUC, September 20, 1973, reprinted in Alvin von Auw, *Heritage and Destiny: Reflections on the Bell System in Transition* (New York: Praeger, 1983), appendix B.
13. Federal Communications Commission, *Statistics of Communications Common Carriers: Year Ended December 31, 1973* (Washington, D.C.: U.S. Government Printing Office, 1975), Table 12, p. 21.
14. von Auw, *Heritage and Destiny*, p. 138.
15. Henck and Strassburg, *A Slippery Slope*, p. 139.
16. *Telerent Leasing Corp. et al.*, 45 *FCC 2d* 204 (1974), *aff'd sub nom. North Carolina Utilities Commission v. FCC*, 537 *F.2d* 787 (4th Cir., 1976).
17. 56 *FCC 2d* 593 (1975); 59 *FCC 2d* 83 (1976).
18. 77 *FCC 2d* 384 (1980) at 446, 447.
19. 77 *FCC 2d* 384 (1980) at 495.

7. Initial Long Distance Competition

1. A more complete account of the early microwave systems is contained in Gerald Brock, *The Telecommunications Industry: The Dynamics of Market Structure* (Cambridge, Mass.: Harvard University Press, 1981), chaps. 7 and 8.
2. 27 *FCC* 359 at 388 (1959).
3. 38 *FCC* 370 at 379 (1964).
4. An account of the litigation is contained in Fred Henck and Bernard Strassburg, *A Slippery Slope: The Long Road to the Breakup of AT&T* (New York: Greenwood Press, 1988), pp. 87–95.
5. Ibid., pp. 102, 103.
6. Quoted ibid., p. 104.
7. 16 *Radio Regulation 2d* 1037 (1969).
8. Henck and Strassburg, *A Slippery Slope*, p. 102.
9. Peter Temin with Louis Galambos, *The Fall of the Bell System* (Cambridge: Cambridge University Press, 1987), pp. 50, 51.
10. 16 *Radio Regulation 2d* 1037 at 1067 (1969).
11. 29 *FCC 2d* 870 at 920 (1971).
12. Federal Communications Commission, *Statistics of Communications Common Carriers: Year Ended December 31, 1971* (Washington, D.C.: U.S. Government Printing Office, 1974), p. 28.

8. Interconnection and Long Distance Competition

1. 29 *FCC 2d* 870 at 940 (1971).
2. Fred Henck and Bernard Strassburg, *A Slippery Slope: The Long Road to the Breakup of AT&T* (New York: Greenwood Press, 1988), p. 160.
3. Ibid., pp. 162, 163.
4. Peter Temin with Louis Galambos, *The Fall of the Bell System* (Cambridge: Cambridge University Press, 1987), pp. 65, 66.
5. Reprinted in *Hearings before the Subcommittee on Antitrust and Monopoly of the Committee on the Judiciary*, U.S. Senate, 93rd Cong. (July 9–31, 1974) (Washington, D.C.: U.S. Government Printing Office, 1974), 4640–4644.
6. 58 *FCC 2d* 362 (1976).
7. Henck and Strassburg, *A Slippery Slope*, p. 168.
8. Ibid., p. 168.
9. FCC decision at 60 *FCC 2d* (1976); court decision at 561 *F.2d* 365 (1977); cert. denied, 434 *U.S.* 1040 (1978).
10. "Execunet II," 580 *F.2d* (1978); cert. denied, 439 *U.S.* 980 (1978).
11. MCI numbers taken from MCI Annual Reports; Southern Pacific numbers taken from "Form P" filed with the FCC; total toll revenues taken

from the sum of MTS and WATS revenues in Table 7.3 of FCC, *Statistics of Communications Common Carriers*, 1988/89 edition. The three numbers are computed on somewhat different bases and are not precisely comparable, but provide an approximation to the relative magnitudes.

12. Computed from restated historical figures in MCI's 1984 Annual Report, p. 20. Return on total assets is computed as "Income from Operations" (before interest) over total assets. Return on stockholder equity is computed as net income over stockholder equity.

13. Southern Pacific Communications' rate of return is computed as net operating income (after taxes and before fixed charges) over total assets as listed in FCC "Form P" (public files of the Industry Analysis Division, FCC). The comparable numbers after 1982 are not available because the reporting requirement was abolished.

14. MCI, 1981 Annual Report, pp. 2, 3.

9. The Divestiture

1. John deButts, "An Unusual Obligation," speech to NARUC, September 20, 1973, reprinted in Alvin von Auw, *Heritage and Destiny: Reflections on the Bell System in Transition* (New York: Praeger, 1983), appendix B.

2. Bill and analysis reprinted in *Hearings before the Subcommittee on Communications of the Committee on Interstate and Foreign Commerce*, House of Representatives, 94th Cong. (Washington, D.C.: U.S. Government Printing Office, 1977), 763–780.

3. Peter Temin with Louis Galambos, *The Fall of the Bell System* (Cambridge: Cambridge University Press, 1987), p. 99.

4. Roger Noll and Bruce Owen, "The Anticompetitive Uses of Regulation: United States v. AT&T," in John Kwoka and Lawrence White, eds., *The Antitrust Revolution* (Glenview, Ill.: Scott, Foresman, 1989), p. 307.

5. Phillip Verveer, "Regulation and the Access Problem: What's Happened and Where Are We Now," in Alan Baughcum and Gerald Faulhaber, eds., *Telecommunications Access and Public Policy* (Norwood, N.J.: Ablex, 1984), p. 86.

6. Noll and Owen, "The Anticompetitive Uses of Regulation," p. 295. Another view of the rationale of the case from a DOJ economist is contained in Tim Brennan, "Why Regulated Firms Should Be Kept Out of Unregulated Markets: Understanding the Divestiture in *US v AT&T*," *Antitrust Bulletin* 32 (1987): 741–793.

7. von Auw, *Heritage and Destiny*, pp. 131, 132.

8. Temin with Galambos, *The Fall of the Bell System*, pp. 206–216.

9. Ibid., pp. 223–230.

10. Ibid., pp. 228, 229.

11. Ibid., pp. 246–248.
12. A detailed account of the efforts to craft a legislative solution is contained in ibid., chap. 6.
13. "Defendants' Pretrial Brief," *U.S. v. AT&T* (December 10, 1980), pp. 199–203, reprinted in C. H. Sterling, J. F. Kasle, and K. T. Glakas, eds., *Decision to Divest: Major Documents in U.S. v. AT&T, 1974–1984* (Washington, D.C.: Communications Press, 1986), vol. 1, pp. 560–664.
14. The MFJ provided that until September 1, 1991, "the charges for delivery or receipt of traffic of the same type between end offices and facilities of interexchange carriers within an exchange area, or within reasonable subzones of an exchange area, shall be equal, per unit of traffic delivered or received, for all interexchange carriers; provided, that the facilities of any interexchange carrier within five miles of an AT&T class 4 switch shall, with respect to end offices served by such class 4 switch, be considered to be in the same subzone as such class 4 switch." *Modification of Final Judgment*, appendix B, section B(3), *552 F. Supp.* 131 (1982), reprinted in Sterling, Kasle, and Glakas, eds., *Decision to Divest*, vol. 2, pp. 1294–1302.
15. "Exchange access" was defined to include "any activity or function performed by a BOC in connection with the origination or termination of interexchange telecommunications, including but not limited to, the provision of network control signalling, answer supervision, automatic calling number identification, carrier access codes, directory services, testing and maintenance of facilities and the provision of information necessary to bill customers." *Modification of Final Judgment*, section IV(F).
16. *Modification of Final Judgment*, appendix B.
17. *Hearings before the Committee on Commerce, Science, and Transportation*, U.S. Senate, 97th Cong. (Washington, D.C.: U.S. Government Printing Office, 1982), pp. 77–83.
18. *Modification of Final Judgment*, section I(B).
19. "Testimony of Gen. William J. Hilsman" (January 25, 1982), *Hearings before the Committee on Commerce, Science, and Transportation*, U.S. Senate, 97th Cong. (Washington, D.C.: U.S. Government Printing Office, 1982), p. 43.
20. "Testimony of William Baxter" (February 4, 1982), ibid., pp. 58–60.
21. Ibid., p. 60.
22. W. Brooke Tunstall, *Disconnecting Parties: Managing the Bell System Break-Up: An Inside View* (New York: McGraw-Hill, 1985), pp. 20–22.
23. Tunstall, *Disconnecting Parties*, is a book-length account of the divestiture process by AT&T's director of divestiture planning. Temin with Galambos, *The Fall of the Bell System*, chap. 7, also contains an account of the divestiture process.

24. William G. McGowan, "Chairman's Letter," MCI 1982 Annual Report, p. 2.
25. "Questions and Answers with the Three Major Figures of Divestiture," in Barry Cole, ed., *After the Break-up: Assessing the New Post-AT&T Divestiture Era* (New York: Columbia University Press, 1991), p. 21.
26. Ibid., p. 32.
27. Ibid., p. 49.
28. Ibid., p. 30.

10. Access Charges: A Confusing Ten Billion Dollar Game

1. "Testimony of Gen. William J. Hilsman" (January 25, 1982), *Hearings before the Committee on Commerce, Science, and Transportation,* U.S. Senate, 97th Cong. (Washington, D.C.: U.S. Government Printing Office, 1982), p. 41.
2. Commissioner Fogarty to Commissioners, Chief, Common Carrier Bureau, and General Counsel, January 21, 1982, reprinted in *Hearings before the Judiciary Committee,* U.S. Senate (March 25, 1982), pp. 5–11.
3. 81 *FCC 2d* 177 (1980); see also Robert R. Bruce, "Entering and Exiting the Access Labyrinth: Regulatory and Judicial Background and Policy Initiatives for the Future," in Alan Baughcum and Gerald Faulhaber, *Telecommunications Access and Public Policy* (Norwood, N.J.: Ablex, 1984).
4. A key FCC staff member on access charges wrote privately to the author: "The proposed realignment of MTS and private line rates would have produced a very radical change. Indeed, I suspect the Commissioners never would have voted for the 1980 Notice if they had realized that they were proposing a huge increase in private line rates. It might have been possible to devise an access charge scheme to fit MTS, Execunet, etc. without touching private line. The NPRM did not do that because some of the staff . . . wanted to use access charges as an additional means to change AT&T rate relationships."
5. "Testimony of William Baxter" (February 4, 1982), *Hearings before the Committee on Commerce, Science, and Transportation,* U.S. Senate, 97th Cong. (Washington, D.C.: U.S. Government Printing Office, 1982), pp. 61, 62.
6. 90 *FCC 2d* (1982) 135 at 140.
7. Ibid., p. 141.
8. An active participant in the debates wrote privately to the author: "The staff opposition . . . was also based on a fear that any plan that resulted in adding a charge to everyone's phone bill that would be described as imposed by the FCC could produce a nasty political backlash. Some thought the Commissioners had underestimated the political risk and might aban-

don the whole thing later if they encountered more trouble than they expected. In fact, the Commissioners (particularly Mark [Fowler] and Mimi [Dawson]) subsequently demonstrated far more backbone than most FCC Commissioners had demonstrated in the past."

9. Senior staff members involved in constructing the plan describe complexity and obscurity as intentional goals in order to limit the number of parties that could seriously enter the debate. They succeeded. It is difficult to understand any of the plans, and especially the 1982 plan, without the assistance of insiders.

10. 93 *FCC 2d* 241 (1982) at 249.

11. Ibid., p. 250.

12. Ibid., pp. 251, 252.

13. Changes in the separations rules must first be considered by a Joint Board of federal and state commissioners. The Joint Board then makes a recommendation to the FCC, which is normally adopted. There is close coordination between the Joint Board and FCC processes prior to official action because the FCC Common Carrier Bureau chief supervises much of the staff work for both processes.

14. "Dissenting Statement of Commissioner Anne P. Jones," *Amendment of Part 67 of the Commission's Rules and Establishment of a Joint Board*, CC Docket 80–286 (released September 26, 1983), p. 2.

15. *National Association of Regulatory Utility Commissioners v. FCC*, 737 F.2d 1095 (1984), cert. denied, 469 *U.S.* 1227 (1985).

11. The Implementation of Access Charges

1. 569 *F.Supp.* 990 (1983) at 997–999, reprinted in C. H. Sterling, J. F. Kasle, and K. T. Glakas, eds., *Decision to Divest: Major Documents in U.S. v. AT&T, 1974–1984* (Washington, D.C.: Communications Press, 1986), vol. 3, pp. 1693–1695.

2. "Testimony of Mark Fowler" (July 28, 1983), *Joint Hearings before the Committee on Commerce, Science, and Transportation and the Committee on Energy and Commerce*, U.S. Senate and House, 98th Cong. (Washington, D.C.: U.S. Government Printing Office, 1983), pp. 67–69.

3. Senator Bob Dole to FCC Chairman Mark Fowler, January 18, 1984.

4. Gerald Brock, "Bypass of the Local Exchange: A Quantitative Assessment," Working Paper 12, Office of Plans and Policy, Federal Communications Commission, 1984.

5. 97 *FCC 2d* 1082 at 1083 (1984).

6. Although the larger OCC discount was forced by congressional pressure, that is not a legally defensible rationale for FCC action.

7. "Brief of Petitioner American Telephone and Telegraph Company,"

AT&T v. FCC (appeal of February 1984 access order) (March 9, 1984), pp. 41, 48, 49.

8. MCI 1984 Annual Report.
9. The depooling rules are in 47 C.F.R. 69(G). The financial implications for individual companies are reported in various editions of the *Monitoring Report* issued by the FCC Industry Analysis Division semiannually.

12. The Dismantling of Structural Separation

1. 77 *FCC 2d* 384 (1980) at 387.
2. *Modification of Final Judgment*, August 24, 1982, Sections II(D) and IV(J), reprinted in C. H. Sterling, J. F. Kasle, and K. T. Glakas, eds., *Decision to Divest: Major Documents in U.S. v. AT&T, 1974–1984* (Washington, D.C.: Communications Press, 1986), vol. 2, pp. 1294–1302.
3. FCC, Industry Analysis Division, "Trends in Telephone Service" (August 1991), p. 18.
4. "Amendment of Sections 64.702 of the Commission's Rules and Regulations (Third Computer Inquiry)," *Notice of Proposed Rulemaking*, FCC 85–397 (released August 16, 1985), pp. 3–6.
5. 104 *FCC 2d* 958 (1986), paragraphs 154–166.
6. Ibid., paragraph 252.
7. "Filing and Review of Open Network Architecture Plans," 4 *FCC Record* 1 (1989). (In 1986, the *FCC Record* replaced the *FCC Reports* series as the official record of FCC actions.)
8. "Report and Recommendations of the United States Concerning the Line of Business Restrictions Imposed on the Bell Operating Companies by the Modification of Final Judgment" (February 2, 1987), pp. 113–115, reprinted in C. H. Sterling and J. F. Kasle, eds., *Decision to Divest IV: The First Review, 1985–1987* (Washington, D.C.: Communications Press, 1988), vol. 4, pp. 2264–2266.
9. Ibid., pp. 147–151 in the original and pp. 2298–2302 in the reprint volume. A participant wrote privately to the author regarding this quote: "All the praise for the FCC was, of course, black humor, given the DOJ's real opinion of the FCC capabilities. DOJ endorsed the FCC only because it would result in the outcome DOJ desired."
10. Under the Tunney Act, a judge must evaluate the public interest benefits of a consent decree agreement reached between the Department of Justice and an antitrust defendant rather than automatically entering the decree at the request of the parties. Because the AT&T-DOJ agreement was formally a modification of the 1956 consent decree together with a dismissal of the DOJ case, there was some legal question concerning whether the Tunney Act applied. Judge Greene decided that the Tunney Act applied to this case, and Baxter chose not to challenge that view.

11. "Questions and Answers with the Three Major Figures of Divestiture," in Barry Cole, ed., *After the Break-up: Assessing the New Post-AT&T Divestiture Era* (New York: Columbia University Press, 1991), p. 25.
12. Ibid., pp. 42, 43.
13. 627 *F. Supp.* 1090 (1986) at 1094–1096, and notes 18 and 21.
14. C. H. Sterling and J. F. Kasle, "Introduction: Reviewing the Breakup Is Also Hard to Do," in Sterling and Kasle, eds., *Decision to Divest IV*, p. I–13.
15. "Opinion," *U.S. v. Western Electric, et. al.* (September 10, 1987), p. 22, reprinted in Sterling and Kasle, eds., *Decision to Divest IV*, pp. 2402–2624.
16. Ibid., pp. 123, 124 in the original and pp. 2524, 2525 in the reprint volume.
17. Ibid., pp. 213–219 in the original and pp. 2614–2620 in the reprint volume.
18. "Petition for Declaratory Ruling of the National Telecommunications and Information Administration" (November 24, 1987), pp. 3, 9, reprinted in Sterling and Kasle, eds., *Decision to Divest IV*, pp. 2770–2803.
19. "Opinion on Manufacturing" (December 3, 1987), pp. 5–14, reprinted in Sterling and Kasle, eds., *Decision to Divest IV*, pp. 2629–2662.
20. *U.S. v. Western Electric et al.* (July 25, 1991), pp. 49–52.
21. Ibid., pp. 54, 68.

13. Competition in Local Service

1. S. 1660, Section 6(e), printed in *Joint Hearings before the Committee on Commerce, Science, and Transportation and the Committee on Energy and Commerce*, U.S. Senate and House, 98th Cong. (Washington, D.C.: U.S. Government Printing Office, 1983), p. 12.
2. See Michael L. Katz and Carl Shapiro, "Network Externalities, Competition, and Compatibility," *American Economic Review* 75 (1985): 424–440; Joseph Farrell and Garth Saloner, "Standardization, Compatibility, and Innovation," *The Rand Journal of Economics* 16 (1985): 70–83; for a review and additional references, see Jean Tirole, *The Theory of Industrial Organization* (Cambridge, Mass.: MIT Press, 1988), pp. 404–421.
3. Jonathan Kraushaar, "Fiber Deployment Update," Industry Analysis Division, FCC (1990 and 1992).
4. *Regulatory Response to Competition*, Opinion No. 89-12, Case 29469 (N.Y. PSC May 16, 1989); *Pooling, Collocation and Access Rate Design*, Opinion No. 92-13, Case 28425 (N.Y. PSC May 29, 1992); see review of issues in G. G. Schwartz and J. H. Hoagg, "Virtual Divestiture: Structural Reform of an RHC," *Federal Communications Law Journal* 44 (1992): 291–294.
5. 7 *FCC Record* 7369 (1992); 8 *FCC Record* 7374 (1993).

6. "Statement of Chairman Alfred C. Sikes Concurring in the Result and Dissenting in Part," 7 *FCC Record* 7369 (1992).
7. 7 *FCC Record* 7369 (1992) at paragraphs 143, 144.
8. 8 *FCC Record* 7374 (1993) at 7421.
9. 7 *FCC Record* 7369 (1992), paragraph 177 and footnote 410.
10. Gerald Brock, "Telephone Pricing to Promote Universal Service and Economic Freedom," Working Paper 18, Office of Plans and Policy, FCC, 1986; "Interconnection Conditions, Access Charges, and Universal Service," presented at the Telecommunications Policy Research Conference, October 1993.

14. Price Caps and Regulatory Boundaries

1. John Haring and Evan Kwerel, "Competition Policy in the Post-Equal Access Market," Working Paper 22, Office of Plans and Policy, FCC, 1987.
2. Kathleen Levitz, "Loosening the Ties that Bind: Regulating the Interstate Telecommunications Market for the 1990's," Working Paper 23, Office of Plans and Policy, FCC, 1987.
3. Ibid., pp. 49, 50.
4. 2 *FCC Record* 5208 (1987) at 5213, 5214.
5. Ibid., p. 5221.
6. Edward J. Markey and John D. Dingell to Dennis R. Patrick, September 28, 1988.
7. Daniel K. Inouye to Dennis R. Patrick, September 28, 1988.
8. Edward J. Markey to Dennis R. Patrick, November 21, 1988, p. 1 of attached legal review.
9. John Dingell and Edward Markey to Dennis Patrick, January 13, 1989.
10. John Dingell Press Release, March 16, 1989.
11. 6 *FCC Record* 5880 (1991).
12. 5 *FCC Record* 6786 (1990) at 6806.

Index